The Paradox of our National Security Complex

How Secrecy and Security diminish our
liberty and threaten our Democratic Republic

The Paradox of our National Security Complex

How Secrecy and Security diminish our
liberty and threaten our Democratic Republic

Richard Otto

Winchester, UK
Washington, USA

First published by Chronos Books, 2017
Chronos Books is an imprint of John Hunt Publishing Ltd., Laurel House, Station Approach,
Alresford, Hants, SO24 9JH, UK
office1@jhpbooks.net
www.johnhuntpublishing.com

For distributor details and how to order please visit the 'Ordering' section on our website.

Text copyright: Richard Otto 2016

ISBN: 978 1 78279 444 8
978 1 78279 446 2 (ebook)
Library of Congress Control Number: 2016951893

A CIP catalogue record for this book is available from the British Library.

Design: Stuart Davies

Printed and bound by CPI Group (UK) Ltd, Croydon, CR0 4YY, UK

We operate a distinctive and ethical publishing philosophy in all
areas of our business, from our global network of authors to
production and worldwide distribution.

CONTENTS

I dedicate this book to my loving wife Carol and to my
beautiful daughter Miranda.

"We are not now that strength which in old days
Moved earth and heaven, that which we are, we are;
One equal temper of heroic hearts,
Made weak by time and fate, but strong in will
To strive, to seek, to find, and not to yield."

Ulysses by Alfred Lord Tennyson

Preface

I originally wrote these articles in the form of lengthy e-mails to family and friends to share with them the information I was discovering regarding dark events in the history of our nation. Over the years, I have edited these essays into a more polished and formal structure in the hope that they might be worthy of publication.

Most of my early research and commentary was in response to the financial collapse we all endured in the fall of 2008. For most of us residing on main street who clearly were not too big to fail, and thus were not the beneficiaries of government bailouts, we are still suffering the consequences of that event.

My focus in those e-mails was on the erosion of the power of labor and its influence on our political institutions, as well as the decline of our once proud middle class who manufactured the products that fueled the global economy when I was a young child. As candidate Bernie Sanders has reminded us, we once were a proud economic power that was the envy of the world. As he pointed out in the 1950s and 1960s, General Motors was the largest employer in the country. Their employees were members of the United Auto Workers Union that negotiated contracts with the auto giant that included a livable wage, health and pension benefits, a safe work environment, weekends and paid vacations to enjoy their lives and their families, and a mediation process to ensure that they were treated fairly when disputes would arise between labor and management. Today the largest employer is Walmart that aggressively deters any mobilization by its employees to organize so they can exercise their right to collectively bargain for better wages and benefits. As Sanders has repeatedly stated on the campaign trail, the workers without any leverage to advocate for themselves are paid starvation wages and are allotted part time hours so the company can avoid any legal obligation to provide benefits. Walmart, however, is just one of many companies who maximize their profits at the expense of their employees.

Although I am still troubled by the inequitable economic model we have been living under for decades that clearly benefits the biggest corporations and the wealthiest in our society, there has also been another trend that is just as disturbing that threatens the viability of our democratic institutions and is diminishing our fundamental liberty once protected by our Constitution. The rise of our military industrial complex, or what I refer to as our national security complex, since the end of **World War II** in many ways encourages this inequality and contributes to the growing disparity between the most affluent in our society and the rest of us. This is the result of a significant diversion of our labor and financial resources to maintain, support and enlarge this colossal war machine. In addition, we have become the leading exporter of military hardware and weaponry in the world that is being used by governments to oppress their people and bomb their neighbors. This has contributed significantly to the global violence that has caused millions to flee their countries in search of refuge, resulting in a worldwide humanitarian crisis. As the numbers of refugees continue to grow, the international community's response has varied as each recipient nation struggles politically, economically and morally to ameliorate this tragedy.

In order to continue to justify the infringement of our liberty for security, the government continues to seek enemies to maintain a state of fear in our society to perpetuate this inequality. This is exemplified by the present war on terrorism that has no clear delineated objectives for its conclusion. As a consequence, we have allowed our public schools to flounder in mediocrity and our infrastructure to deteriorate as we continue to build weapons of war. In addition, we have permitted the transformation of our nation from an influential lender to a debtor nation that is incrementally bankrupting our safety net and earned benefit programs by stealing from future generations. Instead of being respected as an economic power that supports a huge middle class with plenty of opportunities for the working class and the poor to elevate their status, we, at present, are primarily feared by many around the world because of our military power and our willingness to deploy it to allegedly defend our national interests. I say allegedly because in many cases what is referred to as the interests of the nation is in actuality the interest of corporate entities, elite agencies and organizations and not the American people. We are essentially enforcing a "Pax Americana" on the rest of the world by our weapons of war which is exactly what President Kennedy had astutely warned should not be our objective in his commencement address at American University.

In pursuit of the politics of power and empire building, we have sacrificed our well-earned image as a defender of liberty, justice and human rights that we had rightfully fought for in **World War II**. This sacrifice has diminished our credibility when advocating for these principles by undermining our moral standing on these issues. For instance, I often wonder what Russian and Chinese leaders must be thinking when lectured by American politicians on the virtue of laws that promote human rights when the **Central Intelligence Agency** (CIA) has been implicated in some of the most barbaric practices and atrocities ever committed by mankind. We must appear to them as arrogant hypocrites that need to look into a mirror and begin a process of self-examination that might humble our saintly image wrapped in this concept of American exceptionalism. A belief that somehow human frailties have never intruded upon our concepts of power or national policy.

Some of the articles confront the stark contrast of the government and the corporate media's well entrenched views regarding the cause of the Kennedy assassination and the realities of the witness testimonials and the forensic evidence that exists today. It is clear beyond doubt that Kennedy was hit by bullets that emanated from several directions. The fatal shot to his head captured by the Zapruder film on frame 313 originated from an assassin that was located in front of the motorcade. The number of shots and their directions are all supported by the acoustic evidence and the medical observations of the doctors and nurses at Parkland Hospital in Dallas. It has also been established beyond any reasonable doubt that the government covered up any evidence that was indicative of a conspiracy. Although my intent was not to write another volume on this seminal event, you cannot ignore it because it is the most prominent example of how secrecy in government promotes deceit and corruption in the pursuit of absolute power. The successful assassination of the President by those in our national security complex that viewed him as a naïve, treacherous, Cold War liability emboldened them to assassinate others that jeopardized their policy objectives and their power. This is why the Kennedy assassination seeps into many of the essays.

I should confess that since an early age I have admired President Kennedy and his brother Robert. To a lesser degree, I was interested in the successes and failures of their younger brother former Senator Edward Kennedy. I also must concede that I accepted my government's assertion that Lee Harvey Oswald was the sole assassin that ended Camelot that tragic day until I watched Oliver Stone's movie **JFK**. It was the movie that initiated my journey into the abyss. But I was not convinced that something far more sinister had occurred in Dallas until I read **Brothers** by Talbot and **JFK and the Unspeakable** by Douglass. It was a review of Douglass' volume by James DiEugenio that inspired me to read the book. By this time in my late forties, I was determined to assist the effort being made by concerned citizens in their search for the truth.

I was haunted by his death in ways I could not fully understand as a young child. I was only two years old when he was assassinated so it could not be explained by my somber memories of those four dark days in November nor any observations of what the adults in my family had suffered. By 1968, I read every article and magazine I could get primarily fixated on the pictures of a man that appeared to have sad eyes from my perspective. His wit and personality would be unknown to me until I saw specials about him on television when I was a teenager. Anyone who has watched his give and take with the media at those press conferences must admit that there was something special about this man that needed to be remembered and understood by future generations just as Theodore and Franklin Roosevelt, Abraham Lincoln, Martin Luther King, Jr., and our founders should be.

There was an incident that could provide some paranormal explanation for my admiration of President Kennedy. I certainly could not claim as an 8-year-old that I understood his policies or his legacy. On the afternoon of November 22, 1963, I had hit my head on a sharp corner of a coffee table that had been given to my mother by my maternal grandparents, causing a huge gash on my forehead that allowed blood to cover my face. My mother must have been mortified by the event as she quickly loaded me into the back seat of our navy blue Chevy Corvair. We lived in Bethesda Maryland at that time in a small brick cape not far from where my father was a medical intern at Bethesda Naval Hospital. When she arrived, she was confronted by a Marine guarding the entrance who calmly informed her that the President's body had arrived and that they were instructed not to admit anyone until further notice unless it was an emergency. She quickly directed his attention to me and all the blood that was over my head and face. After his cursory observation of my injury, he escorted her to an entrance where she could receive medical attention for her son. She was directed to an examination room that was off a long hallway that formed a T intersection with another. As medical staff attended to my wound, my mother caught a glimpse of Jackie Kennedy from a distance in her bloodstained pink dress surrounded by family and other navy personnel. As most know by now, Kennedy was a doting father that loved children and on many occasions made decisions regarding war and peace based on his concern for the welfare of children and their opportunity to have a good life. I imagined as an adult that maybe he noticed my pain and distress that day and attempted to comfort me. I know it seems irrational if not whimsical, but I have pondered this for years as a possible explanation for my early admiration and concern for his family.

These articles were written separately but when read in the order set forth in this volume provide sufficient knowledge to enhance your appreciation for each successive essay. Each chapter begins with quotes from iconic and revered figures from politics, science, philosophy and literature, acquainting the reader with their observations on the subjects I examine. Some of them were central players in the events I investigate. My intent was to inspire the novice to explore the issues by reading the sources I referenced to enhance their knowledge of policies that are jeopardizing our republic and diminishing our liberty. Through this knowledge, it is my hope that a greater under-standing of our past will be attained, and its importance to our present and to our future as a people and a nation. As to the experts, the descriptions of intrigue, deception, corruption and the struggle for power contained in my brief editorials may not unveil new facts or evidence, but hopefully will provide some interesting observations that will contribute to our under-standing of these dark events.

Because of the informality of the original articles, it has been difficult to assign specific credit for all the facts that are presented in this book. I, therefore, must clearly state that I do not presume credit for any of the ideas or discoveries that do not have specific endnote references unless otherwise specified in the text. My bibliography is a complete listing of all those enlightening resources cited herein.

I must also acknowledge my appreciation to friends and family that were the recipients of my long e-mails that confronted difficult subjects or at a minimum could be described as melancholic. Unlike television, the script writers had not inserted a happy ending that left you with a good feeling after the episode concluded. In addition, I must give my appreciation to all those researchers and directors that risked everything in search of the truth. I have been and continue to be significantly indebted and influenced by the works of James DiEugenio, Lisa Peace, David Talbot, Jim Marrs, Len Osanic, Brent Holland, Professor Peter Dale Scott, Oliver Stone, Sherry Fiester, John Newman, John Barbour, Mark Lane and James Douglass to name a few. To my wife who has endured my research and writing of this book for so long, I not only tender my loving appreciation for her support, but in addition dedicate it to her.

Chapter 1

The Evolution of our Modern National Security Complex

When discussing why the CIA ran amuck with Trento, Angleton stated, "There was no accountability. And without accountability everything turned to shit."
James Angleton

"You know, the CIA got tens of thousands of brave people killed...We played with lives as if we owned them."
James Angleton

"When national security is used as the excuse for concealing essential facts surrounding a disaster, it usually refers to the security of the man who allowed the disaster to occur. Actually, the greater threat to national security is the cynical concealment of such facts from the people."
James Garrison

"War is peace. Freedom is slavery. Ignorance is strength."
George Orwell

When asked by a reporter to describe the purpose of the CIA, Allen Dulles replied, "It's the state department for the unfriendly countries."
Allen Dulles

"When machines and computers, profit motives and property rights, are considered more important than people, the giant triplets of racism, extreme materialism, and militarism are incapable of being conquered."
Martin Luther King, Jr.

"A nation that continues year after year to spend more money on military defense than on programs of social uplift is approaching spiritual death."
Martin Luther King, Jr.

"There is little value in insuring the survival of our nation if our traditions do not survive with it. And there is a grave danger that an announced need for increased security will be seized upon by those anxious to expand its meaning to the very limits of official censorship and concealment."
John F. Kennedy

"...the Japanese were ready to surrender and it wasn't necessary to hit them with that awful thing (atom bomb)."
Dwight D. Eisenhower

"It is my opinion that the use of this barbarous weapon at Hiroshima and Nagasaki was of no material assistance in our war against Japan."
Admiral William D. Leahy

"...we used them as an experiment for two atomic bombs."
Brigadier General Carter Clarke

"The atomic bomb had nothing to do with the end of the war at all."
General Curtis LeMay

"The war might have ended weeks earlier if the United States had agreed, as it later did anyway, to the retention of the institution of the emperor."
General Douglas McArthur

"We cannot, as a free nation, compete with our adversaries in

tactics of terror, assassination, false promises, counterfeit mobs and crises."
John F. Kennedy

National Security vs Dark Secrets
(How our classification system threatens our republic)

An interview of Edward Snowden triggered some thoughts on how our national security state operates. Snowden was posing questions to former KGB officer, President Vladimir Putin, regarding Russia's intelligence programs and if they collected and stored data on their citizens as was done by our **National Security Agency** (NSA). His reply was predictable in that he denied that they had the money or the technology to spy on their citizens as in the United States.

The issue I intend to confront is the expansive classification program we have instituted in this country since the end of **World War II**. Before the war documents were classified and secrets were kept from the public; this certainly was true. However, the dynamics and the scope of this practice has morphed into a beast that undermines our democracy or what our founding fathers called our republic. When Benjamin Franklin was asked after the **Constitutional Convention** of 1787 how he would characterize our form of government – a republic or a monarchy? He responded "A republic, if you can keep it."

Before **World War II**, this country never had a formal infra-structure for intelligence. This was considered by our British allies as a liability as war approached. British intelligence and military officers – which included Ian Fleming the eventual author of the James Bond series – advocated to President Franklin Roosevelt the need for the United States to establish an intelligence capacity worthy of a world power that was commensurate with what the European nations had instituted. Roosevelt was persuaded and quickly formed the **Office of Intelligence**

Coordination. This fledgling agency would be eclipsed during the war by the **Office of Strategic Services** (OSS) which added clandestine operations to its responsibilities.

The euphoria that swept through the world after the surrender of Germany and Japan did not last long. The hopes and aspirations by many at the end of the war were dashed as cooperation between the allies would slowly recede to the tides of fear and mistrust as the world observed the rise of the **Cold War** between the East and the West. This combination of fear and paranoia was memorialized in the passage of the **National Security Act** of 1947. This act reorganized our military that was now headed by the Secretary of Defense. It also created our National Security Council, the Joint Chiefs of Staff and the **Central Intelligence Agency** (CIA). The **NSA** was established in 1952 by President Truman. It is operated under the auspices of the Pentagon and is completely separate from the **CIA**.

As our intelligence communities grew in stature and their influence in the formation of **Cold War** policy was consolidated, as well as supported by the military, the pressure to engage in secret programs and operations began to expand their authority and responsibilities in the safeguarding of our national security. Many of those who originally joined the **CIA** were former **OSS** agents that were well trained in covert operations. This perceived need to be able to confront an adversary as evil as the Soviet Union and its communist allies encouraged policies and programs that could tackle any threat even if it required illegal and unethical action. As former Deputy Director of Plans Richard Bissell conceded in his memoir, "The end justified the means." This clearly meant that secrecy was paramount to the success of any mission or operation. This led to the **doctrine of plausible deniability** which was formalized in **National Security Council 10/2**. Along with this was the establishment of a hierarchy of classification codes that limited access to documents and information to those who had the requisite security clearance. Consequently, the **CIA** was compartmentalized and responsibilities were divided. Information was transferred and shared on a need to know basis. This meant that two employees engaged in the same project while working next to each other would not be able to comprehend that their duties were related.

Many of the programs executed by the **CIA, FBI** and the **NSA** operated under such strict security and secrecy that even the President and Congress were not informed. In many cases, this was an intentional corollary to our classification protocol in that the President or a member of Congress could not plausibly deny knowledge of programs that violated domestic and international laws that they had been fully briefed on. In some instances, Senators told operatives that they had no desire to know the details of their black ops. The consequence of this was that the activities of the **CIA** were not supervised by our elected officials which allowed the proliferation of nefarious practices within the Agency to flourish. The agents in the field and the officers at Langley in many cases were ultra-conservative cold warriors – whose allegiances varied – that wielded tremendous influence on our policy towards the Soviet Union and the developing world. Their alleged mandate was to fight communism by defending democracy around the globe. Their operations in many circumstances achieved neither for their corporate allies were not interested in the rights and liberties of other nations but rather were solely invested in their goal to maximize their profits.

Their desire to enhance the Agency's power and influence caused them to inevitably violate their founding charter by spying on US citizens, public officials, government agencies, journalists and organizations. The organizations that the **CIA** and **FBI** infiltrated and spied on included the NAACP, the Southern Christian Leadership Conference, Students for a Democratic Society, the Non-violent Student Coordinating Committee, the Black Panther Party for Self Defense, the Young

Lords, the Fair Play for Cuba Committee and other associations not considered acceptable by God fearing anti-communists. The **CIA** also formed symbiotic alliances with the mainstream media to further promote its agenda.

All the above evolved into a process in which almost anything can be classified under the ambit of national security. In many circumstances, the government official who determined whether a document would be classified as top secret was involved in its creation or was implicated in the events contained within the memorandum. This has created a dangerous precedent as was discovered by the **Church Committee** in the mid-1970s. Programs and operations in many cases were classified as matters of national security so that misconduct and even murder could remain hidden from the public and the media. Agents of our government who had access or were privy to these documents were confronted with a serious moral dilemma. If they released the documents into the public domain, they would be violating their oaths, as well as potentially humiliating their beloved country or worse. If they chose to be complicit in maintaining their secrecy, people as well as nations would continue to suffer. This is the dilemma that confronted Daniel Ellsberg, Private Bradley (Chelsea) Manning and Edward Snowden.

The case of Frank Olson is an example of how this policy of secrecy has allowed agents within the system to engage in criminal acts with impunity.[1] Olson was the head of the Special Operations Division within the **CIA** which was a top secret research program. Agent Olson was an expert in biological and chemical weapons. He was also involved in mind control projects that included the use of drugs and hypnosis. He therefore was implicated in **Operation Artichoke** which evolved into **MK Ultra**. In addition, he was familiar with **Operation Paperclip** that assisted the emigration of Nazi scientists into the U.S. where they worked in our secret labs. During the **Korean War**, his research was used in top secret programs that involved the use of chemical and biological weapons that were dropped on Chinese troops and North Korean civilians.[2] He eventually became disgusted with how his research was being implemented by his superiors within the Agency and wanted to retire in 1953.

The CIA determined that he was a security risk and that Olson's retirement posed a serious threat to these secret operations. The Agency decided to drug him with LSD without his knowledge. Subsequently, he had a terrible reaction to the drug and became very depressed. His superiors told him they were going to treat his depression with medication and a period of rest and relaxation. He was accompanied to a hotel in Manhattan by another agent. A doctor came by and injected him with a sedative. Shortly thereafter, he allegedly jumped through a closed window and fell 13 floors to his death.[3] The switchboard operator at the hotel received a request by Agent Lashbrook to make a call to Long Island. She connected the call to Dr. Herald Abramson who had earlier administered the sedative. The operator overheard the brief conversation that she included in her statement to the police. She stated that she heard Lashbrook say "Well, he's gone." Dr. Abramson replied "That is too bad" and hung up. It was after this call that Lashbrook finally informed the police. The medical examiner found inconsistencies with the reported events but nevertheless ruled it a suicide.

The Olson Family in 1975 while following the **Church Committee Hearings** became very suspicious of Frank Olson's alleged suicide when they heard CIA operatives discuss assassination programs that included poisons and other techniques to mimic death by natural causes or appear as a suicide. The family began to make their suspicions public and accused the **CIA** of lying about the cause of his death. The Agency reacted by engaging in what is referred to in intelligence parlance as a "limited hangout." They admitted to injecting Olson with LSD but denied they were culpable for his death. The Chief of Staff for

President Ford Donald Rumsfeld and his assistant Dick Cheney were in charge of damage control. They recommended that the matter be settled as quickly as possible in order to avoid the potential of national secrets being disseminated to the public that could severely embarrass the administration. The **CIA** as a result of pressure from the administration paid the Olson family $750,000. President Ford also personally tendered an apology to the family at the White House.

The family had Frank Olson's body exhumed in the 1990s and examined by a coroner to determine the cause of death. The medical examiner concluded that it was a homicide. This is the type of behavior that is being protected by our broad classification program. Below I will discuss three whistleblowers that were unable to remain silent while their government was abusing its power and lying to the American people.

Daniel Ellsberg was a military analyst employed by the **RAND Corporation** who became involved in a top secret Pentagon study of U.S. government decision-making in relation to the **Vietnam War** that would later be called the **Pentagon Papers**. As he assisted in the preparation of that study, he became disturbed by what he discovered in the documents. Essentially, he learned that many in the Johnson administration recognized early on that the war could not be won, that there were many more casualties than were being reported and that President Johnson had lied to Congress and the American people.

He began attending anti-war rallies in 1969 and found himself agreeing with their cause. He was deeply moved by a statement made by Randy Kehler who declared that he was willing to join his friends in prison than go to Vietnam. Ellsberg after the event wrote, "There is no question in my mind that my government was involved in an unjust war that was going to continue and get larger. Thousands of young men were dying each year. I left the auditorium and found a deserted men's room. I sat on the floor and cried." He decided with his friend and colleague Anthony

Russo – who was also a staff member of Senator Edward Kennedy – to make several copies of which one went to The New York Times who subsequently won a Pulitzer Prize for their reporting on the documents. They both were eventually charged under the **Espionage Act** of 1917 and with conspiracy and theft.

U.S. District Judge William M. Byrne, Jr. dismissed all charges on May 11, 1973, because of "gross government misconduct and illegal evidence gathering." It had been brought to his attention that members of the plumbers who would later become infamous for **Watergate** had broken into Ellsberg's psychiatrist's office seeking information to smear his reputation.

Private Bradley (Chelsea) Manning was an intelligence analyst in Bagdad in 2010. He also was exposed to information that appalled his sense of decency. For example, he came upon a video that captured an Aerial Weapons Team engaging a Bongo truck driving up to assist wounded civilians. The team determined that they were enemy combatants and requested permission to destroy the target. Once granted permission, they blew up the vehicle that not only transported adults but was also carrying children. In the video, the team showed no remorse for their mistake. Instead, they made comments such as "dead bastards" and congratulated themselves even though children were among the casualties. This was one of many examples that were included in the thousands of documents that Private Manning had released to Julian Assange's WikiLeaks. Manning defended his action by stating, "I wanted the American public to know that not everyone in Iraq and Afghanistan were targets that needed to be neutralized, but rather they were people who were struggling to live in a pressure cooker environment of what we call asymmetric warfare." He also wanted the public to know how corrupt the government in Iraq was that we were supporting. He was only 25-years-old when a military court sentenced him to 35 years in prison.

The last of the whistleblowers was Edward Snowden, an

American computer professional who was a former employee of the **CIA**, and when he released the documents to The Guardian and The Washington Post was a private contractor for the **NSA**. The reason he released the documents was the same as the others. He was concerned that our government was trampling on our liberties in the name of national security. He stated, "If we do not contest the violation of the fundamental right of free people to be left unmolested in their thoughts, associations and communications – to be free from suspicion without cause – we will have lost the foundation of our thinking society. The defense of this fundamental freedom is the challenge of our generation, a work that requires constructing new controls and protections to limit the extraordinary powers of the states over the domain of human communication." He resides in Russia as a fugitive from justice.

The question we must ask ourselves is as follows: Are the above whistleblowers security threats that our nation must be protected from by depriving them of their liberty, or are they profiles in courage that should be commended for their efforts to confront the goliath that forms our national security state? It seems to me that they were defending our national honor and our individual liberty by reminding our government that it is of us, by us and for us. They could have chosen to remain silent and defer action to someone else. Instead, they chose to risk everything dear to them for an ideal and what is more American than that. Dr. Martin Luther King, Jr. said "It's not the repression of the bad people that hurts, it's the silence of the good." A system that demands their silence is an affront to all those that fought and died at Bunker Hill, Gettysburg, Okinawa and Normandy. These battles were necessary to defend and preserve our fundamental concepts of liberty, as well as to safeguard our humanity.

The classification system we use is too broad. It is not protecting our national security but rather our government's dark secrets that have nothing to do with the ideals that are emblematic of our national pride. We should choose liberty over national security, and should demand that our government is more transparent in the way it conducts its business. It also would be prudent to remember what Benjamin Franklin cautioned; "They that choose to give up essential liberty to obtain a little temporary security, deserve neither security nor liberty."

Black is White
(The National Security State and the case against Edward Snowden)

Brian Williams of NBC interviewed Edward Snowden on May 28, 2014. This exclusive was televised to an audience that was estimated to be six million. The initial response from the media portrayed Snowden as sincere, articulate and intelligent. Many who watched the interview were astonished by Snowden's ability to eloquently respond in a calm and thoughtful manner under what most would consider a stressful event. He clearly was not awed or intimidated by the prospect of addressing a national audience and cogently explaining his actions to the American people. During this interview, he responded to claims by President Obama that he was a low level "hacker" and charges of being a "coward" and a "traitor" by Secretary of State John Kerry. At one point, Williams asked if he thought the government would attempt to kill him. His laconic reply was "yes." This exchange occurred so nonchalantly as though it should be expected. He was also accused by the government of not utilizing proper channels within the **National Security Agency** (hereinafter NSA) to lodge his complaints prior to releasing classified documents to **The Guardian** and **The Washington Post**.

Before he responded to the above accusations, he felt compelled to provide some contextual background for his political views and his government service. He pointed out that –

although he never graduated from high school – he was hired as a computer system analyst by the **Central Intelligence Agency** (CIA) and eventually was trained as a spy. He was involved in several overseas undercover operations in that capacity for the **CIA** and the **NSA**. He further indicated that many of his security system recommendations were adopted by the **NSA**.

When confronting claims that he was a coward, he indicated that after the tragedy of **9/11** in 2001 he entered the Army to become part of their special forces. He unfortunately had to drop out after breaking both legs in boot camp. He added that he wanted to serve and was willing to die for his country. It was after that experience that he began applying for employment in the intelligence community.

When asked if he was planning to return to the United States and "face the music", he answered that he wanted to come home and submit himself to the judicial system that awaits him, but he cannot do so under the present **Espionage Act**. He explained that he would be unable to speak out and mount a full defense to his actions because in spite of what government officials have pronounced the present law will not allow it. The law does not differentiate between those that sold secrets to foreign governments for personal gain and those who return information to the public for the purpose of serving a public interest. His defense would inevitably require access by his defense attorney to classified information that would be denied.

He asserted further that he did go through channels by e-mailing colleagues, his superiors and the **NSA** legal department about his concerns that the **NSA** was overreaching its legal authority by obtaining personal data on U.S. citizens without a warrant. He received no response from his superiors. The legal department advised him "to stop asking questions." His colleagues on the other hand were appalled by his revelations.

When responding to claims that he weakened our national security and was not a patriot, he revealed that he had negotiated agreements with **The Guardian** and **The Washington Post** to not disclose any intelligence that would adversely affect national security. He wanted them to focus on the data collection programs that he opined were unconstitutional and potentially very dangerous to our democracy. These agreements were honored at the time and appear to have had no adverse impact on our nation's security. He confronted the patriot issue by elucidating the difference between someone who blindly follows his government with an individual who is willing to contradict and oppose their government when it makes mistakes or is abusing its power.

He applauded the hard work of the low level employees of the **NSA** and in no way wanted to disparage their contributions to their country. His concerns rested with those in high positions within the agency who were engaged in "power grabs" that were being done without a public debate or the consent of the American people. Snowden added that his observations were recently validated by a federal court review that determined that the surveillance programs were most likely unconstitutional and their scope was Orwellian.

The definition of a security state is one that prioritizes the state and its security interests over all other considerations without any regard of the consequences to the liberties of the individual. This was clearly the paradigm in Nazi Germany and Stalinist Russia. However, all security states are not the same in that their evolution may be influenced by different factors. There are subtler ways of controlling and manipulating public opinion than just brute force as was done in my prior examples. After the revelations of the **NSA** programs appeared in the press, a resurgence in interest of George Orwell's dystopian novel entitled **1984** – regarding a super state called Oceania – was noted by a rise in sales.

The book was intended as a satire of Stalinist Russia, but it also included programs that were primary in Nazi Germany. In essence, the novel confronts issues of infringement of freedom of thought and privacy, as well as censorship and ubiquitous surveillance by government justified by claims of national security. The state is involved in a "perpetual war" with another super state that was being used to justify a constant diversion of labor and resources to defense. This constant state of war allowed the government to validate its power and rationalize the economic inequities that existed.

Oceania was under the control of a privileged inner party elite represented by an individual who was treated as a deity named "big brother" that persecuted all individualism and independent thinking as "thought crimes." These crimes were punishable by a form of spiritual death in that you are reprogrammed to accept the government's pronounced reality or risk becoming an "unperson."

The protagonist, Winston Smith, is an employee of the "Ministry of Truth" which in essence is in charge of propaganda, the media and all entertainment. Its name is misleading in that it has nothing to do with establishing the truth about anything. Winston's duties within the ministry are to edit and revise the historical record so that it is in accordance with the government's version of the past. This is very important for the elite to maintain power. For the government knows, "He who controls the past controls the future. He who controls the present controls the past." The original documents and news reports are incinerated in a "memory hole."

While reviewing the documents, Winston becomes interested in the "true past" which is a crime. His research causes him to cross paths with Julia – a member of an underground group whose purpose is to challenge the government – of which he develops a romantic relationship. Eventually, Winston and Julia are caught and brought to the "Ministry of Love" where both are interrogated and tortured until officers obtain confessions that cause them to betray each other. Their sentence will be death unless they can be reprogrammed.

Officer O'Brien explains to Winston, "We know that no one seizes power with the intention of relinquishing it. Power is not a means; It is an end. One does not establish a dictatorship in order to safeguard a revolution; One makes a revolution in order to establish the dictatorship. The object of persecution is persecution. The object of torture is torture. The object of power is power." He further points out that "black is white" and "2 + 2 = 5." All of these can be true. The author labels this philosophy as "doublethink."

The above reference reminded me of a scene in **JFK** directed by Oliver Stone in which Kevin Costner played James Garrison who was the District Attorney of New Orleans Parish in the 1960s. Garrison – while having lunch with his staff – was discussing the fundamental problem that confronted their investigation of Clay Shaw who was accused of participating in the conspiracy to murder President Kennedy. The concern that plagued his investigation was all the disinformation, fabrication, obfuscation and deception that was being propagated by the CIA and their media assets. This caused his investigative team to use resources on tips that led to nowhere. Garrison told his staff, "We need to think like the CIA. Black is white, and white is black." Nothing could be accepted on face value.

He who controlled the investigation and the flow of information would win the battle for the truth. The CIA controlled the investigation through obstruction and manipulation of the evidence. They, as well as their assets, would bribe, intimidate and in some cases murder witnesses. Many of these deaths were determined by the authorities to be suicides or the result of natural causes.

In any event, Snowden's concerns were well founded in that the historical record – which I am not convinced even he fully appreciated – was replete with examples of government overreach and abuse when the safeguards incorporated within our Constitution were ignored or intentionally circumvented.

The intelligence agencies we are familiar with today are post **World War II** creations that were initially instituted to provide the president with sufficient information to formulate U.S. foreign policy. This became even more critical as the world descended into a Cold War between the West and the East. The **CIA** and **NSA**, as well as the **Federal Bureau of Investigations** (FBI) and **Office of Naval Intelligence** (ONI), slowly expanded their influence and power. By the time President Eisenhower had vainly warned the nation of the "military industrial complex" and its corporate sponsors in his farewell address in January 1961, these agencies had become an essential component of that complex. As the executive branch grew in power as issues related to national security became primary, the other branches became less influential. The separation of powers with the checks and balances the founders intended were constantly under assault by the demands of our growing national security state. The **CIA** and **NSA** were essentially unsupervised as their influence mushroomed in the 1950s.

It is imperative to comprehend who were in positions of power within these agencies and what their objectives were to fully appreciate the threat they posed to our democracy. When the who and why is known, you quickly realize that the dictatorships of Nazi Germany and Stalinist Russia are not just a German or a Russian phenomenon but rather are emblematic of human frailties within all of us. Our political system may not build death camps or employ Stalin type purges to effectuate its agenda, or consolidate its power, for our transformation will be subtle but nevertheless just as effective in controlling our minds and behavior while undermining our fundamental liberty. This is why the **NSA** programs that were collecting data on U.S. citizens is potentially very dangerous. For in the final analysis, the sacrificing of essential liberties for security is a treacherous endeavor that could have catastrophic consequences for future generations. When you consider that these surveillance programs have not resulted in actionable intelligence that enhanced our national security, the sacrifice that our government requests of us seems unnecessary. The programs in place prior to **9/11** did not fail to capture the information required by our government to prevent the tragedy; it was rather the failure of those whose responsibility was to interpret that intelligence that allowed it to occur. Some may say that this intelligence was intentionally ignored for dark policy reasons.

James Jesus Angleton was the Counter Intelligence Chief of the **CIA** from 1954 until 1975 when he was compelled to resign due to revelations to the **Church Committee** that his division administered programs that involved opening the mail of U.S. citizens in violation of the **CIA** charter and U.S. law. He testified that espionage was a "wilderness of mirrors." A treacherous terrain in which "nothing – no identity, no organization, no event – is what it seems." He further stated "It is inconceivable that a secret intelligence arm of the government has to comply with all the overt orders of the government." He believed that his department could obey or not obey orders by our elected officials. This meant he could disregard or even countermand policies he disagreed with while supporting those he opined were in the best interest of the nation.

His friend, Max Corvo, once described Angleton as an "ultra-conservative and a fascist sympathizer." Lisa Pease wrote in Probe Magazine that it was reported that Angleton routinely used information he had gathered through the use of illegal wiretaps to blackmail people into supporting his efforts. She wrote, "No wonder some of the agency associates feared him."

Joseph Trento interviewed Angleton in 1985. He included this interview in his book entitled **The Secret History of the CIA** which was published in 2001 and reissued in 2005. He asked Angleton "How it all went so wrong?" Trento wrote that Angleton responded with no emotion in his voice, but his hand was trembling when he replied "Fundamentally, the founding fathers of U.S. intelligence were liars. The better you lied and the more you betrayed, the more likely you would be promoted. These people attracted and promoted each other. Outside of their duplicity, the only thing they had in common was a desire for absolute power. I did things that, in looking back on my life, I regret. But I was a part of it and I loved being in it ... Allen Dulles, Richard Helms, Carmel Offie and Frank Wisner were the grand masters. If you were in a room with them, you were in a room full of people that you had to believe would deservedly end up in hell." Trento continued that Angleton slowly sipped his tea and added, "I guess I will see them there soon."

Angleton was their colleague and friend, and this is how he described those that transformed the CIA and helped formulate our **Cold War** policy in the 1950s and 1960s. By anyone's account, the **CIA** programs and operations for the most part were an unmitigated disaster. It was as Eisenhower described it "a legacy of ashes" that he left for President Kennedy to confront. Unfortunately for Kennedy, as warned by General Douglas MacArthur, "You are moving into the chicken coup and the chickens are all coming home to roost." President Kennedy tried to grapple with and control the **CIA** and as a result got his head blown off. After all, one does not seize power only to relinquish it later.

If Snowden had not released these classified documents, we would still be blissfully unaware of the constitutional liberties that were incrementally being eroded by a powerful elite within our intelligence community that are unknown to us. Their programs would continue to be protected by claims of national security even though their link would be tenuous at best. As we walked through our malls purchasing items we do not need while driving in vehicles with a multitude of technological wonders that distract us from what is truly important, the republic that our founders secured for us would be transforming in ways that would not benefit the people nor defend the liberties that our national security state was allegedly created to protect. Instead, we would become more like our adversaries than the country that we believed we were born in.

Snowden was not a coward or a traitor. He gave up everything he cared about to defend the liberties he opined that our government was unnecessarily infringing upon in the name of national security. It would have been easier to just stop asking questions as he was advised to do and keep his mouth shut. If he had, he would be in Hawaii with his girlfriend still working for the government as a highly paid computer system analyst. Instead, he resides in a country under the leadership of President Vladimir Putin that represents everything he detests. This is not the actions of a coward but a hero – a patriot!

It would be beneficial for us to remember that our founders were considered traitors by King George III's government. Our founders – as a result – were very wary of central power and argued vehemently whether our nation should even have a permanent professional military. The military industrial complex that now exists would astonish them. They in fact may argue that we have lost the republic they valiantly gave us. The fact that we as a people are discussing these matters gives me hope that our republic will not perish from the earth.

I would like to close with the eloquent warning of Jim Garrison that he iterated in his 1967 Playboy interview. He too was labeled a nut and a narcissist that was dangerous to our society. The reality was different than the caricature that was created by the **CIA** and the mainstream media. In that article, he passionately cautioned us not to be fooled by the reality proffered by our government. In response to the question by the interviewer of how he would characterize his political beliefs, he said:

That's a question I've asked myself frequently, especially

since this investigation started and I found myself in an incongruous and disillusioning battle with agencies of my own government. ... Over the years, I guess I've developed a somewhat conservative attitude – in the traditional libertarian sense of conservatism as opposed to the thumbscrew-and-rack conservatism of the paramilitary right – particularly in regard to the importance of the individual as opposed to the state and the individual's own responsibilities to humanity. I don't think I've ever tried to formulate this into a coherent political philosophy, but at the root of my concern is the conviction that a human being is not a digit; he's not a digit to the state and he's not a digit in the sense that he can ignore his fellow men and his obligations to society.

I was with the artillery supporting the division that took Dachau; I arrived there the day after it was taken, when bulldozers were making pyramids of human bodies outside the camp. What I saw haunted me ever since. Because the law is my profession, I've always wondered about the judges throughout Germany who sentenced men to jail for picking pockets at a time when their government was jerking gold from the teeth of men murdered in gas chambers. I'm concerned about all of this because it isn't a German phenomenon; it is a human phenomenon. It can happen here, because there has been no change and there has been no progress and there has been no increase in understanding on the part of men for their fellow man. What worries me deeply, and I have seen it exemplified in this case, is that we in America are in great danger of slowly evolving into a pro-fascist state. It will be a different kind of fascist state from the one the Germans evolved; theirs grew out of depression and promised bread and work, while ours, curiously enough, seems to be emerging from prosperity. But in the final analysis, it's based on power and on the inability to put human goals and human conscience above the dictates of the state. Its origin can be traced in the tremendous war machine we've built since 1945, the military industrial complex that Eisenhower vainly warned us about, which now dominates every aspect of our life. The power of the states and congress has gradually been abandoned to the executive department, because of war conditions; and we've seen the creation of an arrogant, swollen bureaucratic complex totally unfettered by the checks and balances of the constitution.

In a very real terrifying sense, our government is the CIA and the Pentagon, with the Congress reduced to a debating society. Of course, you can't spot this trend to fascism by casually looking around. You can't look for such familiar signs as the swastika, because they won't be there. We won't build Dachaus and Auschwitzes; the clever manipulation of the mass media is creating a concentration camp of the mind that promises to be far more effective in keeping the populace in line. We're not going to wake up one morning and suddenly find ourselves in gray uniforms goose-stepping off to work. But this isn't the test. The test is: What happens to the individual that dissents? In Nazi Germany, he was physically destroyed; here, the process is more subtle, but the end results can be the same.

I've learned enough about the machinations of the CIA in the past year to know that this is no longer the dream world America I once believed in. The imperatives of the population explosion, which almost inevitably will lessen our belief in the sanctity of the individual human life, combined with the awesome power of the CIA and the defense establishment, seems destined to seal the fate of the America I knew as a child and bring us into a new Orwellian world where the citizen exists for the state and where raw power justifies any and every immoral act. I've always had a

kind of knee-jerk trust in my government's basic integrity, whatever political blunders it may make. But I've come to realize that in Washington, deceiving and manipulating the public are viewed by some as the natural prerogatives of office. Huey Long once said 'Fascism will come to America in the name of anti-fascism.' I'm afraid based on my own experience, that fascism will come to America in the name of national security.

I believe Garrison summed up the threat that our national security state poses to our liberty and our democratic republic as well as anybody. Essentially, in many respects, Garrison and Snowden had similar concerns, although viewing that threat from a different vantage point. It is important to note that Garrison's reputation and his marriage were destroyed because he dared to dissent. He by doing so had committed a "thought crime."

I too used to trust the basic integrity of my government. I believe to continue to do so without sufficient knowledge of the "true past" with a clear appreciation of human frailties is fraught with peril. In addition, we must understand that power that is given or taken without accountability and administered without transparency is dangerous. Therefore, I am not placated, nor comforted, by the assertions of the **NSA** that they are not utilizing the data they have collected inappropriately but are solely using it for the purpose of the public interest. Because I know the past history of intelligence, this has enhanced my ability to comprehend the immediate dangers presented by these clandestine operations.

Snowden in my opinion is no traitor; no more than the voices who confronted Joe McCarthy or challenged our government's proclamations that sending combat troops to Vietnam or Iraq was in our national interest. Andrew Jackson once articulated, "One man with courage is a majority."

Hell's Bottom
(The rise of the Pentagon and the formation of the American Empire)

On September 11, 1941, an event that evidently Osama Bin Laden took note of when setting the date of another act of infamy, the ground at Hell's Bottom began its transformation from a swamp to what would become after the war the symbol of American military power. This project's humble initiative by President Franklin Delano Roosevelt (FDR) was to build a structure that contained all our military branches under one roof. FDR's hopeful vision was an attempt to unify them as war raged in Europe and Asia, threatening to drag us into another World War. A war that Roosevelt recognized we continued to ignore at our own peril.

He eloquently spoke of those dangers as early as 1937 in a speech in Chicago that historians have referred to as his "Quarantine Speech." Roosevelt tactfully described the precarious situation in the world that had significant conse-quences for our security without fully tipping his hand that he had already concluded that in time we would have to enter the fray. He stated "War is a contagion, whether it be declared or undeclared. It can engulf states and peoples remote from the original scene of hostilities." He, however, felt politically trapped by the pervasive view of isolationism that dominated the political landscape of the time. A view that we had been duped by European intrigue and military competition when we needlessly sacrificed resources and lives for their failure to peacefully co-exist in World War I. A large majority of the public and the leaders in Washington were determined not to be drawn into another European war and once again have to bail them out.

Japan's infamous surprise attack on **Pearl Harbor** on December 7, 1941, settled the debate on whether the Axis powers, Germany, Italy and Japan, were a threat – to not only our allies –

but our nation's national security interests as well. As FDR became more involved in the planning and monitoring of our military campaigns in the Pacific, North Africa and Europe, and as his health slowly declined, those that were entrusted with the project began to usurp his limited vision and pursued appropriations from Congress that would permit the design and construction of a building that became the edifice of what President Eisenhower labelled the "military industrial complex." When the building was completed in January 1943, it was named the Pentagon because of its shape as clearly seen from the sky. The Pentagon was the biggest manmade structure until it was surpassed by the completion of the World Trade Towers which were built on the tip of Manhattan in the early 1970s. When the towers tragically collapsed by the design of a small group of terrorists, blinded by hate and obsessed with thoughts of revenge for betrayals not understood at the time, the Pentagon regained its title as the largest building in the world.

FDR, Winston Churchill and Joseph Stalin met in **Yalta** in February 1943 to discuss a multitude of subjects related to their war aims. The most prominent for the Russians was the establishment of a second front. Although the tide was turning against the massive German war machine after their disastrous defeat at Stalingrad, the Germans were able to mount an offensive in the spring of that year. The largest tank battles in history occurred during that campaign. The Russians courageously held the line and continued to combat 200 German divisions at a tremendous cost to their resources and human lives. The Eastern Front had witnessed some of the most brutal and barbaric battles in history that had been ruthlessly waged ever since June 1941 when **Operation Barbarossa** was launched by Hitler. As the Wehrmacht reluctantly retreated, its leaders authorized a scorched earth policy which devastated what was left of Russia's farms, towns and cities. They also mercilessly butchered and raped the Russian people. In comparison, the allied troops in the west were pitted against only 10 German divisions and in some cases much less. FDR was sensitive to this and argued for the acceleration of a plan to invade Northern Europe. Churchill, on the other hand, opined that if we attacked German forces in France too soon it could result in a humiliating defeat which could undermine the morale of their troops. The disaster of the **Dieppe Raid** weighed heavily on their thoughts as they strategized at Yalta. In the end, Churchill had successfully argued for an assault in what he called the soft underbelly of Europe. But first, he contended that they needed to defeat Field Marshall Rommel in North Africa to prevent the German's from gaining control of the rich oil fields that they desperately needed to fuel their massive armored divisions and the Luftwaffe (German Airforce).

Critics of Churchill have suggested that he also wanted to protect the colonial interests of the British Empire. In addition, he may have anticipated that a delay in the formation of a second front in the West would allow Hitler and Stalin more time to destroy each other. It was no secret at the time that Churchill did not trust Stalin any more than he did Hitler. His alliance with Russia was a necessary evil that he tolerated as long as it continued to assist British national interests such as their survival. Roosevelt, to the contrary, confidently surmised that he could control Stalin with tactful diplomacy and by his charm. For Churchill, FDR was deluding himself, for in his estimate, there was no chance of building trust and allegiance with a psychopath. He also fervently believed, as did most at the time, including many American military leaders, that communism was just as big a threat to world liberty as was fascism.

The other issues that were discussed at Yalta pertained to the fulfillment of the principles espoused in the **Atlantic Charter** of 1941. Roosevelt and Churchill wanted assurances from Stalin that Eastern Europe would be granted autonomy after Germany had been defeated. Stalin argued that he was willing to agree to this with exception to those parts of Poland he had obtained when he consummated the **Non-Aggression Pact** with Hitler in 1939. He pointed out that Germany in the first half of the twentieth century had invaded Russia twice with devastating consequences for his country by travelling through Poland. He was determined to have a buffer zone between Russia and Germany that would provide his nation with sufficient warning of future military aggression by the Germans. They also negotiated an agreement that Russia would enter the war against Japan three months after the defeat of German forces.

The execution of **Operation Overlord** which constituted that largest amphibious campaign in history finally provided the second front that the Russians had been requesting for years. The landings in Normandy were a brilliant triumph for the military planners who devised the operation. As commander of all Western allied forces, General Eisenhower's reputation benefited significantly as the troops valiantly began to get a foothold on what had been called the fortress of Europe. He would ride this success all the way to the White House in 1952. The day of June 6, 1944, is fondly remembered as D-Day.

As allied troops pushed into the farmland of France and took control over the coastal towns and villages, it increasingly became apparent to the commanders of German forces who was going to win the war. Because the allies had agreed on terms of unconditional surrender which Hitler never did assent to, the war continued until Berlin had been destroyed by allied bombings and was physically occupied by Russian troops. The Russians lost 500,000 taking the capital of Nazi Germany.

Roosevelt died of a brain hemorrhage in April 1945 where he was convalescing at Warm Springs, Georgia. Ever since he had contracted Polio in his early twenties while swimming at his retreat at Campobello, he occasionally bathed in the warm healing waters of Georgia fed by underground springs. He did not live to see the surrender of Germany which occurred in May.

Stalin who was described by American diplomats as stoic and without emotion uncharacteristically with a trembling voice and a tear in his eye tendered his condolences to George F. Kennan, the U.S. Ambassador to Russia, for the passing of Roosevelt. Just maybe, FDR's charm was having the effect that Churchill had dismissed as impossible and naïve. The death of FDR, as it did with Lincoln, had profound consequences over the long awaited peace and the restructuring of the international community. The joy of victory quickly was replaced with mistrust and suspicion that devolved into a **Cold War** between the West and the East.

Vice President Truman's assent into the presidency was not as smooth as he had hoped. He quickly learned how much FDR had kept from him, regarding many of our top secret programs. One could only imagine what his initial thoughts were as he was briefed on the **Manhattan Project** which was monitored by Lieutenant General Leslie Groves, Jr. and supervised by Dr. Robert Oppenheimer at Los Alamos in New Mexico for the purpose of developing the atom bomb. The success of this highly classified scientific endeavor that had been significantly aided by Albert Einstein's formulas created options for the United States in its war with Japan. The Japanese would eventually surrender in August 1945.

Prior to their surrender, Truman had his first and only opportunity to size up Stalin at **Potsdam**. Churchill initially joined the conference that was convened from July 17 through to August 2, 1945. When he and the conservatives were defeated, the newly elected Prime Minister, Clement Attlee, represented British interests for the remainder of the negotiations. The discussions included post war order, peace treaties and the rebuilding of most of the civilized world in Europe and Asia.

Before Truman was made aware of the successful detonation of the atom bomb in New Mexico, he got Stalin to reaffirm the commitment he made at Yalta to enter the Asian war three months after the defeat of Germany. However, Truman, unlike

Roosevelt, did not trust Stalin and was very concerned about the position that Stalin had taken as he maintained Russian troops in the Balkans, Poland, Hungary, Bulgaria and Czechoslovakia. Stalin essentially reneged on his agreement to withdraw from these countries after the conclusion of the war. He argued that Western Europe had launched assaults against his country on multiple occasions and that these nations were necessary to provide a buffer zone against aggression and that they were a legitimate sphere of Soviet influence. Truman, to say the least, was not impressed with Stalin's position. As a consequence, Truman's perceptions began to harden into mistrust and fear of Russian ambitions.

When Truman was apprised of the triumphant detonation of the atom bomb, his attitude significantly changed from apprehension to one of confidence. He boasted to Stalin of the achievement of American scientists in their development of the most destructive weapon ever built by mankind. Stalin was not impressed and showed little reaction to Truman's announcement. Unbeknownst to Truman, Stalin had infiltrated the secret project and was well informed on the development of the heinous weapon. He, however, was outraged with his advisors after his meeting with Truman because he had not been told the weapon had been successfully detonated. Truman throughout the rest of the conference used the bomb as a club to intimidate the Soviet leader into his way of thinking. Berlin, for example, was divided into four zones; British, French, Russian and American quadrants were negotiated. Stalin who had objected to the French zone because they had not earned it in battle was forced by Truman to assent. In addition, Germany was divided into two nations, East and West Germany. This was done to prevent the German people from becoming a threat to their neighbors in the future.

After Potsdam, Truman immediately recognized that he had made a mistake by getting the Russian leader to reaffirm his commitment to enter the war against Japan. Based on that agreement, the Russian forces would be attacking one million Japanese troops stationed in Manchuria by mid-August. He feared that if Stalin's army advanced into Manchuria and Korea they would continue to occupy these regions and prop up puppet regimes as they had done in Eastern Europe. This would significantly threaten U.S. strategic interests in the region. This led to a debate between the hawks who wanted to use the bomb on Japan to expedite their capitulation, and the doves in Washington who thought the use of the bomb served no legitimate military purpose. And more importantly, they argued its use would be immoral. Many contended that it would be a travesty for this nation to go down in history as the first to use this evil weapon. The hawks countered that if an invasion of Japan was launched it could cost as much as 600,000 lives.

While this debate continued in Washington, American intelligence who had broken the Japanese military coded communications were listening to messages sent to Moscow seeking their assistance in facilitating a negotiated settlement with the Americans. Their primary demands were that Emperor Hirohito would not be tried as a war criminal and that he would be allowed to remain in his present position. They also wanted to maintain the sacred land on which his palace resided. The Emperor was considered a deity in Japanese culture and for them his residence and position was similar to the Christian's worship of Jesus and reverence for the city of Jerusalem. All of these communications were relayed to the military command of General Douglas McArthur who forwarded this information on to Washington.

General McArthur and Allied Commander Eisenhower – who clearly could not be categorized as doves – objected to the use of the weapon. They opined that the Japanese were on the verge of surrendering and that the weapon served no valid military objective. They also argued that it would scar the legacy of our nation permanently. Dr. Oppenheimer who had been a proponent of developing the weapon would join others such as Einstein in his opposition to its use. Unfortunately, his well-argued letters were intercepted by Lieutenant General Groves who sided with the hawks on this matter. Truman was surrounded by powerful advocates for dropping the bomb. Secretary of State James F. Byrnes, Secretary of the Navy James Forrestal and Secretary of War Henry Stimson dominated the discussion in Washington and insured that opponents, such as former Vice President Henry Wallace, had little opportunity to voice their concerns with the President.

Truman eventually decided in favor of the hawks. The question then for Truman and his advisors was where and under what circumstances should the bomb be used. They contemplated dropping it in a remote site while Japanese military leaders witnessed the horrific spectacle of destruction as the signature mushroom cloud climbed thousands of feet above them. They also considered whether the bomb should be dropped on a military target or on a Japanese city. Unfortunately for humanity and the nation's legacy, he chose the latter.

The bomb named "Little Boy" was dropped on the unsuspecting city of **Hiroshima** on August 6, 1945. The bomb in a matter of seconds incinerated 80,000 civilians and many more would die later of radiation poisoning; nothing but their shadows remained burned into the pavement and cement walls, revealing what they had been doing moments before their death. The Empire of Japan did not immediately surrender. As the Russian troops prepared for the invasion of Northern Manchuria, Truman agreed to drop a second bomb named "Fat Man" on the city of **Nagasaki** on August 9th. This bomb instantly killed 40,000 and flattened the city in the blink of an eye.

The colossal Russian force launched its assault against the Japanese on August 9th, causing them to immediately retreat from their fortified positions. The Japanese announced their surrender on August 15, 1945.

The mythology promoted in many generic history books is that the use of the atomic bombs avoided the need for a very hazardous invasion of Japan and was the impetus for their surrender. The reality as pointed out by Japanese historian Tsuyoshi Hasegawa was that "The Soviet entry into the war played a much greater role than the atomic bombs in inducing Japan to surrender because it dashed all hope that Japan could terminate the war through Moscow's mediation." The Japanese were also very aware of the brutality of Russian forces and their defeat of what had been the most intimidating military power at that time when German forces surrendered in May. Because of this, the Japanese military command feared the Russians more than the Americans. In addition, they had significant concerns that if Stalin's military marched into the sacred land upon which the emperor's palace was located they might refuse to return it after the war. This would be a devastating assault on Japanese heritage and culture.

Many U.S. military leaders, as well as former President Herbert Hoover, also argued that the conventional bombing campaign had already had devastating effects on the people and infrastructure of Japan. The fire-bombing of Tokyo for example with the use of incendiary bombs that contained chemicals such as napalm not only burnt the city to the ground but killed over 100,000 civilians. This horrific scenario was repeated in many cities throughout Japan during the war. The atomic bombs were in essence an extension of a bombing campaign that already had achieved its military objectives.

The most prominent reasons I suspect the bombs were dropped were to end the Pacific war expeditiously to prevent Soviet forces from occupying territory that U.S. leaders feared they would refuse to relinquish after the war concluded. The destruction of Nagasaki was a warning to Moscow that we had more than one bomb and that we were prepared to use it more than it was an attempt at securing Japan's capitulation.

The surrender ceremony was held on September 2, 1945, aboard the battleship the *USS Missouri*. General McArthur commanded an interim government until Japan was able to write and approve their new constitution which ironically not only prohibited a large military but guaranteed universal health care to all its citizens. The lessons of the war for the United States was interpreted differently, causing us to move in a conservative direction that was determined to reverse the accomplishments of the **New Deal** and to build a defense establishment that over time would have no rival.

Russia by the end of the war had suffered 27 million dead and countless casualties. A third of their country was destroyed. To compare the devastation by using an American context, it was equivalent of everything east of Chicago. As Stalin solidified his control of Eastern Europe, Russia and its satellite states became the Soviet Union. Although they remained a powerful military presence on the continent of Europe, most of their resources and efforts were focused on rebuilding their destroyed infrastructure and anemic economy. The United States in contrast was essentially unscathed with exception to the damage caused at **Pearl Harbor** and remote Alaskan islands that are part of the Aleutian chain that jut out into the Bering Sea. In addition, we suffered approximately 400,000 deaths. We in essence emerged from the war with a robust economy that witnessed the growth of a huge middle class.

The **San Francisco Conference** of 1946 set up the structure of the **United Nations**. It was agreed that its headquarters was to be built in New York City. The Americans were riding a wave of popular support around the world for their contribution in defeating the Axis powers, as well as their promotion of liberty and peace. We had a marvelous opportunity to shape a post-war world that respected international law and supported the emergence of many nations that wanted autonomy and freedom.

We were in a position to guide these movements and transform them into a world in which the strong were just and the poor were secure. A world in which war was to be deterred and peaceful competition was to be encouraged. This hope that emerged from such great devastation and death would be squandered as we fell victim to the dictates of power born out of mistrust and fear. We had already forgotten the wisdom of Roosevelt in his first inaugural when he said, "...the only thing we have to fear is fear itself – nameless, unreasoning, unjustified terror which paralyzes needed efforts to convert retreat into advance." One could argue we did advance, but I would contend in the wrong direction.

There had been an irrational fear of communism by corporate elites who influenced politics in Washington and other democratic capitals such as London and Berlin ever since the **Bolshevik Revolution** of 1917. The dread of this type of uprising by the people who were not benefitting from capitalistic economic structures for instance influenced the decision of the leadership of the Weimar Republic in Germany to form an alliance with Hitler and his Nazi party to prevent communists from dominating the politics of the Reichstag. A decision that they immediately regretted as Hitler and his cohorts began to solidify their power. This great anxiety of centrally planned economies was also present in Italy, France, Britain, Spain and the United States. In the case of Italy and Spain, they turned to fascist governments as well. In fact, the rise of Benito Mussolini was an inspiration for Hitler to take power in Germany. Francisco Franco in Spain initiated a civil war in 1936 that was aided by German military support that resulted in his coronation in April 1939. Europe by the late 1930s had decided to move in the direction of authoritarian regimes who consolidated their power by forming symbiotic alliances with their military establishments that they used to oppress and intimidate their internal foes. In the cases of Mussolini and Hitler, their ambitions were to expand their nations and create formidable empires that spanned the globe. In essence, these fascist movements were extreme conservative attempts to block the spread of communism.

The dismissal by many capitalists of Marx and Engels' **Communist Manifesto** published in 1848 was predictable for the book focused on the exploitation of the people by a small elite who lived like Gods off of the sweat and toil of the masses. This was Marx's observation of the Czarist Regime in Russia that inspired their book. He and his co-author were not offering another form of elitist control as eventually occurred in Russia and China, but rather were attempting to offer a model of government that would benefit the many not just the few. Stalin and Moa usurped this utopian vision by creating another form of dictatorship from the far left whose power was just as oppressive and brutal as their fascist counterparts.

The reason that corporate elites preferred the fascist regimes is that business entrepreneurship, as long as it benefitted the goals of the party elite, remained private while in so called communist governments their capital and assets were taken over by the state.

This certainly elucidated why so many American financiers and corporate giants before the war invested in the emerging economy under Hitler. Hitler could not have built his vast war machine without their money, their technology and their manufacturing plants. For instance, Allen Dulles was very familiar with German companies such as the chemical giant I.G. Farben, who developed the gases used in Nazi death camps, because of his stint at Sullivan and Cromwell.

This was the largest law firm on Wall Street in the 1930s and 1940s that represented many American and German companies that fueled the rise of the Third Reich. He thus knew many of the Nazi leaders in government and in business and found it easier to socialize with them than some of our allies such as Russia. He strongly believed, as did General Patton and others in

Washington, that after the war communism would be the greatest threat to American security and to the building of an American empire. Because of this, he solicited James Jesus Angleton who was stationed in Italy to create "rat lines" that facilitated the emigration of many Nazi leaders to South and North America. In return, they supported their efforts to defeat communism. They were able to assist Nazis such as Karl Wolff an SS officer who was the liaison between SS commander Heinrich Himmler and Adolph Hitler to avoid their fate at **Nuremburg**.[4] They also recruited Reinhard Gehlen, the head of German intelligence on the eastern front, to join their crusade to combat what became the Soviet Union.[5] They even contemplated saving Himmler, but he was murdered before he could get to the safety of their network. This network was in essence frustrating and interfering with other intelligence operations within the military to capture these Nazi war criminals and bring them to justice.[6]

Dulles was committing treason by negotiating with German leaders in violation of Roosevelt's terms of unconditional surrender as agreed upon by the allies at Yalta. Although Dulles' rat lines may also have been treasonous, the Office of Strategic Services and other agencies were assisting Nazi scientists out of Germany to deprive Russia of the technology they were developing during the war such as the V-2 Rockets and jet propelled fighter planes. Some of these skilled scientists in future years were assigned to the Apollo Program and to the CIA's Special Operation Division supervised by Agent Frank Olson. This program was code named **Operation Paperclip**.

In the United States, Roosevelt's inauguration in 1933 caused significant anxiety among the bankers and industrialists because they perceived his prescriptions for the nation's economic crisis as dangerous to their influence and power, as well as a threat to their lavish lifestyles. This was so intense that business leaders who were members of the **American Liberty League** decided to plan a coup to overthrow his leftist government. In furtherance of their goal, they contacted General Smedley Butler – the most decorated Marine in history – to lead their 500,000-man force derived from members of the American Legion. The reason the general was chosen was to provide some legitimacy to what was in essence an illegal act. This bizarre conspiracy was brought to the attention of the Un-American Activities Committee in the house when General Butler testified about this treasonous plan that for the most part has slipped into the shadows of history. Roosevelt's New Deal was to the conservative right a socialist, and to some even a communist, solution to the economic stressors of the 1930s such that they were determined to dismantle it as soon as they could regain control over the political apparatus of the country. This is exactly what happened after the war.

Roosevelt's declaration to develop a second bill of rights that included the fundamental right of work, a home and health care for all was submerged beneath a wave of anti-communistic fervor that attempted to wash away the accomplishments of his New Deal. His global vision of France, Britain, China, Russia and the United States as the policeman of the world working in cooperation to reinforce international law to prevent another World War was also lost to the demons of human frailty. This crusade founded on fear, mistrust, pride and power led the nation down a treacherous path that we have not entirely recovered from.

By the 1950s, we had the witch hunts of Senator Joseph McCarthy and his side kick Roy Cohn that ruined the careers of many talented and distinguished Americans through innuendo and fictitious allegations. The congress over the veto of President Truman passed the **Internal Security Act** of 1950. This draconian act attempted to eradicate communist influence in American politics and society through coercion and intimidation. The act is generally regarded by legal scholars as one of the most egregious assaults upon freedom of speech and association in our history.

It earned this dubious distinction by making it illegal to pursue a communist agenda while requiring all communist organizations to register with the U.S. Attorney General. Members of these organizations were denied employment in government or in private firms that had contracted with the federal government. Their members were harassed and placed on watch lists as they were surveilled by Hoover's FBI.

Churchill in a speech he orated in 1946 while visiting with Truman in Fulton Missouri had described Stalin's refusal to adhere to his agreement at Yalta as an "iron curtain" that had fallen over Eastern Europe; an iconic phrase that would linger throughout the Cold War era. President Truman was very distressed by what Russia had done in Eastern Europe by propping up puppet regimes that were clearly influenced by Moscow. This was also done in North Korea that eventually led to war on that peninsula. Truman surmised that Russian ambitions went beyond their present holdings and consequently posed a serious security threat to the West. His administration was dominated by hawks that began to steer the President toward a military solution to this perceived threat.

Berlin would remain a source of tension throughout the Cold War. It was an island surrounded by the oppressive communist regime of East Germany. This tension almost erupted into another global conflict when Stalin had ordered the blockade of the city to prevent Western access to their zones that had been sanctioned by a treaty. This led to the **Berlin Airlift** of 1948 that was so successful the Russian and East German leaders eventually removed the barriers. West Germany and especially Berlin became the bulwark of Western resolve during the Cold War. Because of this, the Truman administration decided it was important to rebuild West Germany and make it a powerful example of Western economic principles that when compared with the anemic economy of East Germany would reaffirm to the world the fallacy of their ideas. This resulted in the **Marshall**

Plan in which millions of dollars were invested to jump-start the economy and repair the infrastructure damaged during the war.

Truman's efforts to confront this threat was memorialized in the passage of the **National Security Act** of 1947. This act merged the Department of War and the Department of the Navy into the National Military Establishment headed by the Secretary of Defense. The Act also established the National Security Council (NSC) which was entrusted with constructing a cohesive national security policy for the executive branch. The NSC advisor would become part of the cabinet. In addition, the most ominous segment of this legislation was the creation of the Central Intelligence Agency (CIA) that Allen Dulles and others had been proposing for years. The CIA, however, was not initially the clandestine operational power that it eventually became under the leadership of Dulles in the 1950s. It was fundamentally an intelligence gathering agency that assimilated and interpreted information that was presented to the president to assist his ability to formulate U.S. foreign policy. This new Agency was assigned other powers that were not defined in its founding charter. This was a door that was left open that others who envisioned a more ambitious and aggressive Agency would walk through when the opportunity emerged. And finally, this Act formally set up the Joint Chiefs of Staff (JCS).

The year of 1947 also witnessed the issuance of the **Truman Doctrine** after communist infiltrators tried to influence and manipulate elections in Greece and Turkey. Truman had declared that U.S. military forces would come to the aid of nations that were preyed upon by communist subversion and aggression. While all of this was occurring, U.S. Ambassador to the Soviet Union, George F. Kennan, sent a telegram to Washington that set forth his observations of the internal politics and aspirations of Soviet leaders. He indicated that the Soviets were like a wind-up toy that would continue to move forward until its progress was impeded. He surmised from these observations that the West needed to contain them economically, politically and militarily. Paul Nitze who was the head of the NSC study group used this memo to write **NSC Report 68**. This was the origin of the **Containment Policy** that was approved by the President in 1949. This policy was quickly seized upon by the hawks and transformed, much to the dismay of Kennan, into a military doctrine. This resulted in the building of bases all over the world, the eventual deployment of land based nuclear missiles in Turkey and Italy and the formation of collective security treaties. The North Atlantic Treaty Organization (NATO) was negotiated in 1949, and the South East Asia Treaty Organization (SEATO) was consummated in 1955 under the Eisenhower administration. Russia responded by forming the Warsaw Pact.

The battle to win over the allegiance of the developing world necessitated a more active and aggressive intelligence agency that could compete with their Soviet counterpart, the KGB. These covert operations inevitably required illegal and immoral actions that U.S. leaders could not be directly implicated in. Allen Dulles, Frank Wisner and many in the military, including members of Truman's cabinet such as Secretary of Defense James Forrestal, were staunch proponents of granting specific powers to the CIA that included clandestine operations that the government could plausibly deny knowledge of. Truman relented and signed **NSC 10/2** in 1948. Although Truman's vision of the CIA still remained more limited than Dulles, he had paved the way for the growth of an agency that would be the source of Cold War intrigue with tragic results for many countries seeking freedom and democracy. By the mid-1950s, the CIA was involved in sabotage, covert para-military operations, extraordinary rendition, assassination, dissemination of propaganda and the overthrowing of legitimate governments.

The foundation of our National Security Complex was complete with exception to a few additions. The National Security Agency (NSA) was established in 1952 by Truman.

President Eisenhower authorized **NSC 5412** to expand covert para-military operations that he opined would allow him to reduce our conventional forces. Eisenhower also wanted to invest heavily in our nuclear arsenal to use them in what was called nuclear brinkmanship. He then signed **NSC 5412/2** which was referred to by Colonel Fletcher Prouty as the secret team. This small group within the executive branch was to provide some oversight to covert activities. This purpose was sabotaged by Dulles and his cabal in that their influence and power continued to grow, as it did in the NSA, with little supervision. This lack of accountability and the wake of destruction to American prestige around the globe as a supporter of peace and international law, and its undermining of our Constitution and individual liberty, would all be extracted from the dark corners of our government and brought into the light during the **Church Committee Hearings** of the mid-1970s.

Under the stewardship of Allen Dulles and the support of his brother John Foster Dulles, the stoic and austere Secretary of State for Eisenhower, the CIA quietly assumed its role as a major component of the secret government. Its influence and insidious power infiltrated every agency of government, including the Federal Bureau of Investigations, the State Department, the Congress, the Department of Defense and the entire executive branch. They even formed symbiotic alliances with the media to advance its influence over domestic and foreign policy. Under the umbrella of national security and empowered by the doctrine of plausible deniability, the Agency engaged in what Truman later regretfully referred to as their "strange activities" or what Dulles and Helms fondly named the "department of dirty tricks." These euphemisms masked repugnant actions that were conducted by the covert side of the Agency. These actions included murder, kidnapping, alliances with organized crime and regime change. The governments they ousted were democratically elected by their people such as Mohammad Mossadegh in Iran (1953), Jacobo Arbenz in Guatemala (1954), Achmed Sukarno in Indonesia (1965) and Salvador Allende in Chile (1973). These are just a few examples of the CIA's exploits that had tragic consequences for the people of those nations. In each case, these social democrats who were elected by their people were replaced by brutal dictators or a military junta.

The defense establishment along with its corporate sponsors also had a tremendous impact on government policy and our nation's reputation around the world. Prior to World War II, our nation after a war reverted back to producing consumer goods. Most of the soldiers that in many cases were drafted or were volunteers returned to their communities and resumed their civilian lives. Our department of war was always reduced to pre-war levels. The primary purpose of our military and navy was the defense of the nation. They were used, however, on numerous occasions to squash dissent in Latin and South America against what was perceived to be a threat to U.S. strategic and corporate interests. These were commonly referred to as the "Banana Wars" that General Smedley Butler testified to in Congress. Otherwise, military spending was limited and our influence in most regions of the world was over shadowed by the European powers that had colonial possessions around the globe. We were a growing economic giant but were not considered an elite military power. After the defeat of the Axis powers, this all changed.

Stalin was a dangerous and unpredictable foe. He had murdered and imprisoned more people than even Hitler. He was paranoid and obsessed with maintaining control of the government. Even comrades or close friends could not escape his wrath if he perceived them as a threat to his power. Nevertheless, he had no ambition of launching his colossal conventional army against Western Europe. He had enough to contend with internally with his political and economic problems, as well as his supervision of all the satellite states that he manipulated and controlled like puppets. This, however, was not how our military commanders and national security officers interpreted his motivation and ambition. They too in many ways were paranoid about future Soviet aggression that they strongly believed was inevitable. Our first Secretary of Defense James Forrestal had terrific influence on our emerging post-war defense policy. He, along with Paul Nitze, convinced Truman of this growing Soviet threat. By the 1950s, the defense complex and its co-sponsors engaged in what C. Wright Mills, a dissident professor of sociology, referred to as a form of "crackpot realism." He elaborated in his book **The Power Elite** published in 1956 that "...in the name of realism they have constructed a paranoid reality all their own."[7] It may be a coincidence but Secretary Forrestal was clinically diagnosed as suffering from paranoia. His illness progressively advanced to the point that he committed suicide while being treated at Bethesda Naval Hospital in Maryland in April 1949.

As the military assumed the primary role of enforcing Truman's containment policy, their budgets continued to grow. Many events reinforced this emphasis on defense. The fall of China to the communists, and the successful test of an atomic bomb by the Soviets in 1949 and the invasion of South Korea by the North in 1950 reaffirmed in the minds of Washington policy makers that the communists had plans of world domination. They were so blind and subservient to their political dogmas that they missed an opportunity to thaw the Cold War when Stalin died in 1953.

President Eisenhower was inaugurated in January of that same year. Before the year ended, his administration was able to negotiate a ceasefire that divided Korea at the thirty-eighth parallel. He was determined to maintain the peace but was also adamant that containment of the communist powers was not enough. His Secretary of State John Foster Dulles was the perfect choice to impose Eisenhower's policy to roll back communism where it had entrenched itself. He intended to do this by investing heavily in our nuclear forces and by expanding our covert para-military capacity. This view was reinforced when the CIA with minimal cost and loss of life was able to overthrow the governments in the Philippines, Iran and Guatemala. The fact that these were democratically elected governments apparently did not concern him.

Eisenhower also was hoping that he could cut the growing costs of defense by reducing the necessity of maintaining a large conventional force. Instead, if Soviet or Chinese subverts endangered our allies, we would threaten to launch our whole nuclear arsenal, erasing them from the face of the earth. This policy of massive retaliation, a game of nuclear brinkmanship, under an analysis most favorable to the administration could be considered a bluff and under a more critical inquiry could be categorized as recklessly dangerous.

By the late 1950s, the dynamics of the Cold War encouraged the growth of an unfettered and fanatical anti-communistic executive branch that increasingly subverted the concepts of checks and balances as designed by our forefathers. The power of our national security complex was Orwellian and as such posed a serious threat to our democracy. Our nation's first war hero and president, George Washington, warned that a large army was "inauspicious to liberty" and was "particularly hostile to republican liberty." This is why our founders were not inclined to establish a large military complex because of its innate threat to the government they had created as witnessed by the experience of European history. All of this was either ignored or overlooked by those who were staunch supporters of the growth of our military.

At the end of his administration, Eisenhower would learn of its hazards when his last attempt at peace was thwarted by opponents within his government that opposed his desire to negotiate a Comprehensive Test Ban Treaty with the Soviets. In anger and frustration, he included in his farewell speech his otiose warning of the power of our "military industrial complex" and its cheerleaders which consisted of large defense firms who had gotten fat on government contracts. Because of this, Eisenhower left a foreign policy teetering on disaster as events in Cuba, Indonesia, Vietnam and Laos threatened peace in a larger sense and our commonsense in a more limited view. John Kenneth Galbraith wisely questioned this "crackpot realism" when he asked how this impoverished nation with no navy or air force that was situated thousands of miles from our most western shore could threaten the most powerful nation on earth. Of course, he was referring to Vietnam. This same astute observation could be applied to Laos and Cuba as well.

President Kennedy was a man of his time in some ways and was ahead of his generation in others. He clearly viewed the communists as a potential threat to U.S. security interests and to peace. As such, he came to power with a firm belief that our defense capacity had to be beyond doubt to deter aggression by our adversaries, but more importantly to preserve the peace. Kennedy, however, was not a traditional cold warrior nor was he an uncritical backer of the domino theory. A theory that forecasted the fall of South East Asia if only one nation in that region was overrun by the communists. He had to support many of these concepts in public because of the mass hysteria on this subject by those in power, in the media and in the general public that supported these dogmas. It would be political suicide not to have done so. In private, he often questioned these concepts. His policies in Laos and Vietnam attest to his true beliefs on these fictitious edicts. In addition, his overall view of the nationalists, whether they be democratic, socialist or communist, was not of concern to him as long as they were neutral in the Cold War, supported their people and were not a threat to their neighbors.

This was never more evident than his willingness to meet with President Sukarno of Indonesia at the White House in April 1961 who Eisenhower had considered a communist. His relationship with the recalcitrant founder of Indonesian independence grew into mutual respect. Although relatively unknown by the American public, Indonesia has the fourth largest population in the world, including the largest Muslim population residing within its borders. It is composed of 13,000 islands in the southern Pacific region.

Kennedy in his first year in office was instrumental in assisting Sukarno in obtaining sovereignty over "West Papua/West Irian" from the Dutch and corporate giant Freeport Sulphur.[8] The executives at Freeport Sulphur were "aghast at the potential loss of 'El Dorado'."[9] The company after having much of its assets expropriated by Castro's regime was hoping to recoup its losses with the rich gold deposits discovered in the West Irian region. British MI6 and the CIA were determined to maintain control of these extremely profitable gold mines and oil fields that had been discovered in that area which apparently were not revealed to Kennedy or Sukarno. In addition, as in the Congo, Dulles was determined to prevent the Soviets from gaining access to these riches and was attempting to overthrow the leftist government that had formed an alliance with the PKI which was the Communist Party of Indonesia.

Since the CIA had tried to foist a coup against his government in 1958, Sukarno had turned to the Soviets for military aid and support. Kennedy understood this and was trying to entice his return to the Western camp. He negotiated with Sukarno and secretly supported the UN's effort led by Secretary General Dag Hammarskjold to help unify the nation that the Dutch, the British and the CIA were trying to split.[10] The reason this alliance was covert is that Kennedy did not want to openly defy the interests of two NATO allies. Hammarskjold and Kennedy's long term objective was to terminate the colonial control of the Dutch. In return, the President opined that he could develop a powerful alliance with Indonesia that would enhance the image of the U.S. as a partner of those indigenous peoples seeking freedom and independence. This wave of goodwill might also compliment his plan to disengage from Vietnam, as well as open the door to China a decade before Nixon and Kissinger accomplished this in 1972. Therefore, he adamantly needed Sukarno, who continued to be a very popular figure in the region, to remain in power in pursuit of this larger objective. His wife Dewi for instance attracted significant media attention and was considered one of the most beautiful women in the world. Dulles was zealously opposed to Sukarno's government and was actively sabotaging Hammarskjold and Kennedy's policy.[11]

Hammarskjold was traveling in a DC-6 airplane on the night of September 18, 1961, to Northern Rhodesia, now Zambia, to meet with Katangese separatist leader, Moise Tshombe, in Ndola when his plane inexplicably crashed as it was approaching the local airport. He was optimistic that this meeting might contribute to the cessation of hostilities in the Congo. All 16 passengers died in the crash. The statements of witnesses and some of the crash site evidence supported foul play but the official investigation ruled it an unfortunate accident. Even at the time many questioned the validity of the conclusions of the investigative authorities, including former President Harry Truman. A New York Times article published on September 20, 1961, had quoted Truman as having stated that "Dag Hammarskjold was on the point of getting something done when they killed him. Notice I said 'when they killed him'." He refused to divulge anything further in hope that the press would instigate their own inquiries.[12]

Decades after this mysterious Cold War tragedy, new information has emerged that appears to corroborate Truman's ominous statement. The United Nation's based on this new evidence formed an investigative commission in 2013 to re-evaluate the cause of the crash that aborted the noble mission by Hammarskjold. The panel concluded that there was "persuasive evidence that the aircraft was subjected to some form of attack or threat as it circled to land at Ndola."[13]

There were apparently witnesses that saw a smaller plane chasing a larger one, as well as gunshot wounds that some of the passengers sustained before the plane crashed. The commission further requested the declassification of specific documents that presently are being held within the archives of MI6 and the NSA.[14] In addition, former President Desmond Tutu of South Africa, while chairing the Truth and Reconciliation Commission in the late 1990s, obtained documents that it released to the public that described the development of a plot to eliminate the UN Secretary General. The documents contained correspondence between South African Military, the CIA and Britain's MI5 security service. One of the letters states "...it is felt that Hammarskjold should be removed. Allen Dulles has promised full cooperation from his people."[15] British intelligence agencies all emphatically denied their involvement in such a plot and have proffered that the documents were forgeries created by the former Soviet Union.[16]

Kennedy praised Hammarskjold as a great statesman who would be profoundly missed. He, however, was undaunted by the tragedy in that he continued to maintain diplomatic channels with Sukarno and to support the peace keeping mission of the UN in the Congo. In fact, Sukarno and Kennedy were negotiating a settlement to the Malaysian-Indonesian conflict that broke out in 1963. Sukarno was wrongly perceived as the aggressor in that war by Congress who decided to significantly reduce American aid to Indonesia. Kennedy believed that he could negotiate a settlement that would be reinforced by his visit to the country. The President also opined that he could get the aid package restored to prior levels. He was a very popular leader with the people of Indonesia and was much admired by Sukarno. On November 20, 1963, as he was leaving for Texas, Sukarno and Kennedy agreed upon a presidential visit in early 1964. In anticipation of this visit, Sukarno was building a retreat suitable for the

President and his wife. After Dallas, the visit was cancelled. Sukarno much like Khrushchev slipped into a deep depression for days.

As the events above demonstrate, Kennedy's evolving policy towards the developing world was drastically different than the Dulles brothers, Nixon and Eisenhower. During his abbreviated administration, he met with 28 African nationalist leaders that included nations that declared themselves neutral in the Cold War and some that professed socialist and even communist principles. Eisenhower considered the neutralist nations only one step removed from being communists and treated them as potential adversaries that Dulles and the CIA were assigned to deal with.

The Eisenhower administration also used American aid as a tool to manipulate and strengthen those countries it favored. For instance, the composition of the aid he sent was generally 70 percent military and 30 percent humanitarian. He demanded that those nations use their enhanced military to join the U.S. efforts to combat communists on the continent. He, however, did not consider Africa very high on our strategic priority list and generally left it to the European colonial powers to exploit and control. To buttress this point, Eisenhower had only met with 8 African leaders in his two terms in office. When he did court these African nationalists such as William Tubman of Liberia, they were in some cases patronized and treated as children. Tubman reported that the main thrust of Eisenhower's policies towards his country had been "very offensive to him and his government" and had insulted the "honor of Liberia."[17]

This condescending view was shared by his National Security Council (NSC) that regarded these emerging nations as too incompetent and weak to resist the overtures of the communists. Thus, they were not prepared to be independent sovereign nations.[18] Vice President Nixon at one point during an NSC meeting observed that "some of the peoples of Africa have been out of the trees for only about 50 years."[19] By 1960, Eisenhower became increasingly hostile to the idea of an independent Africa and referred to this movement to sever the chains of colonialism as a "destructive hurricane."[20]

By the end of his administration, the President became so alarmed by the nationalists that he authorized the assassination of Patrice Lumumba in support of Belgium and U.S. strategic interests in the Democratic Republic of Congo.[21] As it occurred in Indonesia, the American government's belligerent posture towards his nation precipitated in his seeking military and economic support from Moscow. Eisenhower and Dulles clearly did not want the Soviets to get control of the enormous uranium and cobalt deposits in the Katanga province. Kennedy in contrast supported Lumumba and was hoping to assist in the unification of his nation, as well as their independence. Because of this, the CIA felt compelled to murder the nationalist leader before Kennedy's inauguration. He was assassinated on January 17, 1961, just three days before Kennedy took power while in the custody of his political adversaries. On February 13, 1961, Kennedy was informed by telephone of Lumumba's death. Jacques Lowe who was the White House photographer took the iconic picture of Kennedy receiving the tragic news. Kennedy's instantaneous response was one of horror as his hand rubbed his forehead and his eyes closed.[22]

In addition, Eisenhower while meeting with his special group formed by NSC 5412/2 in the summer of 1960 told Allen Dulles that he wanted the Cuban leader "sawed off." A phrase that Dulles understood was an order to assassinate Fidel Castro. These were extraordinary directives authorized by a president in that he was setting a precedent that no other chief executive in our history was known to have ever done.[23]

Kennedy in contrast welcomed this development and was determined to be on the side of history of which he clearly surmised would be in support of Africa's independence. He reversed our aid formula so that the overwhelming amount of assistance from the United States was for humanitarian purposes. He allocated just enough military aid to provide for their defense but not enough to threaten their neighbors. He used diplomacy to dissuade the African leaders of fears that Peace Corp volunteers were CIA agents undercover. His strategic objectives for the continent, as well as Asia, was to undo the American image as a proponent of colonialism and transform it into a friendly partner for those seeking autonomy and freedom. Kennedy felt that our prior policy was too aligned with the past. A past that was quickly fading into antiquity and disfavor. He stated "One finds too many of our representatives toadying to the shorter aims of other western nations, with no eagerness to understand the real hopes and desires of the people to whom they are accredited, too often aligning themselves too definitely with the 'haves' and regarding the action of the 'have nots' as not merely the efforts to cure injustice but something sinister and subversive."[24] With this view, he unequivocally moved to position his administration on the side of the future.

Although he had profound concerns about the Soviets and China, he strongly believed that in the long run our common humanity and our common interests would eclipse our differences. He thus was a strong proponent of making the world "safe for diversity." His vision, however, was stalled as his administration confronted crisis after crisis as a result of his predecessor's prior initiatives. The year 1961 as described by him was a very "mean year."

The **Bay of Pigs** would not only setback his strategy for peace but was also a crash course on the political intrigue and power struggles that existed within the executive branch. His failure to ask the right questions as Dulles, Bissel and General Cabell of the CIA deceived him caused Soviet Premiere Khrushchev to question his resolve and judgment.

The Cuban debacle tainted any hope of achieving any

meaningful understanding between the two leaders at their **Vienne Conference** in early June 1961. Although Kennedy tried to convince Khrushchev that the Cuban matter was a mistake, the Soviet leader was unable to accept the President's explanation. Instead, he viewed him as too young and inexperienced to lead a world power. He entrapped Kennedy in a long diatribe regarding the merits of communism that Kennedy was not prepared to debate. When the discussion did include matters of substance such as Berlin, Khrushchev threatened to negotiate a separate peace treaty with East Germany which would abrogate the rights of France, Britain and the United States to have troops in West Berlin. Kennedy retorted that the United States commitment to defend the interests of its allies would become hollow if the U.S. relinquished our rights that had been secured by a treaty and left Berlin. He firmly declared his determination to defend our interests and to uphold our obligations even if it meant a war. A war that he emphasized would be started by Moscow not Washington.[25]

The reason Khrushchev was so concerned about Berlin was the large exodus of citizens from the East fleeing across that porous border to the more prosperous West. This was not only a great source of embarrassment to the Soviet leadership but was causing a significant brain drain as the most educated escaped to the West in search of liberty and better employment opportunities. As the summit concluded, Kennedy asked what the medal was that was pinned to Khrushchev's jacket. He proudly told Kennedy it was a peace medal. Kennedy caustically remarked "I hope you can keep it." After the summit, Khrushchev decided against his threat to establish a separate peace treaty with his ally and instead authorized the building of a wall that would divide the city, separating friends and families. Kennedy understood that this was a terrible development but in private conceded it was better than a war.

The construction of the Berlin Wall was for many military

leaders intolerable and a blatant reminder of a failed policy imposed on them by their commander-in-chief. General Lucius Clay, Kennedy's representative in Berlin, without authorization from the White House, initiated secret preparations to tear the wall down. He ordered Major General Albert Watson to have army engineers construct a replica of a segment of the wall. This was done so that U.S. tanks which were outfitted with bulldozers could employ different tactics in destroying the structure. Their rehearsals were done in the middle of a forest to conceal their activities. While they engaged in their maneuvers, Soviet spies watched. Their intelligence was immediately forwarded to Moscow. Khrushchev and his military commanders began to develop counter-measures to defend the wall. He intuitively recognized that these provocative acts were not ordered by Kennedy.[26]

Once General Bruce Burke who was the commander of U.S. forces in Europe discovered Clay's subterfuge, he terminated the operation. This, however, did not end the matter. General Clay who was determined to achieve his objective on October 27, 1961, instructed 10 American M-48 tanks with bulldozers mounted on the front to move up to Checkpoint Charlie which was located in the heart of Berlin. The Soviets who were well informed had already stationed their tanks on the side streets of East Berlin. The Soviets immediately brought up 20 more heavy tanks to reinforce their position. General Clay responded by ordering 20 additional U.S. tanks to the front line. As the tanks faced each other for 16 hours, Kennedy diligently opened up back channels to Soviet leaders. He had his brother Robert deliver a message to Khrushchev that specified that if he pulled his tanks back we would reciprocate within 24 hours. The Soviet leader obliged, and the tanks retreated.[27] Kennedy then phoned Clay and told him "to get them God damn tanks out of sight."

Kennedy once again was placed in a dangerous predicament by his obstinate military who were itching for a fight. The de-escalation by both leaders avoided what could have escalated to a nuclear war. Soviet documents that were declassified decades later revealed that if the American tanks came any closer to the border the Soviet tank commanders were instructed to fire. Sergei, Khrushchev's son, would comment many years later that "It seemed to father that other forces, bypassing the president, were interfering."[28]

The assessment of Kennedy that Khrushchev had formed after the infamous Bay of Pigs – among other matters – emboldened the Soviet leader to place nuclear missiles in Cuba. He not only did this to aid the defense of an ally but also to give the Americans a taste of their own medicine. In the late 1950s, we had placed missiles in Italy and Turkey that instilled great anxiety amongst the Soviet leadership. Consequently, he commenced this gamble that he quickly regretted as the crisis unfolded in October 1962.

He recognized as the Cold War threatened to become hot that he had terribly misjudged Kennedy. Fortunately for humanity, Kennedy held his ground against the warmongers in Washington that were proponents of an invasion of Cuba while bombing the missile sites. This was for Generals LeMay and Power the pretext they had hoped for to justify their implementation of a preemptive war that permitted them the opportunity to eradicate Russia and China from the face of the earth. Kennedy ignored the bellicose proposals by the generals but nevertheless stood firm on his position on the removal of the missiles, proving his metal to Khrushchev.

The most important facet of Kennedy's statesmanship was his determination to defend U.S. strategic interests by fulfilling the proclamation of the **Monroe Doctrine** of 1823, and yet not doing so in a way that humiliated his adversary. By doing this, he did not provide ammunition to the hawks in Khrushchev's government to foist a response that would assure Armageddon. We know this because of a secret recording system that Kennedy had installed after the Bay of Pigs. The tapes revealed that in many instances Kennedy was not only thinking one step ahead of his advisors, but was also attempting to anticipate potential responses by the Soviets for each action as he directed the discussions of the ExCom meetings. In many of those discussions, he stood alone seeking a peaceful resolution to the crisis.

The reality that confronted both leaders during that sobering event caused each of them to re-evaluate what was in the best interest of their people and humanity. The last year of Kennedy's presidency was a dramatic shift in our priorities and long term goals as a nation and a people. He took major risks that threatened his re-election and ultimately his life. He did so because he believed that our nation was commissioned by history to honor those promises unfulfilled at our founding and to contribute to mankind's greatest cause – that of peace. When he delivered his American University oration at their commencement ceremony on June 10, 1963, he outlined his path to peace. Only twenty-four hours later, he delivered his civil right address to the nation, announcing his submission to Congress of the most comprehensive civil rights bill since the end of the Civil War. In both speeches, he was not only appealing to the "better angels of our nature" but was knowingly risking his presidency.

Kennedy, in contrast to most presidents, backed up his speeches with bold action. After his commencement address at American University, he immediately assigned senior diplomate Averill Harriman the task of negotiating a Comprehensive Test Ban Treaty and sent him to Moscow. In addition, Kennedy travelled the country in an attempt to persuade public opinion that overwhelmingly was initially opposed to it. He also courted both houses in Congress to overcome the skepticism of the treaty that dominated the discussions held on Capitol Hill. By the end of the summer, Kennedy had moved a reluctant nation one step closer to peace. The senate in September ratified the agreement, and the President signed it. Kennedy, however, was not able to achieve the cessation of underground testing because of an impasse that could not be circumvented on the number of on-site inspections that the military demanded and the Soviets were willing to accept. Nevertheless, the **Partial Test Ban Treaty** of 1963 which prohibited testing above ground and beneath the ocean was a major achievement for Kennedy, and the first agreement signed by the two super powers since the inception of the Cold War.

He followed this up with his support of an accord to send much needed wheat and grain to Russia because of austere weather conditions that significantly reduced their supplies. The hawks in the Pentagon and state department were appalled that he was signing legislation that was in essence feeding the enemy. They also were equally perplexed when Kennedy authorized **National Security Action Memorandum 271** on November 12, 1963, in which he instructed the director of NASA to prepare for a policy that would include the possibility of a joint lunar moon landing with the Soviets. This was all part of his overall strategy to forge greater trust and cooperation between the two nations. Khrushchev had decided to accept Kennedy's magnanimous offer when he received the dramatic news emanating from Dallas.

Kennedy was assassinated because he was countermanding the paranoid orthodoxy that our national security complex not only thrived on but needed to justify its existence. This is why his policies have been submerged beneath an ocean of obfuscation and why the circumstances of his death remains a convoluted mystery as though we were attempting to unlock the secrets of Stonehenge. A cryptic and intricate dark occurrence even though the whole crime was captured on film on a beautiful sunny day and only lasted for 5.6 seconds. A mystery at least to those who have not taken the time to remove the curtain of deception and dampen all the noise intended to divert and distract the examiner from those facts that stubbornly remain. For over five decades, this concerted subterfuge has been successful. And thus, our future was hijacked by their treachery and our history for those now looking back has been written by the victors. Or in this case, the traitors that sealed his fate.

After Kennedy's death, the national security complex regained control of the executive branch to advance its agenda. President Johnson unwittingly complied with their mandates as he developed the policy that sucked us into Vietnam. A debacle that took decades for our nation to politically, socially and psychologically overcome. It consumed the idealism and promise of the 1960s for a better world and with it Johnson's Great Society. By the 1970s, Nixon and Kissinger would grudgingly end the war for political reasons.

Although President Johnson successfully pursued Kennedy's domestic agenda, his tone and approach in our foreign policy was drastically different than his predecessor. This was clearly demonstrated by his response to Greek leaders regarding the growing crisis between Greece and Turkey over the Mediterranean island of Cyprus that descended into a civil war in 1964. The United Nations had to send a peace-keeping force of 6,500 troops whose mission was to last for three months. They remained there until the early 1990s.

When the Greek Ambassador to the United States, Alexander Matsas, protested to Johnson that U.S. policy was breaching the Greek Constitution, prior agreements and was not supported by their parliament, Johnson retorted "Fuck your parliament and your constitution! America is an elephant. Cyprus is a flea. Greece is a flea. If these two fleas continue itching the elephant, they may just get whacked good...We pay a lot of good American dollars to the Greeks, Mr. Ambassador! If your prime minister gives me talk about democracy, parliament and constitution, he, his parliament and his constitution may not last long..."

This was also true with his dealings, or lack thereof, with Fidel Castro. Castro, desperately hoping that the initiative of Kennedy was not aborted as a result of the events in Dallas, outlined the concessions his nation was willing to make to end the hostilities between the two countries in correspondences he sent to the new president in late 1963 and early 1964. In spite of the pleadings of former Ambassador William Attwood and other progressives in his administration, Johnson never responded to Castro. The assassination attempts sponsored by the CIA continued well into 1965, and the sabotage and violence committed by anti-Castro groups with the support of the U.S. continued for decades.

The largest reversal of course occurred in Vietnam. Kennedy had resisted the demands of his national security team to send combat troops to Vietnam for three years. Johnson immediately began to setup the necessary policy perquisites that he surmised were essential to inject U.S. combat forces into that nation only 48 hours after Kennedy's death. He did this over the objection of some of his advisors that supported Kennedy's decision not to Americanize the war. One of those was Vice President Hubert Humphrey. He wrote a prophetic letter in 1965 pleading with Johnson to reconsider his evolving policy towards that belea-guered nation. He pointed out that since Kennedy's death the situation has gotten worse and that if we got enmeshed in Vietnam it would become a quagmire for our military that would be extremely difficult to extricate ourselves from. Johnson responded to this heartfelt correspondence by advising his National Security Advisor, McGeorge Bundy, to ban Humphrey from all security meetings involving Vietnam and to have his speeches monitored to avoid any hidden references to disengagement and peace.[29]

Another prime example of Johnson's repudiation of Kennedy's approach was his policies towards Indonesia, the Caribbean, Latin and South America. The CIA sponsored another coup in Indonesia in 1965 that resulted in a military junta whose leader

was General Suharto. Former President Sukarno, who Kennedy had planned to visit in 1964, was placed on house arrest until his death three years later. The death squads that were formed to rid the country of the PKI and its leftist supporters resulted in the murder of hundreds of thousands of innocent Indonesians. This policy of imperialism was never more evident than Johnson's intervention in the Dominican Republic's civil war in 1965.

The Dominican Republic had been ruled by the brutal regime of Rafael L. Trujillo since 1930. Like most of the brutal dictators in Latin and South America, he was imposed on the Dominican people by the United States. He was tolerated by the Roosevelt administration that was attempting to reform our relationships with our southern brethren by instituting his **Good Neighbor Policy**. This policy was ignored by President Eisenhower's administration, but was reinvigorated by Kennedy's **Alliance for Progress**.

Trujillo, however, was assassinated by officers within his own military with the assistance of the CIA in May 1961. Although he had been a loyal ally of the U.S., his actions in 1959 and 1960 had made him a liability and source of embarrassment to Washington. The year of 1960 was a very harsh year for the regime. The Dominican Republic was suffering from a severe recession and his government was under heavy criticism by the international community for their complicity in the attempted assassination of Venezuelan President Romulo Betancourt. A naval officer from Venezuela conceded that the bomb used in the botched assassination was made in the Dominican Republic. This was in essence an act of retaliation by Trujillo against Venezuela for their insistence that the **Organization of American States** (OAS) censure the Dominican regime for "flagrant violations of human rights."[30] The OAS eventually did censure his regime followed by several Latin American countries, including the U.S., suspending diplomatic relations.[31]

Trujillo also attempted to alleviate the growing economic

crisis by attempting to expand sugar production that would be shipped to the U.S. markets. He had hoped that this could be accomplished by taking over a significant portion of the sugar quota previously allotted to Cuba. He had lobbyists in Washington convince Congress to approve an increase from 27,000 to 250,000 tons. President Eisenhower immediately placed a punitive excise tax on this imported sugar that September.[32] He did this after the OAS voted to impose economic sanctions against Trujillo's regime and severed diplomatic relations.[33] Eisenhower, while all of this was occurring, may have authorized Trujillo's assassination as he had done with Lumumba and Castro that same year.

After his assassination, a military junta ruled the nation until elections were held in 1963. The Kennedy administration had backed the candidacy of Juan Emilio Bosch who was a social democrat. The CIA on the other hand vehemently opposed Bosch. Once Bosch took power, he immediately began to implement social democratic reforms, causing a backlash within the business community and his own military. They began disseminating propaganda that he was a communist.

On September 25, 1963, twenty-five senior military officers sponsored a coup and instated Donald Reid Cabral as the new president. The Kennedy administration did not protest much publicly but internally was disappointed with the emerging developments within that nation. Kennedy was assassinated before any cohesive policy was developed. However, many in his inner circle supported the idea of getting Bosch back into power. The Johnson administration supported the CIA's position and wanted to implant another puppet as head of the country. When Cabral was removed from power in an uprising supported by the people who demanded the return of Bosch, the Johnson administration began to implement **Operation Power Back**.[34]

Johnson in order to justify U.S. military intervention told the public that the operation was necessary to "protect American lives."[35] The administration proclaimed that the developments in the Dominican Republic were part of a communist conspiracy that implicated our national security interests.[36] To further the hysteria that was created by his administration, he claimed that "1,500 innocent people were murdered and shot, and their heads cut off..." He further asserted that a "thousand American men, women and children" had pleaded for their government's assistance.[37] Of course, none of this was corroborated then and is not supported in the documentary record now.

Fanning insightfully wrote that "Johnson was becoming well-accustomed to lying to the American public, particularly in the lead-up to war. Only a few months prior, he claimed that North Vietnamese patrol boats had twice attacked an American destroyer to justify an attempt to declare formal war on Vietnam. Johnson himself later suggested that the incident might even have involved shooting at 'flying fish' or 'whales'."[38]

As 40,000 U.S. Marines took control of the Dominican Republic, the Johnson administration backed the conservative reformer Joaquin Belaguer over the leftist Bosch. Belaguer defeated his opponent in a controversial election that was the result of tremendous intimidation and coercion imposed on the nation's electorate by the United States and its assets.[39] This action was the impetus for the **Johnson Doctrine** which declared that the United States was not going to tolerate another Cuba in our hemisphere. As Fanning pointed out, this was the blueprint Reagan imitated two decades later to justify his invasion of Grenada.[40]

President Johnson was an enigma of great proportions. He was described by historian Robert Dallek as a "flawed giant."[41] In spite of his intense insecurities while supporting one of the largest egos in Washington, he could have been considered one of our great presidents. This could have been his legacy if he had not invaded Vietnam. However, it must be noted that he was one of the most corrupt politicians to occupy the White House. He also was quite capable of being ruthless if he viewed you as a threat to him or his policies, and was a prolific womanizer in ways that made Kennedy appear as a boy scout. His presidency was followed by another severely flawed and corrupt politician who also was quite competent in the administration of government.

Prior to the ceasefire Nixon negotiated with North Vietnam in 1973, and the chaotic extrication of U.S. civilian and military personnel during the Ford administration in 1975, Nixon employed tactics that would even make the supporters of nuclear brinkmanship in the Eisenhower administration blush. His madman theory that he utilized on occasion bordered on insanity. The basic premise was that if the North Vietnamese leaders thought he was emotionally unstable that they might conclude he was capable of authorizing the use of nuclear weapons to win the war. In furtherance of his reckless experiment in diplomacy, he authorized the Strategic Air Command to order B-52s that had thermonuclear bombs on board to fly towards the Soviet Union and in some instances North Vietnam. He then canceled the order at the last possible moment. This was all done to encourage North Vietnam and their Soviet ally to agree to discuss a resolution of the war. He was also hopeful that these dangerous bluffs would induce them to accept concessions that they otherwise would not have considered. One might wonder what the Soviet leaders were thinking as they monitored these large bombers on their radar screens flying towards their targets.[42]

Kissinger had actually praised the President for having the "guts of a riverboat gambler." In fact, both of them, as you listen to the Nixon tapes, had an enigmatic cavalier attitude towards these monstrous weapons. In one of their recorded conversations regarding their potential use, Nixon stated "The nuclear bomb. Does that bother you? I just want you to think big, Henry, for Christ's sake!"[43]

In addition, the Defense Readiness Condition or DEFCON is a warning system developed by the JCS to be used by our armed forces. This protocol consists of five levels. Each level represented a graduated stage of alert, depending on the severity of the perceived nuclear threat. For instance, DEFCON five specified there was no imminent threat whereas DEFCON 1 indicated the situation was severe and required the U.S. nuclear forces to be fully ready for their deployment. The U.S. has only reached level two on four occasions.

Two of them occurred while Nixon was engaged in his extreme form of nuclear brinkmanship. The third occasion was also emblematic of how dangerous these large stockpiles of weapons posed to not only peace but to the survival of mankind, depending on who was in power. As the crisis of the Yum Kippur War was escalating, the Soviets in October of 1973 issued an ultimatum to the White House. Ambassador Anatoly Dobrynin with clarity announced that if the U.S. did not join a peace-keeping mission with their military in an attempt to end hostilities between the Egyptian and Israeli forces they would take unilateral action. Kissinger, as the Secretary of Defense, immediately contacted Nixon who was inebriated at the time. The President was drinking heavily more often as the Watergate scandal began to swallow his administration and his legacy. Kissinger decided to assemble an NSC meeting without him or his Vice President. As a response to the Soviet declaration, he ordered DEFCON 2.[44]

The other event that triggered this level was the **Cuban Missile Crisis**. The Soviets on the other hand at no time during the entire Cold War era ordered a comparable alert status to their nuclear forces.[45]

The Nixon administration, however, was able to open the door to China and negotiate détente with the Soviets. He also consummated that **Strategic Arms Limitations Treaty** (SALT I) that for five years restricted the number of ICBMS the United

States and the Soviets had to 1972 levels. This intermission in the Cold War was brief because it was founded upon concepts of convenience and power and not mutual cooperation, understanding and acceptance that was contemplated by Kennedy and Khrushchev.

The 1970s ended with an ever expanding security interest in the oil fields of OPEC, as well as the ghosts of past policies supported by our growing secret government which instigated major investigations by congressional committees as their nefarious activities were unveiled by audacious investigative reporters and whistleblowers.

The reforms that were instituted after the **Church and Pike investigations** led to the formation of the Senate and House intelligence committees. This was all part of the **National Intelligence Reorganization and Reform Act** of 1978. The revelation of assassination programs compelled President Ford to sign executive order 11905 in February 1976 which was an attempt to reform and to provide additional supervision of our intelligence agencies that included a ban on political assassinations. Carter would strengthen this order in 1978 when he removed the word "political." Although these changes in the law did curtail the assassination programs, they did not eliminate them. They remained an option for those elements in our intelligence organizations whose allegiance was to the secret government that operated under the ambit of national security. Consequently, their actions were classified. By the 1980s, many of these reforms were ignored as the Cold War was reignited by the Reagan administration. This not only resulted in an arms race but implicated our intelligence agencies and our military in multiple proxy wars primarily being fought in regions considered strategically important to our security such as Latin America, Northern Africa and the Middle East.

The other ramifications of past programs were on the network news throughout the decade. The hostages that were taken from our embassy in Tehran in 1979 by Islamic extremists as retribution for Carter's reluctant decision to permit the Shah to receive medical treatment in the U.S. for an undiagnosed abdominal ailment was the lead story throughout the year and continued until the presidential campaign the following fall. A dictator that Ayatollah Khomeini and his cohorts knew the Unites States had imposed on their people in 1953. The news of Pol Pot and the tragic rise of the Khmer Rouge in Cambodia and the lingering pain inflicted by the death squads that haunted the jungles of Indonesia were a constant companion for the viewer of the nightly newscasts.

The brutal government in Indonesia for instance continued to arrest and incarcerate political dissidents and other innocent civilians that they considered a threat to their regime. Dewi Sukarno wrote to President Gerald Ford on July 24, 1975, pleading with the President to intervene and help secure the release of all the political prisoners. She unequivocally asserted that those that were being held were innocent of the charge of treason.

She then went on to describe the immoral and illegal acts perpetrated against her husband's government by the CIA. She requested a full explanation of why this had been done to her country. She wrote "Both in 1958 and in 1965, the CIA directly intervened in the internal affairs of Indonesia. In 1958, this monstrous action led to civil war. In 1965, it led to the ultimate takeover by a pro-American military regime, while hundreds of thousands of innocent peasants and loyal citizens were massacred in the name of this insane crusade against international communism...ten years later... tens of thousands of true patriots and Sukarnoists are locked up in jails and concentration camps...American companies and aggressive foreign interests are indiscriminately plundering the natural riches of Indonesia to the advantage of the few and the disadvantage of the millions of unemployed and impoverished masses."

She waited in earnest, hoping the United States would at least attempt to negotiate the release of her fellow countrymen, knowing that she would not receive an answer to her question or an apology. As she anticipated, President Ford remained silent and ignored her letter. Like Ho Chi Minh's' correspondence in 1967 to President Johnson, she not only had articulated the absurdity and injustice of this American policy but had spoken the truth.

Another major event was the Russian invasion of Afghanistan in 1979 to reassert control over another Islamic state that bordered their country, and President Carter's response to this act of aggression of not allowing our athletes to compete in the summer Olympics in 1980; an act that appeared to punish the athletes more than it deterred the Soviets.

He also issued the **Carter Doctrine** which stated that if the flow of oil from the Middle East to the West was interrupted this would implicate the national security interests of the United States. The military began to focus on that region to satisfy the President's decree by developing strategies to protect our strategic interests. A policy that would spark an obsession from one administration to the next whether they be Republican or Democrat. This highly prized energy source was the twentieth centuries' version of the gold rush of the late nineteenth century.

As the political campaign that fall began, Carter and Reagan bantered back and forth over who was more prepared and tough enough to defend our national security interests as we entered the 1980s. This debate occurred at the end of a decade that witnessed the proliferation of nuclear weapons to nations such as India and Pakistan. This troubled Carter tremendously, but his personal concerns did not manifest itself into a cohesive policy.

While the candidates debated the fate of the nation and humanity, Father Daniel Berrigan and his brother Phillip initiated what became the **Plowshares Movement** when they and six others, in protest of nuclear weapons on September 9, 1980, broke into a General Electric plant in King of Prussia, Pennsylvania. Once inside the large defense contractor's facility, they began to damage the nose cones for several nuclear weapons. They also poured blood onto numerous documents and files. This courageous act of civil disobedience was reminiscent of their symbolic protest against the Vietnam War when he and his brother with seven others used homemade napalm to burn 378 draft files in Catonsville, Maryland. They became known as the Catonsville nine. Father Berrigan because of that act served three years in prison. The name of their anti-nuclear movement was inspired by Isiah 2:4. "They will beat their swords into plowshares and their spears into pruning hooks...nor will they train for war anymore."

Ronald Reagan's successful bid for the presidency in 1980 shamefully began by his announcement to seek the Republican nomination in Philadelphia, Mississippi. A town whose infamy was well known to the rest of the nation as the location where three civil right activists had been abducted and brutally murdered by the Klan in 1964. This tragedy had been the inspiration for the film **Mississippi Burning** which featured William Dafoe and Gene Hackman who portrayed two FBI agents that were assigned the unenviable task of solving the murders. Reagan in his speech asserted his support for state rights in his attempt to steal the South from the Democrats.

He ironically at the time was considered a liberal by the Koch bothers and their business associates such that they vehemently opposed his candidacy. And yet, Reagan ushered in a new era of conservatism that ended the smoldering vestiges of what was left of the idealism of the 1960s and the 1970s. His new political base reclaimed all those conservative Democrats that President Roosevelt had enticed into his party in the early 1930s. The South and much of the mid-west became red states that the Republican party still rely upon today. The once proud members of the counter culture and the social movements that were inspired by their activism retreated to a life of commercialization and accumulation of material goods they once had vainly denounced. The 1980s is inauspiciously referred to as the 'me' decade.

Reagan's objective was to rebuild the respect and prestige of our nation that he opined had been significantly damaged not by Vietnam or the nefarious actions of our intelligence agencies or Watergate, but rather by the liberal media, the misguided protestors, as well as the weakness of the Carter administration that was primarily responsible for its decline. The taking of our hostages in Iran, the failed rescue attempt, the feeble response by Carter to the invasion of Afghanistan by the Soviets and the growth of our federal government encouraged by liberal programs all epitomized to him why our nation was so impotent in achieving our national objectives at home and around the world. Because of this, he surrounded himself with hawks and fiscal conservatives that supported his agenda to rebuild the military and reinvigorate our intelligence agencies. On the domestic front, he attacked labor, programs of social uplift and promoted tax cuts that primarily benefited the most affluent in our society. This was all justified under a theory – now debunked – called supply-side economics or what admirers and critics have labelled **Reaganomics**. He brought in George H.W. Bush, Edwin Meese III, John Poindexter, Casper Weinberger, Colonel Oliver North, William Bennett, David Stockman and appointed William Casey as the Director of the CIA to help him implement these policies.

He immediately requested additional funds to increase the defense budget and augment our presence in the Middle East. In addition, he intended to expand and modernize our nuclear arsenal that included in 1983 his **Strategic Defense Initiative** (SDI) which was a missile defense system that was in theory capable of defending the United States from a surprise Soviet nuclear attack. This program, dubbed 'Star Wars', naturally implanted images of the iconic film trilogy directed by Steven

Spielberg that mesmerized audiences in the late 1970s. The Soviet leaders were not amused by the attempts to link this provocative program to the magic of Hollywood's special effects technology. Their military suspiciously regarded it as an attempt to obtain a first strike capacity that reinvigorated an intense arms race.

Although Reagan was considered the great communicator and perceived as a grandfatherly figure, his bellicose language and precipitous nuclear build up received intense scrutiny by international and domestic proponents for peace and nuclear disarmament. One of those who took notice was Randall Forsberg a young graduate of the prestigious Massachusetts Institute of Technology (MIT). She initiated "A Call to Halt the Nuclear Arms Race" that inspired a movement that caught the Reagan administration by surprise. Her lonely voice eventually culminated in one million followers who gathered in Central Park in 1982, demanding the abolishment of nuclear weapons. This movement was branded the **Freeze** campaign.[46] Reagan for the first time was being booed at rallies by their members. This had a profound effect on him that eventually resulted in a revision of his policy in his second term. He, in essence, was a reactor not an initiator for this change.[47]

Reagan, however, was not an enlightened Cold War warrior as a result of these social movements that were formed in response to his belligerent and imperialistic policies. He continued his hawkish foreign policy by backing a regime change in Nicaragua and by defending the ruthless government in El Salvador that terrorized the people of that destitute nation. He also supported the brutal regime in Guatemala that was murdering thousands of their people. Much of this senseless violence was focused on many of the indigenous villages and their inhabitants. This combination of military aid to vicious insurgents attempting to overthrow leftist governments, and the sponsorship of murderous dictators as the CIA provided support and trained their security forces, foisted terror and intense suffering on the societies of that poor region. The vestiges of hope inspired by Kennedy's Alliance for Progress was a distant memory that for some was a myth induced by the imagination of elders who always reminisced about the good old days.

Reagan's most ignominious intervention in the internal affairs of the Caribbean was his invasion of the small island of Grenada in 1983. The administration, in an attempt to implicate God, duty and country, painted this military action as a rescue mission to save the lives of medical students from communist insurgents while attending a local medical school. Many of these students were U.S. citizens. This unnecessary action more likely was intended as a diversion from the tragedy that had befallen 241 Marines that died when a bomb went off at the U.S. Marine Corps barracks in Lebanon.[48] In addition, this was an opportunity for Reagan to topple the revolutionary government that had an alliance with Cuba. In fact, the Cubans were constructing an airstrip at the time of the invasion.

Reagan authorized 7,000 troops to assault the island. There was more resistance than they had anticipated. The government troops were no match for the heavily armed U.S. forces, but the poorly armed Cubans fought ferociously. 29 U.S. soldiers died, and 100 were wounded during the conflict. This intervention had been opposed by the Organization of American States and by our ally British Prime Minister Margaret Thatcher. Nevertheless, the administration used Orwellian phrases to justify its policy. They alleged that the new Grenadian government posed a threat to the entire region. A small island whose population consisted of 100,000 residents. Congressman Dick Cheney of Wyoming applauded the action and continued to perpetuate the myth that it was a rescue mission not an invasion as proposed by the critics. The UN General Assembly on the other hand by a margin of 10 votes to 1 "deeply deplored" the "armed intervention in Grenada."[49]

The reality was that the students were never at risk. The dean of the medical school polled the students and 90 percent wanted to remain. In fact, General Edward Trobaugh, commander of the 82nd Airborne Division, informed visiting congressmen that there was no indication that the medical students had been threatened.[50] In my opinion, the whole event was a ruse to overthrow another leftist government. This was all part of Reagan's hemispheric strategy to rid Latin and South America of communism. His definition of a threat to our national security was any government that he deemed governed from the left on the political spectrum.

His administration's strategy in the Middle East was also wreaking havoc in that region as well. He sold arms and reinforced Saddam Hussein's military during its war against Iran. His administration did this even though Hussein was dropping chemical weapons not only on Iranian forces but also on the Kurds in Northern Iraq. In fact, Donald Rumsfeld, as his special envoy in 1983, publicly praised the dictator while also extending additional American military aid.

The CIA was also funding and supplying weapons to mujahedeen fighters in Afghanistan to prolong and undermine the Soviet military campaign to tame the country. Many of these rebels would constitute what would become the Taliban in the 1990s that instituted an extreme element of Islam called Sharia Law. One of those fighters, a citizen of Saudi Arabia, was Osama Bin Laden. His perceived betrayal by CIA agents planted the seeds of hate that grew into a monstrous organization that threatened the West and sparked this endless war on terror.

Reagan also authorized the sale of arms to a designated enemy of the United States for the release of American citizens in violation of a congressional act, and members of his adminis- tration diverted some of those funds to the Contras in Nicaragua in violation of the Boland Amendment. When these activities were unveiled in the media by serendipity, it threatened his presidency in ways reminiscent of Watergate. The **Iran-Contra** scandal was more egregious in many aspects than Nixon's attempt to cover-up an ill-advised and botched burglary of the Democratic headquarters located in the Watergate Hotel in Washington D.C. He should have been impeached but for the agreement reached with the Speaker of the House Tip O'Neill. This unspoken accord may have been the impetus for Reagan's support of legislation to reform Social Security and catapult its viability into the future. He certainly was not a proponent of the programs of the New Deal.

The main thrust of Reagan's appeal to conservatives and his legacy as memorialized by historians is his participation in the tearing down of the **Berlin Wall** and the end of the Cold War in 1991. He deserves some credit for these historically important events, but maybe not as much as he has received. Mikhail Gorbachev became the Soviet leader in 1985. He rose to power at a time when the Soviet economy was in a serious recession. The burden of maintaining an arms race with the United States was consuming 20 to 40 percent of their budget. An expenditure that he recognized that they could not continue indefinitely. He decided to meet with Reagan in Geneva in 1985. Their talks were fruitful as they discussed a reduction in the numbers of intermediate missile arsenals in Europe. Both leaders were hopeful that future talks could lead to an arms reduction accord that could significantly lessen the tensions between their respective nations. They agreed to meet again in October 1986 in Reykjavik, the capital of Iceland.

The **Reykjavik Summit** would begin auspiciously on October 11, 1986. Both leaders were anticipating historical achievements that would advance the aspirations of humanity and peace. However, the Soviet leader's goals were far more ambitious than his American counterpart. He was hoping to end the Cold War and begin a new chapter in American and Soviet relations. In a letter he sent to Reagan prior to their summit in 1985, he alluded to this intent when he referenced Kennedy's American University speech when he wrote that they needed to "proceed from the objective fact that we all live on the same planet and must learn to live together."[51] For him, this was not just an opportunity to eliminate a class of weapons as the agenda of the summit suggested but rather was a meeting that he hoped would achieve peace.

Gorbachev noted as the meeting began that Reagan had multiple index cards he held in his hand. Gorbachev sat at the table and immediately offered to eliminate all intermediate missile stockpiles held by both countries while allowing Britain and France to maintain their arsenals. He added that they should cut strategic offensive weapons by 50 percent, freeze short term missiles, halt all nuclear testing, allow for on-site inspections consistent with American prior demands and limit SDI testing to labs for 10 years. Reagan appeared unprepared for such a comprehensive offer and fumbled through his cards searching for assistance on how to respond. His advisors were divided. One advisor, Paul Nitze, told him that this was everything they could have hoped for and advised him to take the deal. Another more conservative aid, Richard Perle, reminded him that if he agreed to this it would limit his Strategic Defense Initiative if not terminate it.[52] Gorbachev quietly listened to their exchange and offered a sixth month grace period before the agreement would take effect. This would allow the continuation of SDI funded research outside a laboratory setting. Reagan sat in silence for a few moments. SDI was a multibillion-dollar program that had become one of his pet projects. He looked up and rejected the offer.

At the afternoon session, the two leaders met in an attempt to breach the impasse they confronted in their morning discussion. Reagan counter-offered to agree to share SDI technology once it became operative. Gorbachev in frustration retorted that he could not sell such a deal to the Politburo; an agreement that essentially allowed the United States to militarize space in violation of prior treaties. He added angrily that "I cannot take your idea of sharing SDI seriously. You are not willing to share with us oil well equipment, digitally guided machine tools, or even milking machines. Sharing SDI would provoke a second American revolution. Let's be realistic and pragmatic."[53] This contentious exchange caused the expert negotiating teams to spend most of the night trying to hash out an agreement acceptable to both sides.[54]

The two leaders resumed their parley the following morning. They were unable to resolve differences on the test ban or any type of Anti-Ballistic Missile accord. In frustration, Gorbachev requested to adjourn their morning session. The SDI program continued to present difficulties for both sides. Their last discussion that afternoon ended in disappointment as another opportunity for real peace was squandered. As they were walking out, Reagan accused Gorbachev of intentionally placing him in that position by expanding the perimeters of their discussion to include the SDI program. Gorbachev immediately understood that Reagan was questioning his sincerity and offered to go back to the table and sign the deal. Reagan somberly declined.[55]

Gorbachev after the summit realized that he was going to have to take significant unilateral action to propel the process to a more prosperous conclusion in the future. He immediately initiated a reduction in defense spending which included the disastrous campaign in Afghanistan. He began the withdrawal of Soviet combat forces in that austere nation in May 1988 and completed that mission in February 1989. He also implemented **Glasnost** which tendered liberties to the Russian people that they were not accustom to, including freedom of speech. In addition, his policy of **Perestroika** restructured the economy by decentralizing it to combat stagnation and to encourage investment and growth.

Reagan passively observed these changes occurring within the Soviet Union and offered to further discuss what had been proposed at Reykjavik. The result was the **Intermediate-Range Nuclear Forces Treaty** that was agreed to by both leaders in December of 1987. This treaty was the first and only agreement reached during the Cold War to eliminate a whole class of weapons. More specifically, the agreement abolished nuclear and conventional ground launched ballistic and cruise missiles with intermediate ranges. The U.S. Senate ratified the treaty on March 27, 1988. The momentum of this magnanimous agreement ultimately led to the removal of the Berlin Wall in November 1989, the reunification of Germany in 1990 and the end of the Cold War in 1991.

Reagan exited the White House as the unequaled champion of the conservatives. He represented to the right-wing of his party what Franklin Roosevelt had meant to the progressive wing of the Democrats. His legacy, however, for most was highly controversial and contentious. As for the man, Reagan headed home to his beloved ranch in southern California while suffering from the onset of Alzheimer's. A degenerative disease of the brain that impairs the person's ability to socially interact with others and to remember the past. He was, as one of his biographer's described him, a compassionate man. A man that would give you the shirt off his back if he thought it would help. And yet, he had no understanding or empathy for those who were negatively impacted by his policies. Of course, the devil is always in the details. And for Reagan, he remained in his ivory tower among the high minded platitudes that composed his politics and myopic world view with little interest of how it was to be implemented. And more importantly, what it meant to those unable to overcome the realties that came with it. Those mischievous devils the details evoked. Those annoying minutiae that he was destined not to remember as his disease progressed. A past that many modern scholars have concluded further entrenched the influence and power of our national security complex while encouraging the inequitable economic structure we are inflicted with today.

Reagan from my vantage point ushered in an anti-communistic crusade reminiscent of the zealots of the late 1940s and early 1950s that destroyed the careers of prominent new dealers such as Alger Hiss and economist Harry Dexter White.[56] As this conservative attack on the New Dealers gained momentum while ratcheting up the fear of communism and its insidious influence in our government, politicians such as Richard Nixon, Lyndon Johnson, Joseph McCarthy and the Dulles brothers would quietly steer the nation away from the post-war vision of Henry Wallace and Franklin Roosevelt.

The consequence of Reaganomics resulted in the largest transfer of wealth from the working and middle classes to the most affluent in our society. His form of voodoo economics, as George H.W. Bush referred to it before becoming his vice presidential running mate, created the largest deficits the nation had witnessed since its founding. His form of deregulation and unfettered support for Wall Street encouraged the greed and avarice witnessed in the late 1980s as investors such as Michael Milken scammed the system. And finally, his constant attacks on unions and the rights of workers to collectively bargain for fair wages and benefits initiated precipitously the decline of union membership and their influence on the American market place. All the triumphs of labor heroes such as Walter Reuther and Cezar Chavez were partially washed away, reversing a trend that had been forged by the blood, sweat and toil of those who successfully initiated a movement to confront the oppressive managerial policies wielded by management during the **Gilded Age**. A period that the Koch brothers intensely desire to return to; a time in which the Robber Barons and their supporters controlled the politicians, the parties, the laborers and the markets. Justice Louis D. Brandeis, an eminent jurist of the time, astutely observed that "We can have democracy in this country, or we can have great wealth concentrated in the hands of a few, but we can't have both."

His successor George H.W. Bush would quickly realize how accurate he had been regarding his predecessor's economic theory when he had to increase taxes contrary to his pledge in his campaign against Michael Dukakis to offset the huge federal deficits. The fiasco of the Financial Savings and Loans scandal was also a reminder of the foxes guarding the chicken coup that Reagan thought was good business. And lastly, he had to deal with the growing threat that Reagan's ally Saddam Hussein and his powerful military posed to his neighbors in what is still a very troubled and violent region of the world.

As Hussein's tanks rolled into Kuwait, President Bush built a coalition to oppose Iraq's violation of another state's sovereignty. The coalition forces which included many Arab states – in what has been named **Gulf War I** – swiftly dismantled Iraqi forces, compelling them to retreat back into Iraq. We, however, wisely chose not to overthrow Hussein's regime and engage in nation building. Dick Cheney ironically in 1994 prophetically described to the media why he believed we made the right decision not to invade Baghdad and remove Hussein's oppressive regime. He indicated that if we proceeded our coalition would not have followed. We, in essence, would be alone. He wisely rhetorically asked himself in interviews "What were you going to replace it with?" He said it was a very volatile and unpredictable area of the world. Iraq without the regime to hold it together could explode into sectarian violence that could tear the nation apart, causing great insecurity and instability in the region. He concluded that it would have become a quagmire for U.S. military forces.

Bush's secretary of state, James Baker III, was also credited with the diplomacy that resulted in the unification of not only the city of Berlin but all of Germany. The United States agreed not to place troops or weapons of mass destruction (WMD) in the eastern region of Germany. President Vladimir Putin in a speech in 2007 alleged that the Americans had also pledged not to enlarge NATO membership by encouraging states of former Soviet Republics in the East to join. Gorbachev in response indicated that this was not entirely accurate. He added that there was no express agreement as such. The talks at the time focused primarily on the eastern portion of the country. He did state, however, that the addition of NATO members from the East was not consistent with the spirit of the agreement that all the participating parties had assented to. It was nevertheless in my opinion a provocative act that unnecessarily created anxiety for those in charge of Russian security and stressed our relationship with Russia at a time when building the bridges of trust was imperative for solidifying our affiliation into the future.

In spite of Bush's success repelling Iraq from Kuwait, as well as his contribution to the culmination of the Cold War, a relatively unknown governor from Arkansas defeated him in the fall of 1992. His loss was primarily because of a recession that lingered through the political campaign; proving once again that the economy will trump foreign policy success in most elections. Many that had voted for Clinton had hoped that he would be the Kennedy of their generation. He clearly did not live up to that wishful expectation with maybe the sole exception of his salacious extramarital affairs.

Clinton's attempts to impose major changes in our society while curbing military spending was dashed when he tried to push the military to accept homosexuals into their ranks. The backlash from this resulted in the disappointing **Don't Ask, Don't Tell** policy that Obama thankfully repealed. He also assigned his wife the task of developing sweeping reform in our health care system. Her proposals stirred up such controversy and dissent that the Clintons slowly backed away from their own policy. In addition, he championed the **North American Free**

Trade Act (NAFTA), claiming it would stimulate the economy and create jobs. Many union officials and economists have concluded that NAFTA has been a disaster for the American worker. As a result of this agreement according to the Huffington Post in 2014, one million jobs have been lost or outsourced to other signatory nations. Many corporate supporters such as General Electric, Chrysler and Caterpillar all promised in consideration for the passage of the act that they would hire more American workers. These corporate giants instead cut numerous jobs in the United States and outsourced them in search of lower labor costs. This agreement also according to the analysts considerably exacerbated the nation's trade deficits.

As to the military budgets, Clinton did not have much success there as well. It certainly did not assist his cause that the generals did not respect him. He had avoided the draft for Vietnam by enrolling at Oxford in England which clearly did not engender much reverence by the JCS for their commander-in-chief. Consequently, the hawks that surrounded the president, which included the first lady, dominated foreign policy discussions which insured that the Pentagon budgets remained the same throughout his two terms.[57]

After the disastrous mid-term elections for the Democrats in 1994, Clinton decided to move to the right and govern as a centrist. He, in many instances, usurped the policies of the neocons much to their consternation and made them his own. He passed the infamous crime bill in 1994 that placed 100,000 new police officers onto the streets of many cities and created mandatory minimum sentences that clogged our prisons with non-violent offenders who were addicted to alcohol and other illicit substances. He also passed what professor Robert Reich has written was the draconian **Welfare Reform Act** of 1996, as well as his **Telecommunications Act** of that same year. This change in the law over time permitted six large corporations to gobble up all our media outlets. In addition, he regrettably repealed the **Glass-Steagall Act** of 1934 which was an important component of the New Deal's restructuring of our financial institutions to prevent another stock market crash.

This act prohibited depository banks from acting like an investment bank by using the funds of their depositors to invest in speculative ventures that could jeopardize the financial security of the bank. The repealing of this legislation contributed significantly to the circumstances that caused the financial collapse of 2008. Clinton, however, was able to balance the federal budget, leaving his successor with budget surpluses.

Clinton, in spite of the Monica Lewinsky scandal and his impeachment by hypocrites in the house, left office with relatively high approval ratings and has remained a popular political figure. I believe this can be primarily explicated by the booming economy of the 1990s that he presided over. As with Reagan and the end of the Cold War, he does deserve some of the credit. I would proffer, nonetheless, that most of this growth benefited Wall Street, large corporate conglomerates and what Bernie Sanders refers to as the "billionaire class." For most of America, with exception to those who were employed by health care and high tech industries, the wages of the average worker remained stagnant as the compensation packages of management rose exponentially. Many Americans maintained their life styles and paid for their children's college tuitions by tapping the equity in their homes and by adding to their credit card debt. It was in many ways a Ponzi scheme that was not sustainable. When the 2008 financial crisis occurred, millions of families had no savings or ability to extend their debt to survive the loss of a job or an employer reducing their hours. The result was a deluge of bankruptcy filings and foreclosures throughout the nation.

Michael Dukakis at the New England Association of Drug Court Professionals' (NEADCP) conference held several years ago at the University of Massachusetts in Boston stated "that you could blame me for the Bush administration. If I had beaten the father, you never would have heard of his son." The administration of George W. Bush was a contentious matter for many Americans right out of the gate. If the Supreme Court had been composed of progressives, the count in Florida would have continued, revealing that Albert Gore, Jr. had won the state of Florida and as a result had secured the election.

A Gore administration would have taken the country in a much different direction. He would have continued to pay down the debt and initiate environmental programs to confront climate change a decade before the social movements that exist today began to impact the policies of nations around the globe. It is also abundantly clear that if **9/11** occurred on his watch he never would have invaded Iraq. His administration would have focused on Afghanistan where the conspirators plotted a tragedy. I would suggest as well that the financial collapse of 2008 might also have been avoided. Hence, the 2000 election was another opportunity for the nation to reverse its current path and rebuild the republic our founders valiantly gave us. This opportunity was lost for a multitude of reasons, but I would suggest primarily as a consequence of the insidious power wielded by an elite that continue to push the nation away from a government that is beholden to the people. A government that is committed to the welfare of the governed.

The Bush administration was composed of elitist neo-conservatives whose mission was to enrich the "job creators" and embellish the selfish interests of Wall Street and corporate giants by unleashing the nation's immense military power on the rest of the world. A war machine that had no rival in the annals of human history. Their economic program was essentially Reaganomics on steroids. Bush signed two of the largest tax cuts in history that primarily benefited the top one percent while placing the burden of funding the nation's financial obligations on the working and middle classes. The consequence of this trickle down policy that intentionally ignored the lessons of the past enlarged the chasm between the few at the top and the many imprisoned by the inequitable system at the bottom.

This group of neo-cons composed of Dick Cheney, Donald Rumsfeld, Paul Wolfowitz, Michael Hayden, John Ashcroft and George Tenet were staunch proponents of this concept of "American exceptionalism." A belief that we were inherently different than other nations because of the nature of our founding. Because of our historical mission to spread liberty and democracy, we were in a profound sense thought to be superior to the rest of the world. This myopic view enabled them to dismiss the heritage and culture of other nations in dogged pursuit of their objectives. The irony was that the policies they promoted reaffirmed that we were no different in the use of power than the colonial powers that proceeded them.

As the Bush administration took control of the apparatus of the executive branch, they began to explore options on how to deal with Saddam Hussein in Iraq long before Al Qaeda ever became the symbol of terror. One of the first major actions by the President – in addition to his first tax cut – was to create the **National Energy Policy Development Group** (NEPDG). Vice President Dick Cheney was appointed as the chairman of the **Energy Task Force** that was formed after NEPDG was in operation. The purpose of this group on the surface appeared mundane and legitimate. Their mission was to develop a national energy policy that included affordable and environmentally sound energy for the nation. Because its activities were classified and thus not available for scrutiny by the media or the public, their real intent remained a secret. In an article written by Michael Klare in January 2004 entitled "Bush-Cheney Strategy: Procuring the Rest of the World's Oil", he reported that as a result of a Freedom of Information (FOI) lawsuit documents that were released in the summer of 2003 revealed more nefarious purposes for this task force. Among these documents was a map of Iraqi oilfields, pipelines, refineries and terminals. In addition, there were two charts describing meticulously Iraqi oil and gas projects, and "foreign suitors for Iraqi oilfield contracts." These documents were dated March 2001 which was several months prior to **9/11**.

Klare surmised that the documents unequivocally revealed that the Bush administration's primary objectives were not to prevent future terroristic acts nor curtail the proliferation of WMD as espoused after 9/11, but rather was to substantially increase the flow of oil from foreign suppliers to the U.S. This is probably why they ignored warnings from the outgoing Clinton administration regarding intelligence that suggested that a plot to attack the United States was being developed. Instead of following up on these disturbing reports, Cheney and his task force were busy carving up oilfields in Iraq with his corporate cabal.

And then, it happened! The unimaginable destruction of the twin towers; the iconic symbols of America's financial power. Many sat in horror as they watched two jetliners crash into the upper floors of the buildings hundreds of feet above the streets below. Thousands perished as the towers collapsed spewing toxic dust all over lower Manhattan. The Pentagon was also hit by another jet. The fourth plane crashed in a Pennsylvania field because of the heroics of passengers that sacrificed their lives, preventing the large jet from reaching its intended target which may have been the White House. As this tragedy unfolded on our televisions, Bush was informed of the attack while sitting in an elementary classroom, attempting to mask the horror that had been quietly reported to him by an aide. Just like Pearl Harbor and the Kennedy assassination, this was not only a black seminal moment for a generation but an event that would transform our national priorities and objectives towards a darker future. It stirred up instinctive emotional responses from the most primitive parts of our brain that immediately desired revenge and vengeance for this senseless act of violence. It resulted in the beefing up of our security and the influence of our national security complex at the expense of our commonsense and our liberty. In fact, the Bush administration used it to justify its invasion of Iraq, as well as Afghanistan where Osama Bin Laden and his cohorts plotted this ghastly act against humanity.

The **Patriot Act** was signed by President Bush on October 26, 2001. The objectives were to enhance domestic security and deter future terroristic acts. Bush also approved the **Homeland Security Act** of 2002 whose director was elevated to the status of a cabinet member. Both paved the way for the ubiquitous surveillance programs administered by the NSA and the development of CIA black sites in remote locations around the world that administered their Enhanced Interrogation Techniques (EITs) that included water boarding, sleep and food deprivation, isolation and other methods that were developed to elicit actionable intelligence from their victims. The Bush administration openly discussed the EITs in press conferences and speeches as though these methods were a legitimate and useful tool to prevent and combat terrorism. The rest of the world, as well as the Geneva Convention, called it torture.

Bush also promoted the **Unitary Executive Doctrine** that allegedly derived its legal framework from Article II of the Constitution. The basic premise is that the president has complete control over the executive branch and has emergency powers during war that enables him to suspend constitutional mandates to protect the national security of the United States. He used this authority to further his power to wage his war on terror that had not been declared by Congress.

As our troops were landing in Afghanistan to engage the Taliban and Al Qaeda forces, Bush, Cheney, Tenet and Rumsfeld were building a case to invade Iraq. They recruited Colin Powell, a distinguished military leader with impeccable credentials, to present their case to the United Nations. He unwittingly used specious intelligence gathered by the CIA and other sources to prove that Iraq had WMD that posed a serious threat to the region and U.S. security. The result of this massive political campaign brought about the **Iraq Resolution** that was enacted by a joint resolution of Congress that authorized the president, if he deemed it necessary, to use military force against Iraq. The act was not passed unanimously, but its support was overwhelming. A few senators who had learned from history, and some who had been in the senate during the passage of the **Gulf of Tonkin Resolution,** voted against the legislation such as Ted Kennedy and Bernie Sanders. The results were the same as it had been in 1964. The United States needlessly invaded another country with disastrous results for not only our people but the citizens of Iraq and the region.

Bush left behind one of the worst legacies of modern times if not American history. He accumulated with the Republican dominated Congress the largest deficits that any generation had ever seen, squandering surpluses that his predecessor had left for him. The United States was bogged down in two wars that were not achieving their objectives despite claims to the contrary by his administration. The unnecessary war in Iraq, and the sectarian violence that resulted, contributed to the formation of the Islamic State (ISIS) that is even more radical than Al Qaeda. His push to defang our environmental regulations did immeasurable harm to our ability to confront climate change which arguably was the most serious threat to our security. He further deregulated our financial structures in pursuit of dubious free markets uninhibited by government interference that when combined with the repeal of the Glass-Steagall Act by Clinton created the perfect storm. A storm that grew bigger by the greed and avarice of Wall Street who resembled pigs at a trough rather than prudent fiscal managers. The collapse of our financial markets in the fall of 2008 was the worst economic crisis our nation had suffered since the **Great Depression** of the 1930s. The depression was an austere and desperate time that had also been caused by speculative ventures by the wizards of Wall Street that contributed to the **Stock Market Crash** of 1929.

To add salt to the wounds of the average American, Main Street was compelled to save Wall Street so that the financial and insurance giants that were too big to fail did not drag us off the cliff. And once Wall Street received tax payer moneys, they partially used it to enhance executive compensation and to pay out huge bonuses to their top executives. These acts of depravity and greed were justified by claiming this was necessary to retain their best talent. This talent that had led us to the brink of disaster.

In addition, his policies of EITs, drone attacks, the imprisonment of alleged combatants at Guantanamo and other CIA black sites without any judicial oversight ravaged the nations moral integrity and credibility as the globe observed our actions with disdain and disbelief. As he walked out the door of the White House, he left an Orwellian government that wrapped its actions in the American flag as it claimed to spread democracy and liberty around the globe by supporting policies that diminished the respect for international law while encouraging the development of an oligarchy at home with little regard to the liberties ordained in our Constitution.

The 2008 election had the potential of transforming our government by making it more responsive to the needs of the governed while holding the national security complex accountable to the people. The president elect, Barrack Hussein Obama, intended to do this by instituting reforms that encouraged a more open and transparent government. He was a constitutional scholar from Harvard with an understanding of history not witnessed since Kennedy had occupied the presidency. His election was historic in many ways but most prominently because he was the first African American to hold that office.

A barrier had been breached in a society with a racist past that had permeated our social, economic and political structures that were irrefutable except by an extreme element in our society that refuse to be enlightened. It was as though the nation had finally resolved its racial discord and was now ready to accept our differences and embrace our common humanity. Even the Supreme Court declared in its dubious decision in 2013 that repealed section 4 of the 1965 **Voting Rights Act** – which required specific states whose state policy was historically racially structured – had been reformed. This meant that they no longer were required to seek prior approval from the Justice Department or a federal court for amendments or revisions to their voting laws. We now are painfully aware that the justices were not responding to social progress but rather political edicts. As for those who had naïvely wished it so by Obama's ascension to the presidency, we quickly learned that change is never that easy, and the past is never dead.

His first two years in office were absorbed by left over wars and a financial crisis that was on the verge of becoming another depression. Obama immediately proposed the **American Recovery Act** to stimulate a sluggish economy by investing in our infrastructure and to assist those that lost their jobs by augmenting and extending their unemployment benefits. He also made loans to Chrysler and General Motors so they could survive the bankruptcy process that confronted them. Ford fortunately was able to restructure their finances from within by tapping into their European division.

The President's agenda to reform our economy did not end there. He courageously tackled our broken health care system that was consuming 17 percent of our Gross Domestic Product (GDP) when many of our competitors had congruent, and in some cases better outcomes, with far less costs to their citizens. Many of these nations had instituted universal health care programs or what critics in the U.S. have referred to as socialized medicine.

The President in an attempt to reach across the aisle seeking bi-partisan support for health care reform decided to sponsor legislation that kept the same rotten for profit system in place with reforms that made it more fair and equitable. He prohibited insurers from denying coverage for pre-existing conditions or terminating policies when the insured needed it most. He also included provisions that allowed children to be covered under their parents' plan until the age of 26. He also enhanced federal support for Medicaid and encouraged competition to reduce costs. But most importantly, he had to compel the young and the healthy to participate otherwise the whole program would collapse under its own weight. The act accomplished this by imposing graduated penalties that would become more onerous each year the tax payer filed their taxes without proof of healthcare coverage. The primary objectives of this complex piece of legislation was to reduce costs and extend health care coverage to millions of Americans that had none.

The outcomes so far have been mixed. Senator Sanders in his campaign has remarked that it was a good first step in a path that should lead us to universal health care. Wendell Potter, a high ranking Cigna executive now whistleblower, has concluded that Obama Care is a "windfall" for the health insurance industry in that millions of healthy Americans are now mandated to purchase their product.

The **Affordable Care Act** never received bi-partisan support even though the financial penalties for not having health insurance was originally an idea proposed by the Heritage Foundation; a conservative think tank that advanced this concept as an alternative to the government plan proposed by Hillary Clinton in the early 1990s. In fact, Republican Governor Mitt Romney of Massachusetts signed health care reform legislation that was the inspiration for Obama Care. Nevertheless, the Republicans argued that the penalties were a tax, that the bill was socialized medicine at its worst and that it contained death panels that could authorize the death of loved ones contrary to the wishes of the family. This of course was propaganda for the gullible who refused to do their homework by consulting objective critiques by legitimate media sources.

The Republicans did this primarily for political reasons for they did not want Obama, a Democrat, to receive credit for another landmark legislative achievement. In essence, the bill which was eventually signed by the President after the Democratically controlled house and senate passed it was a market-based solution to our inequitable and costly health care system. For progressives, it was better than what we had, but had little resemblance to what they had envisioned. Although the act made insurance carriers behave more responsibly, there was no public option. Even worse, the President had obviated any public debate on the merits of universal government financed health care. It was one of many disappointments his progressive base would endure as the mid-term elections rose above the horizon, and for that matter, his entire presidency.

As in 1994, the mid-term elections were a major setback for the nation and Obama's presidency. The Republicans energized by the Tea Party and its propaganda that demonized the President's accomplishments combined with disheartened progressives who failed to vote took over both houses of Congress. Their objective was not bi-partisanship nor a desire to govern the nation, but rather to obstruct the President's agenda and to prevent his re-election. The result was the most obnoxious and inept congressional periods in our history. They made Truman's 'do nothing' Congress look like workaholics. More disturbingly, the public refused to punish this childish behavior. As a result, the nation's problems festered and in some cases got worse. Because of this impasse, Obama used executive orders to address domestic issues such as immigration and climate change while he focused on foreign policy.

The **Iraq War** began in 2003 and officially ended in 2010.

Although, you could make a reasonable argument that it never came to a conclusion. The United States forces in that war suffered 4,491 deaths and tens of thousands of U.S. casualties. It has been determined that approximately 200,000 Iraqi's lost their lives of which 173,000 were civilians. The financial burden incurred by our nation was $1.7 trillion that does not include the $490 billion for the care of the veterans that fought that war. Some recent studies have estimated that the cost of treating our disabled veterans could rise to $6 trillion in four decades. All of this was incurred and suffered for oil.

Obama, as promised, slowly pulled our troops out while refocusing on the neglected war being waged in Afghanistan, America's longest military campaign. He approved a troop surge in that nation that initially appeared to have some positive results. As the troop levels were dramatically reduced after their mission had been completed, the Taliban reclaimed control over large sections of that besieged nation. A nation that has been embroiled in military conflict for decades. The government is inefficient, incompetent and corrupt. We have spent hundreds of billions of dollars in an attempt to rebuild the nation to no avail. Much to our dismay, there are still U.S. soldiers dying in that forgotten war today.

On May 2, 2011, **Operation Neptune Spear** managed by the CIA resulted in the death of Osama Bin Laden in his Pakistani hideout by Army Special Forces and Navy seals. President Obama proudly announced the successful conclusion of that operation to the nation. A feat that had eluded Bush and Cheney for years. A film entitled **Dark 40** told the story that led to the death of America's most wanted nemesis. The CIA and its public relations department had significant influence on the final script which included scenes of agents obtaining actionable intelligence through the use of EITs that led to the identification of an Al Qaeda currier. The Senate Intelligence Report on Torture concluded that no actionable intelligence had been obtained through the use of torture and a recent article by Seymour Hersh came to a conclusion that differed from the administration's version.

Hersh, who was interviewed by Amy Goodman on Democracy Now, indicated that his source had reported that Pakistani officials had known for years where Bin Laden was hiding. They finally divulged that information to American intelligence assets that enabled the operation that resulted in his death.[58] In any event, this should have ended the undeclared war on terror. The head of the snake and the master mind behind the diabolical plot that caused 9/11 was now dead. This unfortunately did not happen, and it appears that the war will continue indefinitely.

Bush had instituted the use of drone technology in the war on terror. Obama rather than reviewing its efficacy enhanced the program significantly. The administration has promoted these drone strikes as a cleaner and less costly way to wage war as we try to kill our way to a resolution. The idea of capturing these alleged terrorist combatants and bringing them to justice has been tossed aside in favor of a secret operation that allows the President, his military advisors and CIA officials to act like judge, jury and executioner as they meet each week to determine who will be assassinated. According to Jeremy Scahill and intercept staffers who wrote the recently published book **The Assassination Complex**, the legacy of Obama will significantly be tarnished by this assassination program. The President, as Bush did with torture, has made assassination of our enemies a normal tool in our arsenal to defend our national security.[59]

Four whistleblowers who resigned from the drone program described on Democracy Now the nefarious aspects of this operation. They indicated that the military sets up booths at video-game shows and promotes this program as a way to be employed as a gamer. The simulations that are used by the military to train drone operators in many ways mimics the violent video games being sold to our children by toy and electronic manufacturers. The reality is far more serious and the outcome much more deadly than the games played in our living rooms.

One of the whistleblowers indicated that at one point they were instructed to kill everyone in white because they most likely were Taliban. As they operated the drone and released its missile, they watched as those that were hit succumbed to their injuries and died. For most in this assassination operation, the death of alleged combatants would be cheered each time a target was determined and successfully murdered. While for some, they questioned the efficacy and the morality of the entire program.

Farea Al-Muslimi is a U.S. citizen from Yemen who has become a political activist that has denounced the effectiveness of the drone program. While he was a student in America, he travelled occasionally back to his village in Yemen to visit with family and friends. He often got into discussions defending the United States. He had gradually convinced his village that the U.S. was more than just its military and the CIA. It was for the most part a good country. This all changed when a drone strike hit his village. The Obama administration reported that they had killed terrorist combatants, but Al-Muslimi and those that resided in the village knew differently. Innocent people were also murdered by the strike. In a few seconds, the image of the U.S. that Al-Muslimi had successfully portrayed to his home village had drastically changed, reversing everything he had accomplished over several years. He concluded based on his experience that the drones are terrifying the civilians and empowering the militants. They are in essence enhancing the recruitment of extremist organizations.[60]

The drone program, therefore, is undermining our security as it unintentionally creates more enemies than we can kill. It is also perpetuating a very negative image of our nation that instills fear, resentment and finally hatred.

The Iraq War and the lessons learned should have been self-evident to Obama and Secretary of State Hillary Clinton. I surmise from their disastrous intervention in Libya that maybe the administration had extrapolated a different understanding. Muammar Gaddafi had ruled Libya since 1969. He had been a thorn in the side of Washington since his ascension to power. When a jet liner fell out of the sky over England, often referred to as the Lockerbie bombing, the Reagan administration without much proof assigned blame to Libya. This resulted in his nation being bombed and economic sanctions imposed by Britain and the U.S. in 1986. Consequently, he was viewed as a dictator of a pariah nation that had to be isolated.

Gaddafi in 1999 decided to restructure his economy by encouraging privatization and by seeking rapprochement with the West. Just maybe, he was mellowing as he grew older. He also embraced Pan-Africanism and in fact helped establish the African Union. Nevertheless, the Arab spring in 2011 would drastically change the viability of his regime and would ferment opposition to his government. As nations such as Egypt erupted, anti-Gaddafi revolts that were primarily sponsored by the National Transitional Council (NTC) pushed the nation into a civil war. With staunch support from Secretary Clinton, Obama convened NATO forces led by the U.S. to militarily intervene on behalf of NTC militants to oust Gaddafi. The immense bombing campaign eventually resulted in the collapse of Gaddafi's government. He ultimately was captured and killed by rebel forces.

The outcome as in Iraq was not in doubt as far as the military action was concerned. The problem that confronted the administration was what was going to fill the void that was inevitable after the regime was toppled. As in Iraq, no viable replacement has asserted itself, and the nation has descended into chaos. It is now reported that 2,500 Islamic State (ISIS) militants have joined other extremists to rule most of Libya. The weapons from

Gaddafi's fallen military have been dispersed throughout Northern Africa wreaking havoc with its neighbors. As Obama admitted in an interview with CNN, one of his biggest regrets was his failure to develop a cohesive plan after the regime was destroyed.

We have a protracted and enigmatic relationship with the ruling family of Saudi Arabia. Their oppressive and brutal rule had disgusted President Kennedy to the point that he tried to avoid meeting with their representatives whenever possible. President Obama appears quite comfortable with this regime that has imprisoned and sentenced to death hundreds of political opponents to their authoritarian rule. In fact, 16 out the 19 terrorists involved in 9/11, including Osama Bin Laden, were citizens of Saudi Arabia. It is also alleged that the regime has financially backed some of these extreme militant groups that we are fighting.

The Obama administration recently approved a $30 billion arms deal that included 84 Boeing F-15 fighter jets and more than 100 attack helicopters. The deal may reach as much as $60 billion over the next decade as we assist in the modernization of their naval fleet. This is by far the largest arms accord in U.S. history. Another billion-dollar agreement was reached in 2015 to assist their efforts against ISIS and in Yemen.

The civil war being fought in Yemen started in 2015. It has pitted Houthi forces with those loyal to former president Ali Abullah Saleh against those aligned with the new government of Abd Rabbuh Mansur Hadi. Since Houthi militants have taken the capital, Hadi has fled the country. This was the catalyst for Saudi Arabia to launch a military campaign with the support of the U.S., using airstrikes with the objective to restore Hadi's regime. While attempting to bomb their way to a palatable solution, the Saudi's have cruelly shelled hospitals, schools and residential neighborhoods, causing 6,500 deaths of which 3,218 were civilians. They are using cluster bombs as part of their arsenal supplied by the U.S. to achieve their goal. This weapon has been banned by the international community and has spurred calls for a UN investigation. Why we are supporting this affront to humanity remains a mystery. I understand that the Saudi's are an important ally to offset the influence of Iran, but that should not be a reason to support this barbarous military assault on the beleaguered nation of Yemen.

The administration's policy in Europe is also posing significant barriers for peace. The U.S. defense strategy there is undermining the spirit of the agreements Reagan and Bush had with Gorbachev by installing a ballistic missile defense shield in Poland and Romania. The alleged purpose of this provocative shield is to prevent Iranian missiles from hitting Europe. It is more likely that this defense program that ironically mimics the capabilities of SDI that caused such contentious debate between Reagan and Gorbachev is now being utilized as a modern tool to contain Russia's perceived military ambitions under Putin. The Russian leader has vowed to neutralize this new threat and has threatened that this will lead to another arms race.

Obama on the other hand has used diplomacy to curtail the development of nuclear weapons by Iran and has opened the door to Cuba by ending our troubled and unjust policy towards that impoverished nation, fulfilling a long forgotten effort of rapprochement initiated by Kennedy in 1963. This was an achievement that was heartedly welcomed by his progressive base.

The Obama legacy will be full of contradiction and disappointment, as well as achievement and visionary success. He, for instance, prevented the Keystone Pipeline and yet authorized Gulf to drill in the pristine and fragile eco-system of Antarctica. He has used his executive power to keep families together while sponsoring policies that has labelled him the deportation president. He has tried to confront the weapons of war while enhancing our military presence throughout the world. He is the first president to visit Hiroshima and has given speeches on nuclear disarmament while contemporaneously investing one trillion dollars over the next three decades to modernize our nuclear arsenal.

He also has engaged in regime change and is presently attempting to undermine Assad's government in Syria. The resulting refugee crisis has essentially been ignored by his administration. So far, only 1800 have been resettled in the U.S. while over 20,000 have been accepted into Canada.

He has inadvertently supported a policy of apartheid sponsored by Netanyahu's government towards the Palestinians as his administration continues to send billions of dollars of military aid being used in part to oppress the residents in Gaza and the West Bank. Obama has also permitted Israel to continue to expand the settlements in Palestine in violation of prior agreements and international law without much rebuke from his administration. Even the Israeli Defense Minister Moshe Yaalon resigned in May 2015 because he no longer had faith in Netanyahu's government. In addition, he cited the growth of extremism, violence and racism in Israeli society that was seeping into the military as a consequence of Netanyahu's policies. He opined that this was a dangerous development and was very concerned about the future of his country.

And finally, he advocated for a more open and transparent government as a candidate and has administered one of the most secretive administrations in history. He has prosecuted more whistleblowers than any of his predecessors and has knowingly supported NSA ubiquitous surveillance programs that threatened our liberty in the name of dubious security objectives. Nevertheless, to be fair, I will concede that he will be judged as an above average president. However, the missed opportunity of 2008, and all its promise, will be what I remember most.

The military budget of the United States was $680 billion dollars in 2010. This does not include defense related programs such as nuclear weapons research, maintenance, cleanup and production. The Pentagon's budget also does not encompass expenditures related to prior wars, Veteran pensions or the State Department's financing of foreign arms sales and military-related development assistance. All totaled our nation spends approximately $1 trillion on defense. This is more than the top ten military budgets combined in the world. China for instance spent $145 billion on their defense in 2015. The U.S. military also has bases all over the globe, as well as Special Forces stationed in dozens of countries training their security forces. In addition, the CIA has procured various secret drone bases hidden from public scrutiny on several continents. And lastly, we are the largest arms dealer in the world.

These enormous expenditures have become so enmeshed in our economic structures that like an addict we immediately go into withdrawal when we attempt to reduce our spending on defense. The Congress quickly learned this lesson after austerity measures went into effect as a consequence of sequestration in 2013. Many towns, cities and communities that had major defense related industries immediately developed adverse economic repercussions from these draconian cuts. The Congress expeditiously carved out exceptions that allowed the defense expenditures to be reinstated while drastic reductions in budgets for programs that ameliorated the social ills of our society remained. This form of Keynesian economics through military spending is bleeding our nation drop by drop until there is nothing left to rebuild our dilapidated infrastructure, reorganize and enhance our public schools, combat climate change and invest in renewable and bio-friendly energy, educate our workforce for the future, upgrade our mass transit system, reform our prison and judicial structures and maintain and expand Medicaid, Medicare and Social Security. Although the defense of the nation is an important obligation of government, its primary duty is to administer and maintain those aspects of our society that contribute to the wellbeing of our people while in pursuit of life, liberty and spiritual fulfillment.

We claim this colossal war machine is necessary because as a world power we have strategic interests all over the earth. Although this may be true in a superficial sense, the reality is that we are a neo-colonial power that by design enforces our will on the rest of the world by our military presence and by clandestine operations sponsored by the CIA that interfere with the internal affairs and sovereignty of many nations. This imposition has generated significant anti-American sentiment and has produced many enemies as a consequence of this corporatist and militaristic global orthodoxy that dominates our political objectives today. In simple terms, we are protecting an empire rather than defending our republic. This misguided and dangerous development threatens world peace which places great stress on our security. As our enemies grow and become bolder, the need for security increases at the expense of our liberty. It is a cannibalistic process in which the hawks in each nation feed off of one another, justifying the diversion of resources to defense while reducing programs that benefit the governed. This is the paradox of our national security complex.

Martin Luther king, Jr., stated that "A nation that continues year after year to spend more money on military defense then on programs of social uplift is approaching spiritual death."

Chapter 2

JFK's Urgent Quest for Peace

For all the sad words of tongue and pen,
The saddest of these,
"it might have been".
John Greenleaf Whittier

"I cringe whenever I hear progressives ding Kennedy's foreign policy record... They do so out of ignorance not of their own making, but of one studiously foisted upon them. It is important to remember, especially with President John Kennedy, that history is written by the victor. Kennedy wasn't killed once. He was killed posthumously so that all he was trying to do, and stood for, would be washed away. By making him less than who he was, his assassination would seem less necessary. By painting him as a rabid cold warrior, no one would suspect cold warriors of having killed him."
Lisa Pease

"I ask you," LeMay said to an Air Force colleague, "would things be much worse if Khrushchev were the Secretary of Defense?"
General Curtis LeMay

"His greatest, most heroic aspirations for a peaceful, demilitarized foreign policy are the forbidden debates of the modern political era."
Robert F. Kennedy, Jr.

"If I tried to pull out completely from Vietnam, we would have another Joe McCarthy Red scare on our hands, but I can

do it after I'm re-elected."
President Kennedy to his aid Kenneth O'Donnell

"I think if Kennedy had lived, we would be living in a completely different world."
Sergei Khrushchev

"I object to violence because when it appears to do good, the good is only temporary. The evil it does is permanent."
Mahatma Gandhi

"The United States, as the world knows, will never start a war. We do not want a war. We do not expect a war. This generation of Americans has already had enough—more than enough –of war and hate and oppression. We shall be prepared if others wish it. We shall be alert to try to stop it. But we shall also do our part to build a world of peace where the weak are safe and the strong are just. We are not helpless before that task or hopeless for its success. Confident and unafraid, we labor on—not toward a strategy of annihilation but towards a strategy of peace."
John F. Kennedy

"I come to this magnificent house of worship tonight because my conscience leaves me no other choice. I join you in this meeting because I'm in deepest agreement with the aims and work of the organization which has brought us together: Clergy and Laymen Concerned About Vietnam. The recent statements of your executive committee are the sentiments of my own heart, and I found myself in full accord when I read its opening lines: 'A time comes when silence is betrayal.' And that time has come for us in relation to Vietnam."
Martin Luther King, Jr.

"Those that make peaceful revolution impossible will make violent revolution inevitable."
John F. Kennedy

"If we do not act, we shall surely be dragged down the long, dark, and shameful corridors of time reserved for those who possess power without compassion, might without morality, and strength without sight."
Martin Luther King, Jr.

"The danger which troubled my husband was that war might be started not so much by the big men as by the little ones. While big men know the need for self-control and restraint, little men are sometimes moved more by fear and pride."
Jacqueline Kennedy

"...we're going to bomb them (Vietnamese) into the stone age."
General Curtis LeMay

"I think there are many times when it would be most efficient to use nuclear weapons. However, the public opinion in this country and throughout the world throw up their hands in horror when you mention nuclear weapons, just because of the propaganda that's been fed to them."
General Curtis LeMay

"There are no innocent civilians. It is their government and you are fighting a people, you are not trying to fight an armed force anymore. So it doesn't bother me so much to be killing the so-called innocent bystanders."
General Curtis LeMay

"Native annalists may look sadly back from the future on that

period when we had the atomic bomb and the Russian's didn't…That was the era when we might have destroyed Russia completely and not even skinned our elbows doing it."
General Curtis LeMay

"Force is all conquering, but its victories are short lived."
Abraham Lincoln

"…overgrown military establishments, which, under any form of government, are inauspicious to liberty, and which are to be regarded as particularly hostile to Republican liberty."
George Washington

"I spent 33 years and 4 months in active military service…And during that period I spent most of my time as a high-class muscle man for big business, for Wall Street and the bankers. In short, a gangster for capitalism."
General Smedley Butler

Resisting the Tide
(The dilemma JFK confronted in Vietnam and his policy to withdraw)

Over the decades since his tragic death admirers and critics have debated the policy Kennedy would have pursued in Vietnam if he had served a second term. The subject was reinvigorated by an avalanche of declassified documents that the government was compelled to release after Congress passed, and President George H.W. Bush signed into law the **JFK Records Act** of 1992. This had all been made possible by an innocuous paragraph that was included at the end of Oliver Stone's provocative movie about the assassination in 1991. The commentary listed at the end of **JFK** indicated that thousands of documents remained in the government's possession and were not scheduled to be released for decades. The public's overwhelming response to demand the release of these documents influenced Congress to act. But before all this occurred, John Newman would reenergize the debate when he became a consultant for Stone's controversial film and published his prophetic book entitled **JFK and Vietnam: Deception, Intrigue, and the Struggle for Power** in 1992.

His research spanned a decade before he published the book. The basic premise of his study was that President Kennedy was never enthusiastic about the prospect of American combat forces being injected into Vietnam. Newman concluded based on everything he discovered in preparation for his volume that Kennedy was withdrawing from Vietnam and on the day he was assassinated that was the policy of the United States.

Newman's credentials were impressive and could not be easily ignored or dismissed by those who rejected the evidence he proffered in support of his conclusion. Newman at the time he completed his insightful book was preparing for his retirement from the military which occurred in 1994. He joined the faculty at the University of Maryland where he taught classes on communism in the Soviet Union and China among other courses from 1995 until 2012. He currently is an adjunct Professor of Political Science at James Madison University. Prior to his academic career, he was a military intelligence officer for two decades who had been stationed in Thailand, Philippines, China and Japan. He eventually became the executive assistant to the director of the **National Security Agency** (NSA). He clearly was well informed on the politics and the history of Southeast Asia, as well as the broader region.

By associating his book with Stone's controversial film that had ignited a firestorm of reaction from historians, the mainstream media and the CIA, he naturally became embroiled in this vitriolic national debate. Although his tome did not address the assassination of Kennedy which was the focus of the movie, his research did contribute to the motive for the killing of Kennedy that was adopted by Stone.

Stone through his cinematic artistry had presented to the American public a visually compelling explanation for the assassination. In essence according to Stone, Kennedy was considered a treacherous **Cold War** liability because he refused to Americanize the war and had decided to withdraw by December 1965 which infuriated the military brass at the Pentagon and the covert sector of the CIA. In addition, the corporations that had become part of our military industrial complex were expecting a war that would add millions if not billions of dollars to their coffers. None of these anticipated profits would be realized if Kennedy's policy of withdrawal was implemented.

President Clinton in compliance with the **JFK Records Act** commissioned the **Assassination Records Review Board** (ARRB) to facilitate the release of millions of classified documents that were relevant to Kennedy's presidency and his assassination. This board was formed in 1994 and would continue its work until 1998. They were instructed not to reinvestigate the murder but were authorized to organize the documents and to conduct interviews of witnesses to this history which were recorded. This treasure chest of documents would not only supplement our understanding of the events in Dallas in 1963 but would reform our image of the man and his policies. Policies that were consistent with those originally espoused after his death by Manchester, Sorensen, Salinger and Schlesinger, Jr. who were often dismissed as Kennedy apologists.

The documents more specifically supported Newman and Stone's portrayal of him as a peacemaker as opposed to the cold warrior promoted in many books published after 1970. These critical views of him were probably influenced by a multitude of factors. The most prominent I suspect was to tarnish his martyred image to offset the intense criticism the hawks and their policies had been subjected to because of **Watergate**, the investigation of the **CIA** and its nefarious activities and the catastrophic legacy of **Vietnam** as our policy was reduced to ashes. Kennedy was not going to be spared and allowed to remain a hero of our generation. He, therefore, had to be implicated in this disaster as had been Eisenhower, Johnson and Nixon. By obfuscating his true Vietnam program, one of the primary motives for his public execution would remain hidden from the public. This was most likely the major impetus for editing the **Pentagon Papers** and for the publication of numerous tomes that perpetuated the myth that President Johnson's policy towards Vietnam was consistent with Kennedy's objectives. Many historians unwittingly supported this false history because of their reliance on documents that were censored, as well as their ignorance of evidence that remained classified. Their inference that the war was inevitable because of the political paradigms that dominated in the 1950s and 1960s was logical, and yet indoctrinated the public with a false understanding of Kennedy's **Vietnam** policy.

History would repeat itself in the 1990s after Newman's book and Stone's movie. The CIA and its media assets encouraged negative tomes that battered Kennedy's policies, as well as his character. This included Seymour Hersh's specious book **The Dark Side of Camelot** (1997) and **A Question of Character** by Thomas Reeves. As to the assassination, Gerald Posner wrote his book supporting the conclusions of the **Warren Commission** entitled **Case Closed** which was first published in 1993.

The real legacy of Kennedy's administration refused to be distorted by the mythology of his critics. No matter how malicious his detractors would write of him, the public continued to hold Kennedy in high esteem. In many polls, he is rated comparable to George Washington, Franklin Roosevelt and Abraham Lincoln. He is clearly viewed by the public as the best president since the end of **World War II**. This is remarkable considering he was only in office for 1,036 days.

The question posed by many is this admiration by the public warranted? The answer to that question in my opinion partially rests upon Kennedy's Vietnam policy. If he was intending to withdraw as argued by Newman, Stone and many others he then cannot be implicated in the largest foreign policy disaster, not only of the twentieth century, but of our entire history. And if he truly was a peacemaker at a time when many within our government were advocating for a war, even if it resulted in the use of nuclear weapons, his courageous stand for peace against the colossal power of the Pentagon and the CIA certainly would justify the public's continued admiration of the man and his leadership.

The revelations that were unearthed in the millions of documents were not kind to Kennedy's critics. Many historians that included Robert Dallek and Howard Jones, as well as Economist James Galbraith (son of economist and U.S. Ambassador to India John Kenneth Galbraith), Professor Peter Dale Scott, Daniel Ellsberg and others were convinced that the record supported the position that Kennedy would not have escalated our involvement in Vietnam as his successor Lyndon Johnson. There were also numerous books that have been published in the last 20 years that concluded that Kennedy was withdrawing from Vietnam. This included **Brothers (The hidden history of the Kennedy years) (2007)** by Talbot and **JFK and the Unspeakable (Why he died and why it matters) (2008)** by Douglass that came to the same conclusion of not only Newman but Stone's film as well.

Before Newman's book was published, there were many distinguished politicians, historians and journalists such as David Halberstam who wrote **The Best and the Brightest** which was a critical analysis of Kennedy's Vietnam policy that supported Newman's view. Halberstam opined that Kennedy was too much a student of history to embroil the nation in the quagmire that Vietnam eventually would become after his death.

He stated in an article in the 1990s on **Vietnam** that "I have never believed that John Kennedy would have sent combat troops to Vietnam." The majority leader of the Senate at the time, Mike Mansfield, based on conversations he had with the President was adamant that Kennedy was getting out.

More recently two video documentaries were released that portrayed Kennedy not as a traditional cold warrior but as a peacemaker. The first documentary was **Virtual JFK** that was accompanied by a book that was primarily written by Professor James G. Blight of Brown University. This video was directed by Kasi Masutani and released in 2008. Essentially, Blight used a counterfactual analysis of Kennedy's actions when armed forces were recommended by his national security team to project what he may have done in Vietnam if he had not been assassinated. The conclusion reached by Blight and others who worked on this documentary was that Kennedy was a different type of president than Johnson. Throughout his administration when a crisis presented itself, he would seek a diplomatic solution in lieu of the bellicose recommendations by his national security team. He did it in Cuba after the **Bay of Pigs**, in Berlin in the summer and fall of 1961, in Cuba during the missile crisis and in Laos and Vietnam on multiple occasions.

I think the historical record as it presently stands is unequivocal that Kennedy's desire to negotiate an end to the **Cold War**, to eliminate nuclear weapons and to improve the quality of life in the developing world compelled him to view conflict through a global perspective. By doing this, he was always concerned about how his actions in one region would impact these broader aspirations. If for example he authorized the invasion of Cuba when it became clear the mission at the **Bay of Pigs** was failing, or he had bombed the missile sites and invaded Cuba in October 1962 as recommended by his national security team, he anticipated reprisals by the Soviets in Berlin that not only would threaten the peace but could escalate to a world war. This was also true of Laos and Vietnam. An invasion of either nation would be viewed by the developing countries as another form of Western imperialism. It would also jeopardize his strategy for peace. As he said in his inaugural address, it was his administration's goal not to create a new balance of power but a new world of law "where the strong are just, the weak secure and the peace preserved."

Johnson was more concerned with his image as a strong leader. He was adamant that Southeast Asia would not become a communist bastion on his watch as China did during the Truman administration. His focus, therefore, was more influenced by domestic politics, and the image he wanted to project to the American people. He was just as concerned with how his senior military advisors thought of him and was eager to demonstrate his willingness to adopt their recommendations for Vietnam. Whereas the domestic political realities for Kennedy did not govern the policies he formulated, but it did influence the strategy he employed to implement them. Kennedy for instance used the upcoming election in 1964 to lend cover to his withdraw plan while pretending to hold the line in Vietnam. Johnson on the other hand used the 1964 election as a way to present himself as the peace candidate while preparing for war. Both, however, recognized that any appearance of weakness as it related to national security would provide the Republican's with an issue that could result in Senator Barry Goldwater's coronation.

Blight further indicated that Kennedy had learned his lesson when he deferred to the **CIA** and the **Joint Chiefs of Staff** (JCS) in April 1961 that resulted in the **Bay of Pigs** fiasco. After that debacle, he questioned and analyzed every recommendation for the use of military force in ways that Kennedy admitted to his advisors would not have occurred if it was not for the Cuban disaster. Kennedy further stated to friends that the military always expect to be successful and paint "rosy scenarios" that are not an accurate assessment of the situation on the ground. He was determined not to be betrayed again by the deception of the **CIA** or the unrealistic hubris of the military brass.

The second documentary was released in 2013 entitled **JFK: A President Betrayed**. This film was directed by Cory Taylor and narrated by Morgan Freeman. Contrary to most of the documentaries on Kennedy's policies and his assassination, Taylor's film incorporated material that was part of the declassified documents, JFK tapes and oral histories that had come to light in the 1990s. He also interviewed the Soviet and American interpreters at the Vienna Conference in June 1961 between Khrushchev and Kennedy. These unique interviews included Soviet officers in Cuba during the missile crisis and many of the children of parents that participated in advancing the agenda of the **New Frontier**. This included economist and Chair of the LBJ School of Public Affairs James Galbraith, Norman Cousins' two daughters Candis and Andrea, and Arthur Schlesinger's son Robert.

Unlike most of the rehashed information that was aired as part of the fiftieth anniversary of the assassination that permeated the networks and major cable stations, this film more accurately assessed the internal power struggle related to war and peace that characterized much of Kennedy's presidency. The film even correlated the actions of Kennedy's opponents, and some in his inner circle, that betrayed his administration, his agenda and his trust to the motivation that led to the events in Dallas.

There were also two important volumes that were published that were written or inspired by prominent members of Kennedy's cabinet. The first was **In Retrospect** by former Secretary of Defense for Kennedy and Johnson, Robert McNamara, which was published in 1995. As pointed out by James DiEugenio, there were three significant admissions by McNamara that added to our understanding of the war and Kennedy's intentions. McNamara conceded that the **Vietnam**

War was a huge mistake; he had determined that the war could not be won as early as April of 1966; and that President Kennedy would not have Americanized the war and escalated it as his successor did.[61]

McGeorge Bundy, the National Security Advisor for both presidents, after reading McNamara's book in 1996 decided that he should re-evaluate his record as it related to the war as well. He had always been an unrepentant supporter of Johnson's decision to send combat troops until he reviewed the whole record and his role in it. After he examined the documentation, Bundy was astounded on how steadfast and resistant Kennedy was to the pressure imposed upon him by the Joint Chiefs of Staff (JCS), the CIA, former President Eisenhower, the State Department and his national security advisors who all recommended the deployment of combat troops to reverse the bleak situation in Vietnam.

Bundy solicited the assistance of Gordon Goldstein, a renowned scholar on international affairs, to write a book on his role in the war. Bundy unfortunately died before it was completed. Goldstein had to research a good portion of the book entitled **Lessons in Disaster** on his own with the complete support of Bundy's wife. It was published in 2008.

Goldstein reported that throughout 1961 and 1962 the president was bombarded with different rationalizations for sending troops to Vietnam. In fact, he had rejected at least ten different proposals. Much of Kennedy's national security team was enamored with the **Domino Theory** that had been introduced to the public in a press conference of Eisenhower's in April 1954. The original idea was most likely endorsed by the CIA and adopted by John Foster Dulles who was Eisenhower's Secretary of State and the brother of Allen Dulles who was the Director of the CIA. The essence of this fictitious doctrine was that if Laos was lost to the communists than all of Indochina would fall like dominoes into the communist sphere which was centered in

Moscow and Peking (now Beijing). When it was clear that Kennedy was not interested in a war in Laos, Vietnam became this magical domino.

President Kennedy gave lip service to this idea in public but privately never fully accepted it. Otherwise, he would have relented and authorized the troops that were requested by the military and the CIA. His position to neutralize Laos and Vietnam by seeking an acceptable political solution placed him in an extreme minority within his administration. The only consistent support he had was Under Secretary of State for Economic and Agricultural Affairs George Ball, U.S. Ambassador to India John Kenneth Galbraith, his special assistant and speech writer Theodore Sorensen and his brother Robert who was the Attorney General.

The advice that Kennedy received at his National Security Council meetings concerned him to the point that he asked Sorensen and his brother to join the discussions.[62] Asking Sorensen to participate was a significant indication on how displeased Kennedy was with his national security advisors. Sorensen had been a conscientious objector during the **Korean War**, and his mother was a Quaker with pacifist views. Kennedy originally requested that Sorensen not attend these meetings so that the JCS were not offended. Apparently, this no longer concerned him.

To fully appreciate the dilemma that Vietnam presented his administration and the origins of Kennedy's views on that belea-guered nation, it is necessary to review the history since the end of **World War II**.

Ho Chi Minh was educated in France before he rose to power on a wave of nationalism that was enveloping the globe in 1946. He had been inspired by the words of Jefferson in the **Declaration of Independence** and the agreement reached by Churchill and Roosevelt on the turbulent North Atlantic called the **Atlantic Charter** in 1941 to seek independence. Minh quoted

Jefferson in his inaugural speech in Hanoi. He, however, was not attempting to build a democratic republic such as ours. He was significantly influenced by Marx and his **Communist Manifesto** of 1848. While he was consolidating his power, the French were eager to regain control of their colonies that they temporarily had abandoned after Hitler's panzers had overrun their defenses and forced them to sign a humiliating armistice. They would quickly focus on their former colony in Southeast Asia after the war.

Minh sent a telegram to President Truman in February 1946 requesting American support. He wrote "...I...earnestly appeal to you personally and to the American people to intervene urgently in support of our independence and help making the negotiations more in keeping with the principles of the Atlantic and San Francisco Charters." Although the Truman administration was not initially enthusiastic with the French decision to send troops to their former colony in an attempt to rebuild their battered prestige, it would eventually assist its ally. After all, Minh was a communist which was akin to a terrorist today.

Minh's primary objective was independence and for him this was non-negotiable. Historically, Vietnam had been dominated by China, the Europeans and the Japanese. They had a turbulent history with their large neighbor to the north and had no past relationship with Russia. Nevertheless, they had to form military alliances with those powers to assist the defense of their country from the modern weaponry of the French. By the early 1950s, the French would have 250,000 troops in Vietnam.

In 1951 as a congressman, Kennedy and his brother Robert travelled to Vietnam to observe the French's struggle and to assess the situation. They met with U.S. diplomat Edmund Gullion who had been stationed in Saigon since 1949. He warned Kennedy that it would be a mistake for the U.S. to get involved. Kennedy was so impressed with the astute assessment of the situation by Gullion that he appointed him years later as the Ambassador to the Democratic Republic of the Congo where another war of independence was being fought against a European colonial power, Belgium. Kennedy initially wanted to assign him to South Vietnam, but Secretary of State Dean Rusk vehemently opposed Gullion's appointment. After his consultation with Gullion and his own observations of the dire predicament of the French, he returned to the U.S. as an outspoken opponent to our ally's effort to maintain colonial control and subvert the aspiration of the Vietnamese people to be independent. In a major statement on Vietnam, he opposed the U.S. getting involved in this "hopeless internecine struggle" where the enemy is everywhere and nowhere at the same time.

As the war dragged on, the French people began to waver in their support of their government's policy in French Indochina. The public's displeasure over the costs of this never-ending conflict would come to a head when General Giap's troops surrounded 15,000 French at **Dien Bien Phu** in 1954. The Eisenhower administration would contemplate the use of nuclear weapons to assist the French. The plan that was devised was called **Operation Vulture**. The JCS, Vice President Nixon, Secretary of State Dulles and the CIA supported the plan. Eisenhower eventually rejected it when he could not get the British to join the effort. When Senator Kennedy heard about it, he immediately attacked it. The French, without a way out and with dwindling public support, decided to surrender. It was a major victory for General Giap and his men.

The ceasefire that was negotiated between the French and the Vietnamese resulted in the **Geneva Accords** of 1954. The agreement had separated the country into two zones divided at the seventeenth parallel. The northern section was governed by the Viet Minh whose leader was Ho Chi Minh, and the southern zone was administered by the State of Vietnam. The accord further specified that free elections would be held in 1956 to determine the government of a unified Vietnam. The United States and South Vietnam never expressly agreed to the general election. The Eisenhower administration was concerned that the North with its military alliances with the Soviet Union and China would win the election, and this was unacceptable politically and militarily. If Vietnam – even if determined by a free election – went communist, the administration feared that Laos and Cambodia would follow creating a domino effect that significantly threatened U.S. strategic interests in the region.

As the CIA propped up Ngo Dinh Diem (hereinafter Diem) and his government, Eisenhower approved 685 military advisors to train the South Vietnamese Government's (SVG) military forces which became part of the **Military Assistance Advisory Group (MAAG)**. It became clear to the North that the election specified in the Geneva Accords was not going to take place. They began to prepare for another war.

The Vietnamese issue for the Eisenhower administration, as the events in Laos deteriorated, became enmeshed in the military strategic struggle of the **Cold War** that made a negotiated settlement an untenable option. Because the civilian leadership was hesitant to engage the Soviets directly which could easily escalate to a nuclear war, the military and the CIA were constantly seeking areas where they could engage the enemy in proxy wars such as Vietnam. As the **Cold War** progressed and the fear of Soviet intentions became the obsession of policy makers in Washington, collective security treaties were formed to deter the actions of the communists. These security accords in essence were a natural corollary to the containment program discussed in **National Security Council Report (NSC) 68** and as articulated in the **Truman Doctrine** of 1947.

The **North Atlantic Treaty Organization** (NATO) was consummated in 1949 to deter Soviet aggression in Europe. The Soviet response was to establish the **Warsaw Pact**. In Asia, the Eisenhower administration negotiated the **South East Asia Treaty Organization** (SEATO) in 1955. The members included the United States, Australia, France, New Zealand, the United

Kingdom, East Pakistan (now Bangladesh) and Thailand. Cambodia, Laos and South Vietnam were not official members. They were made part of the agreement by reference in that they were granted military protection.

President Eisenhower in his attempt to contain communism and deter it from further adventurism in the developing world significantly expanded covert paramilitary operations and invested heavily in our nuclear force. In fact, his ambitions were more aggressive than the policy set forth by the Truman administration. Eisenhower's goal as articulated by his Secretary of State, John Foster Dulles, was to roll back communism in Eastern Europe and in other regions where it had a foothold. They intended to do this not only through covert actions that included regime change and assassination, but also a nuclear brinkmanship that would be used as a club to intimidate the Soviets and their allies.

By the time Kennedy was inaugurated, the CIA had not only assassinated the charismatic national leader of the Democratic Republic of the Congo, Patrice Lumumba, but had also attempted with its Mafia assets to murder Fidel Castro of Cuba. The CIA had also successfully overthrown the governments of the Philippines, Iran, Guatemala and had attempted to sabotage the regimes in North Vietnam, Syria, Cuba and Indonesia. In fact, Cuba, Vietnam and Laos were major issues that were getting worse from a political and military perspective very rapidly. Eisenhower had apprised Kennedy that he might have to send combat forces into Laos to prevent the Pathet Lao from taking control of that government. He was also briefed by the CIA and Eisenhower on **Operation Zapata** which consisted of 1400 Cuban exiles that had been trained by the CIA in preparation for an eventual invasion of Cuba. In Vietnam, the Diem regime had narrowly avoided a coup. This was the precarious situation that confronted Kennedy as his administration was getting ready to take power.

The young President quickly realized that his peace initiatives had to be set aside until he could assess the predicament he was confronted with in Cuba and Southeast Asia. The first crisis he addressed was in Laos, and shortly thereafter it was the CIA-backed operation for Cuba. Laos had been engaged in a civil war for years between the communists and the anti-communists. The major leaders in Laos were General Phoumi Nosavan who was backed by the CIA; Souvanna Phouma was a neutralist; Prince Souphanouvong was the communist half-brother of Phouma; and Kong Le was a former paratrooper who briefly allied with the communists or the Pathet Lao.[63] The two primary armies that participated in the Laotian civil war were the Pathet Lao and the Royal Laotian Army supported by the U.S. and led by Nosavan.[64]

The JCS and the CIA recommended that 60,000 combat troops should be sent into Laos to stabilize the situation. The military felt that if the communists could be defeated in Laos the U.S. could prevent the domino effect and contemporaneously take control of the **Ho Chi Minh Trail** that was primarily in Laos. This trail was the source of most of the supplies that the north was sending to the Viet Cong in the south who were trying to topple Diem's oppressive government.

The CIA had multiple interests in Laos that included defeating the Pathet Lao and elevating the right wing General Nosavan as the head of a new government. The Agency also wanted to maintain control of its major source for opium. The Laotian climate was one of the best places on earth to grow the plant that produced the drug. It was part of the golden triangle which also consisted of Thailand and Burma. The CIA was trading weapons and supplies to militia groups who were willing to fight the communists in exchange for opium. The Agency used its planes and resources to develop and expand opium markets that would not only benefit the CIA but these right wing militias as well. The CIA combined its profits from these drug transactions and added them to their congressionally-approved secret "black budget" to help fund their black ops in the region.[65] The drug money was not only making the Agency rich but also enhanced their influence and power significantly in Southeast Asia. For instance, the CIA transported 1,146 kilos of raw opium in November 1963 in one of their Air America planes to South Vietnam, netting a $97,410 profit for the Agency and General Nosavan.[66]

Kennedy decided to reject the military solution and assigned senior diplomat Averill Harriman the task of negotiating a neutral coalition government that would include the communists. It was an arduous assignment that would consume over a year of Kennedy's abbreviated administration. Nevertheless, Harriman much to the CIA's astonishment and dismay was able to negotiate a settlement that was signed by 14 nations in Geneva.

The **Declaration on the Neutrality of Laos** in July 1962 was heralded as a major achievement by Kennedy to maintain the peace in the region. This accord would not last long. The CIA immediately began to sabotage the diplomacy reached in Geneva by instigating violence and suspicion among the members that participated in the fragile alliance that formed the coalition government. The Agency's ultimate objective was to force Kennedy to respond to events they initiated that would necessitate the introduction of combat troops.

Before the agreement was consummated in Geneva, the CIA backed Royal Laotian Army led by General Nosavan began to concentrate its forces of fifty-two hundred troops at Nam Tha, the provincial capital of Laos. It was situated only twenty miles from the Chinese border. This was done against the explicit orders of Kennedy not to provoke a battle with the Pathet Lao. The administration's warnings were ignored by General Nosavan. The Pathet Lao could not resist and sent a large army to destroy the right wing armed force that had been created by the CIA.

The **Battle of Nam Tha** in May 1962 was a disaster for General Nosavan in that his Royal Laotian Army was obliterated. The CIA anticipated that this disaster would compel Kennedy to respond with military force in order to prevent a communist takeover of the country. Initially, it appeared as though their plan to sacrifice Nosavan's troops was a success. Kennedy did dispatch the seventh fleet to the Gulf of Thailand and sent U.S. troops to the Thailand-Laotian border in an attempt to bluff the communists back to the negotiating table.[67]

His most senior advisors in Washington recommended to the President that if this did not achieve a ceasefire that he may have to authorize the use of tactical nuclear weapons and air strikes against the Pathet Lao. Much to the dismay of the President, they also advised that if North Vietnam or China intervened that both nations should be bombed and if necessary attacked with nuclear weapons.[68] Fortunately for Kennedy, his deception worked in that he was able to get the Soviets to convince the Pathet Lao to stop their offensive. As part of the agreement that was reached in Geneva, the Soviet and American troops were withdrawn.

The CIA was incensed that their plan had backfired. As a result of their miscalculation of Kennedy's resolve, Nosavan and his CIA cohorts were rendered powerless to resist Kennedy's pressure to join the coalition government. They had to salvage what little leverage they still possessed through negotiation. Kennedy's successful gamble had preserved his opportunity to neutralize the country and remove it from the chessboard of the **Cold War**. Contrary to his expectant plans for Laos in 1963, he was compelled to confront major impediments to his Laotian settlement by events fomented by CIA operatives that jeopardized the brittle alliance that formed the government.

The Laotian government disbanded on April 1, 1963, when Foreign Minister Quinim Pholsena was assassinated after the Pathet Lao had murdered one of Kong Le's neutralist officers.

Pholsena was considered a reasonable progressive that Kennedy was hoping would hold the frail alliance together. It was a major setback in Kennedy's plan to neutralize Laos.[69] Pholsena's wife said that she had "no doubts" who was behind her husband's murder. She indicated that the assassins were instigated and backed by the CIA. In fact, the CIA after the collapse of the coalition government rounded up scores of known progressives and had them arrested.[70] As the war was reignited in the spring of 1963, the JCS renewed their recommendation to introduce combat troops into Laos. The President refused further rupturing his tenuous relationship with the military brass and the CIA.

The President – as the chaos continued – initiated back channel communication with Soviet diplomats to restore order, permitting the violence to subside long enough for diplomatic efforts to succeed. Ironically, Kennedy's objective in Laos was more compatible with our **Cold War** rival than major elements of his own government.

While all of this was occurring in Laos, Kennedy was faced with similar problems in Vietnam. Even in the beginning of his administration, and most certainly after the debacle at the **Bay of Pigs**, Kennedy was very reluctant to Americanize the war. He sent Walt Rostow and General Maxwell Taylor to South Vietnam to assess the situation in October 1961. This mission resulted in the **Taylor-Rostow Report** that was filed that November. The report recommended that the U.S. needed to deploy combat troops, increase counterinsurgency operations and bomb the North.

Kennedy believed that our role was limited to providing support and guidance to Diem's military force. If the war was to be fought, they would have to fight it. This was at variance with his national security team that had already concluded that South Vietnam (SVN) would lose without the U.S. military being deployed as the main force against the Viet Cong. By November 7 of 1961, and in accordance with the **Taylor-Rostow Report**, the

JCS, his National Security Advisor, his Secretary of Defense and the CIA presented a grave summary on SVN's chances of success without U.S. intervention. They warned that if SVN was taken over by the communists this could result in a rapid extension of communist control over the whole region. They further projected that the strategic implications for the U.S. would be "extremely serious." This memo conceded that the struggle would be long and hard with a strong possibility of Chinese intervention as occurred in Korea. The number of troops recommended to Kennedy to avoid this scenario was 205,000. They declared that our policy should be to commit to the primary objective of preventing the fall of SVN to the communists.[71]

Ambassador Galbraith and Undersecretary Ball strongly opposed the above proposal. Ball said it would be a "tragic mistake" to adopt this as our policy.[72] Kennedy was troubled by the memo. His frustration with the advice he received was apparent when he told Arthur Schlesinger, Jr. who was the resident historian in the White House, "They want a force of American troops." He continued. "They say it is necessary in order to restore confidence and maintain morale. But it will be just like Berlin. The troops will march in; the bands will play; the crowds will cheer; and in four days everyone will have forgotten. Then we will be told we have to send in more troops. It's like taking a drink. The effect wears off and you have to have another...The war in Vietnam could only be won so long as it was their war. If it were ever converted into a white man's war, we would lose as the French had lost a decade earlier."[73]

As the Vietnam issue was debated between Kennedy and his national security team, Kennedy arm-twisted his Secretary of Defense to change his position to provide some cover for his view just prior to his meeting with his national security advisors on November 11, 1961.[74] Robert Kennedy indicated that his brother's position was made with clarity. The President told his staff, "We are not sending combat troops."

This meeting was only a minor prelude to what transpired just four days later which would become a seminal moment during Kennedy's administration on Vietnam. With his entire national security team assembled on November 15, 1961, Kennedy according to historian James Blight was like a "chess master" countering every argument presented by his team in favor of U.S. military intervention.[75] In fact, as reported by Goldstein, he essentially "eviscerated" their proposal to deploy combat troops more forcefully than he had ever done before. Although the President was primarily alone in his view, he was not intimidated.[76]

The result of the meeting was **National Security Action Memorandum (NSAM) 111** which was his final position on the matter; no combat troops would be sent to Vietnam. He did increase the number of military advisors and approved sending some planes and helicopters to be used to train SVN forces as part of **Operation Farm Gate**. By the summer of 1963, there were 16,000 military advisors under the command of General Paul Harkins who was in charge of **MAAG**. Kennedy established the **Military Advisory Command Vietnam (MACV)** on February 8, 1962, as a response to increased U.S. military assistance to SVN. General Harkins commanded this new agency as well.

The day after his Vietnam meeting Kennedy delivered a key foreign policy speech at the University of Washington in Seattle in which he modified the rhetoric of global activism in his inaugural. This speech according to Sorensen was Kennedy's archetypal expression of his foreign policy that incorporated a new realism on the limits of American power that he had learned over the course of his first year in office.[77] He declared "We must face the fact that the United States is neither omnipotent or omniscient...that we are only six percent of the world's population, that we cannot impose our will on the other ninety four percent, that we cannot fight every wrong or reverse each adversity, and that therefore there cannot be an American solution to every world problem." He discussed the dichotomy of appeasers and warmongers. He emphatically stated that his administration would be neither. His policy was to ensure that our adversaries understood our determination to use force if necessary to defend our liberty if attacked and our vital interests abroad. However, he reiterated his position that "we have nothing to fear from negotiations at the appropriate time, and nothing to gain by refusing to take part in them." This was most likely an admonition to his national security advisors in Washington in as much as it was an attempt to educate the public on his policy.

Ambassador Galbraith in April 1962 proposed a political solution for Vietnam similar to what had been done in Laos. Galbraith recommended that Harriman should apprise the Soviets of our determination to prevent the Viet Cong from overthrowing Diem's regime. The Soviets should also be asked to ascertain from North Vietnam whether they were willing to broker an arrangement with the Viet Cong to cease all combat operations in return for an American withdrawal. He added that we could also offer liberalization of trade relations between North and South, as well as a non-specific agreement to confer about the unification of Vietnam after a period of tranquility. Kennedy was intrigued by the proposal and asked Harriman to respond and authorize Galbraith to approach Soviets with his plan. Harriman would never send that response. Unknown to Kennedy, he was not in favor of settling the Vietnamese issue as he had done with Laos.

It may have been because of the tenuous nature of his negotiations prior to Geneva. He was also discouraged by the inability of the Soviets to pressure the Pathet Lao to shut down the Ho Chi Minh Trial. This eventually became part of a separate agreement with Soviet diplomat Georgi M. Pushkin that was known as the **Pushkin Agreement**. Pushkin died a year after the Laos neutrality accord was consummated. After his death, no one inside the Kremlin enforced the pact he had negotiated with Harriman. Consequently, the supply line for the Viet Cong through Laos was never shut down. Harriman as a result was heavily criticized and in some circles in the Pentagon the trail was renamed the Harriman Highway. This all might have been the impetus for his lack of enthusiasm for Galbraith's proposal.

In spite of Harriman's failure to follow through with Kennedy's instructions, the President ordered McNamara to prepare a plan to withdraw. Despite vociferous objections by the JCS and the CIA, McNamara in May 1962 instructed the defense department to begin formal planning and budgeting for a phased withdrawal consistent with the Galbraith plan. McNamara informed General Harkins at a conference in Hawaii that May. It was reported that the General was completely caught off guard by McNamara's request to develop a plan to withdraw.

The CIA and the defense department – ever since it had been made clear that Kennedy was not enthralled with the situation in Vietnam – had decided to encourage him by providing false intelligence that indicated that SVN was making progress against the Viet Cong. Air Force Colonel James Winterbottom, Jr. sent the doctored statistics to the White House after consulting with General Harkins. The real intelligence that accurately assessed the situation was sent to Vice President Johnson and his special assistant Colonel Burris. Johnson was chosen to receive this uncensored intelligence because ever since his trip to SVN in early 1961 he had been a strong proponent for the deployment of American combat troops. He was viewed by JCS and CIA as an important ally in the administration.

The defense department engaged in bureaucratic stall tactics to frustrate the development of a withdraw plan. They eventually presented a plan in the spring of 1963 that called for a phased withdrawal that would be completed by 1967. McNamara told them that their timetable was unacceptable and requested that they prepare a plan that would be completed more expeditiously.

While this tug of war continued, the Diem regime was under tremendous political pressure from domestic groups, as well as the Kennedy administration to reform his policies by democratizing his government. His regime was especially intolerant of non-Catholic religious organizations. Diem was educated in France and was a practicing Catholic. When he returned to his home country, he had little regard for Vietnamese culture or tradition. Those that benefited from his policies were the elite that resided in the major metropolitan centers of the country such as Saigon. The villagers and farmers were ignored and in some cases persecuted. This was never more evident than his disdain for the Buddhists.

This intentional policy of discrimination resulted in the **Hue Rebellion** in May 1963. Diem had issued a law that no flags other than the national flag of SVN could be flown in public. The Buddhists were celebrating Buddha's birthday which was an annual traditional celebration that involved displaying their religious flags. Diem demanded that the flags be removed which caused many to protest in the streets. A bomb went off during a major rally at a radio station killing many of those standing outside protesting Diem's draconian law.[78] The initial reports which some alleged were leaked by the CIA blamed the police and the SVG for the tragedy. This resulted in further erosion of support for Diem's regime and enhanced the influence of the Viet Cong. Diem and his brother suspected that the CIA may have been behind the bombing. The forensic evidence that was collected, and the injuries sustained by the victims were indicative of a plastic explosive that only the Agency was in possession of at the time.[79]

The CIA was becoming disenchanted with their protégé because of his failure to unite the country against the Viet Cong. They also felt betrayed when Diem's brother, through back channels with the North, attempted to negotiate a ceasefire with the expectation of a U.S. withdrawal. Diem and his brother were becoming very wary of the 600 CIA agents roaming their country. The CIA was aware of Diem's desire to end the war. This may have triggered rogue elements within the Agency to set off the bomb and create an international incident that might compel Kennedy to respond. Kennedy did not take the bait.[80]

The Buddhists responded to this tragedy by setting themselves on fire to protest Diem's policy. These public suicides would continue into the summer. Kennedy and his advisors were terribly concerned that Diem was losing what little support he had to maintain control of the country. The CIA and some of his advisors began promoting a coup. CIA Agent Lucien Conein reached out to disgruntled generals who had quietly revealed an interest in overthrowing Diem's government. Ambassador Lodge joined the effort to support the generals. Kennedy remained resistant but did not reject the plan. He decided to allow for its preparation while attempting to get Diem to make the economic and political reforms that he had been pushing for since the beginning of his administration.

The military continued to provide positive reports on the progress being made against the Viet Cong. This was being done even while Diem's political future was becoming more precarious each month. Kenneth O'Donnell, a top aide for the President, stated that JFK, just like Galbraith, had abandoned all hope for a military solution as early as the spring of 1963.

The words of General Douglas MacArthur continued to resonate in his thoughts. Upon the eve and early days of his administration, the iconic general warned Kennedy that you could send one million soldiers into the jungles of Vietnam and still be out numbered.[81] He added that "Anyone wanting to commit American ground forces to the mainland of Asia should have his head examined." This insight had been fermented by his participation in Korea when UN coalition forces led by MacArthur had invaded the North after successfully repelling the enemy from the South, prompting the introduction of one million Chinese combatants whose primary purpose was to prevent the U.S. dominated offensive from occupying an ally that bordered China. Consequently, what was once called a conflict by the Truman administration evolved into a bloody war of attrition that ended in a stalemate.

With MacArthur's incisive counsel fortified by his own observations of the disaster that had befallen the French a decade earlier, and with his own visceral repulsion of war foisted upon his soul by personal experience, Kennedy pressed for a way to extricate our nation from the immense gravitational force that threatened to compel us into the abyss. He did this knowing he was resisting the tide that other powerful agencies were determined to follow despite the calamity that awaited them on the shore.

The President in August 1963 decided to send the JCS Chairman General Maxwell Taylor and Defense Secretary McNamara on a fact finding mission to Vietnam. He did not trust the intelligence he was receiving from **MACV**. With this innate understanding, he surmised that he could transform this subterfuge that the Pentagon had anticipated would deflate his resistance to military escalation and convert it to a rationale for disengagement. Thus, their mission was in actuality a ruse by Kennedy to make his decision to withdraw appear as though it was based on recommendations made by the military.[82] While Taylor and McNamara were in Vietnam, Kennedy had his brother, Colonel Fletcher Prouty and Lt. General Victor Krulak prepare the analysis that became known as the **McNamara-Taylor Report**. This report was handed to Taylor and McNamara upon their arrival in Hawaii. They were told to review it and become familiar with its recommendations by the time they landed in Washington. This document that was classified for decades became the basis for Kennedy's withdrawal plan.[83]

James Galbraith reviewed the declassified Kennedy tapes of

that October. He indicated that McNamara in the October 2, 1963, meeting was advocating for a specific timetable for the phased withdrawal. He stated, "We need a way to get out of Vietnam, and this is my way of doing it." It was at the October 5, 1963, discussion that Kennedy officially approved the recommendations contained in the **McNamara-Taylor Report**. JFK at the end of the tape says "Let's go on ahead and do it." He continued "without any reference to victory." According to Galbraith, this meant that the withdrawal plan was not contingent on victory or positive reports from Vietnam. This also was not a ploy to obtain concessions from Diem. The plan was to be implemented covertly in such a way as not to arouse suspicion from Diem's government or the American public. The withdrawal that had been decided upon was unconditional and was not predicated on any success militarily.

The result of these discussions was **NSAM 263** which Kennedy signed on October 11, 1963. The end of the second paragraph addressed the withdrawal of one thousand advisors by that December. This was made public in a press release by McNamara and in a press conference by Kennedy. The beginning of the second paragraph would remain classified until the 1990s. Until the sections referenced in the **McNamara-Taylor Report** could be reviewed, their implications could not be fully understood. It was this portion of Kennedy's order that set forth the timetable in which the phased withdrawal would be completed. The recommendation affirmed by Kennedy was that all U.S. personnel would be withdrawn no later than December of 1965. As Colonel Prouty had pointed out in many interviews, the use of the phrase all "U.S. personnel" as opposed to all "military personnel" was intentional. This meant that Kennedy wanted all CIA employees to be removed as well. He had learned his lesson in Laos. If the CIA remained, they could frustrate his policy objectives if not destroy them.

Diem and his brother's government were overthrown by a

military coup d'état on November 1, 1963, that was supported by the CIA, the JCS, anti-Diem employees at the State Department and Ambassador Lodge. The idea of a coup came to fruition on the weekend of August 24 and 25, 1963, while Kennedy and many of his top advisors were out of town. Ambassador Lodge and Agent Conein sent three cables that weekend indicating that the generals were ready to go forward and that all they needed was support from Washington. This was all that Hilsman, Harriman and Michael Forrestal of the State Department needed. They immediately sent a cable back on the 24th. The cable stated that Diem should be given an opportunity to oust his brother Nhu from his government. If he refused, the cable instructed Lodge and Conein to apprise the generals that the U.S. would no longer support Diem.

It was Forrestal's responsibility to get the cable approved that would later be referred to as simply **telegram 243**.[84] He contacted Kennedy at his home in Hyannis to get him to clear the cable. Kennedy was annoyed with the urgency of dealing with this issue by phone over the weekend. He inquired why it could not be discussed that Monday with his national security team. Forrestal told him that they needed to respond and that the matter could not wait. The President then told him that if he could get approval from CIA Director John McCone and JCS Chairman Taylor it could go out. He probably told him this because he knew McCone would not approve it.[85] The cable went out even though it had not been discussed with McCone. In addition, Forrestal later claimed that Taylor had approved it which was not entirely accurate.

Kennedy arrived that Monday, and after he was apprised of what happened he stated to Forrestal "This shit has got to stop!" Forrestal then offered to resign. Kennedy abruptly responded, "You're not worth firing. You owe me something, so you stick around."[86] In Vietnam, Lodge told the generals they had the green light. Once again, Kennedy's instructions to give Diem a chance to get rid of his brother and reform his policies were never reported to him. In addition, Kennedy had ordered that if the coup went forward Diem and his family were to be safely escorted out of the country. Kennedy, however, was still hoping for a diplomatic solution. When the coup did occur, Agent Conein and Ambassador Lodge in blatant disregard of that order provided the location of Diem and his brother to the generals. They were assassinated on November 2, 1963. As reported by General Taylor, Kennedy went white as a sheet when he was informed of their murders during a National Security Council meeting.

He now was more determined than ever to withdraw. He ordered that a conference in Hawaii be held with all his top advisors on November 20 and 21, 1963, to discuss how we got into Vietnam and to further develop the plan to get out. He also scheduled a meeting with Ambassador Lodge that was set for that Monday after he returned from Texas. His intent was to fire him not pat him on the back and allow him to return to his post as Johnson did. As he was leaving for Texas, he told Senator Wayne Morse to stop criticizing his Vietnam policy because he was in agreement with the Senator's position which was to withdraw.[87]

The disastrous coup and the assassination of Diem and his brother was the worst foreign policy setback for Kennedy since the **Bay of Pigs**. Once again members of his administration had betrayed him. He eventually tacitly approved the coup naïvely thinking he could manage events inside a country that was not only thousands of miles away but was controlled by the CIA. This lapse in judgment maybe partially explained by the timing of these events. He was still in mourning over the death of his son Patrick who died on August 9th at Boston Children's Hospital while he was holding his son's small hand just three weeks before the infamous cable was sent. The tragedy had revitalized the President's marriage as they both struggled to cope with their grief. This meant that his weekends in Hyannis – which had always been vital to Kennedy – had taken on a new significance that he hoped would provide refuge for both of them from the constant intrusions that were inherent in his position.

He also was very engaged in his effort to get the senate to ratify the **Partial Test Ban Treaty** he had negotiated with the British and the Soviets which was the keystone in the arch of his strategy for peace. This, in my opinion, were the reasons he was so irritated by Forrestal's call especially when he asserted that the events in Vietnam required an immediate response. Under normal circumstances, he would have consulted with top advisors before making his decision and would not have delegated the issue to McCone. The tragedy of all this is that if his staff had followed his instructions most likely the cable never would have been sent because McCone was unequivocally against a coup. Although McCone was the CIA Director, the covert sector of the CIA viewed him as an illegitimate Kennedy appointee who had replaced their true leader, Allen Dulles.

As the coup faded into the past, Kennedy stated in a press conference on November 14, 1963, that the goal of his administration was to "bring Americans home." He had provided the media and the public glimpses of his intent to withdraw as his fatal trip to Texas approached. Unfortunately for him and the nation, he would not live to follow through with his plan.

The debate continues for those who are unfamiliar with the man or his record. James Galbraith stated that the proposition that JFK was withdrawing from Vietnam is no longer a controversial position and is widely accepted by historians and the public.[88] It is quite clear that the withdrawal he had implemented before his death was unconditional, and therefore was not contingent upon military success or failure. When you link this with actions Johnson employed that violated important tenets of Kennedy's Vietnam program, the changed objectives of his successor can be clearly understood.

This change in the course of our policy directly led us into the disaster that General MacArthur had forecasted to Kennedy. For instance, the authorization of **Oplan-34A** by Johnson – which was an offensive covert action in the Gulf of Tonkin managed by the CIA and supported by the Navy – violated one of Kennedy's primary prohibitions which was that U.S. forces were not to be involved in operations inside of North Vietnam. It becomes clear – when reviewing the entire record – that if Kennedy had lived there would not have been an incident that would have triggered a **Gulf of Tonkin Resolution**. In addition, Kennedy had already accepted that he might become one of the most unpopular president's in history because of the collapse of SVN. This meant that negative events that may have occurred in 1964 and 1965 would not have deterred him from completing his objective because he had already accepted defeat as a possible consequence for his decision to withdraw. It was more important to him to preserve the peace in pursuit of his broader goal of detente with the Soviets that he opined would result in a significant reduction of our nuclear arsenals. He understood that none of this could be achieved if the U.S. was bogged down in a guerrilla war in the jungles of Southeast Asia.

Gareth Porter in stark detail in **Perils of Dominance** published in 2005 described Kennedy's precarious position within his own administration. Kennedy while in complete isolation and with virtually no support devised "Machiavellian ruses" to frustrate the "national security bureaucracy" determined to challenge the communists in a war. They considered any negotiated settlement as an act of appeasement no less egregious than what Prime Minister Chamberlain had done at Munich in 1938 with Hitler. The only option that was acceptable had to be obtained by force unless the Soviets were willing to totally capitulate to U.S. demands. In addition, they did not perceive or appreciate the different shades of communism as it evolved in different nations around the globe. They saw it simply as a monolithic political movement that was orchestrated by Moscow and Peking (now Beijing).

The basic premise of many at the Pentagon – which included General Curtis LeMay – was that war with the Soviets was inevitable. This meant that the U.S. should be prepared to fight at a time when our military strength was overwhelmingly superior to our adversary.[89] Their obsession in achieving military victory over the communists resulted in the development of a top secret plan for a preemptive war with the Soviets. This plan was kept within the archives of the **Strategic Air Command (SAC)** that had been directed by General LeMay until he was elevated to the JCS by Kennedy in 1961.

SAC's new leader was General Thomas Power who was described by LeMay as emotionally unstable and a sadist.[90] General Power on many occasions would reinforce that assessment of him. When briefed by William Kaufman of the **RAND Corporation** on the prudence of avoiding civilian targets, Power retorted, "...why are you so concerned with saving their lives (the communists)? The whole idea is to kill the bastards!" He added in frustration, "Look. At the end of the war, if they're two Americans and one Russian, we win!" To which Kaufman caustically replied, "Well, you better make sure that they're a man and a woman."[91] This paled in comparison to his behavior during the **Cuban Missile Crisis**. On October 22, 1962, as the crisis was mounting, General Power ordered that the SAC be placed on **DEFCON 2** in preparation to strike targets within the Soviet Union. This provocative act to go to the precipice of nuclear war was done without notifying or consulting with the White House.[92]

When discussing Power's secret plan at a National Security Council meeting, U.S. Marine Commandant David Shoup asked what if the Chinese were not complicit with the actions of the Kremlin? General Power replied that he was hoping that question would not come up for he had not considered it. He added that it would "screw up the whole plan" if China was not included. Defense Secretary McNamara was horrified by the brutality and lack of thought that went into the development of SAC's plan. This top secret document that had to be pried out of their archives simply was a list of hundreds of Soviet and Chinese cities targeted for annihilation, waiting for a pretext to trigger its activation. They estimated that 400 million would perish and 40 million others would sustain severe injuries. They did not evaluate the collateral impact of radioactive fall out to our allies, our nation or the rest of the world.[93] McNamara much to the consternation of Generals LeMay and Power diligently modified the plan by shifting the targets from the cities to military infrastructure and assets. He also integrated multiple contingencies that provided the President with alternative actions before authorizing Armageddon.

He recommended similar changes to the **Single Integrated Operational Plan (SIOP 62)** which had been sanctioned by the Eisenhower administration in early 1961. This was our nation's general plan for nuclear war until 2003. Since 1961, it has been modified many times by each succeeding administration. The SIOP in essence provided the president with a variety of targeting options, and specific instructions on launch procedures and target sets against which nuclear weapons would be launched. **SIOP 62** was based on the **massive retaliation doctrine** that had been promoted by Secretary of State John Foster Dulles. The crux of that doctrine was that our entire nuclear arsenal would be launched against the Soviet Union presumably for a major transgression such as an attack on Berlin. McNamara's efforts culminated in **SIOP 63** which was approved by President Kennedy. This revised policy allotted Kennedy a range of graduated options before invoking nuclear war.

The transformation of our national strategy required that both plans be consistent with Kennedy's overall objective which was to provide the president with a flexible response to Soviet actions. Much of the brass at the Pentagon were outraged by what they considered civilian intrusions on their sphere of influence. This wrestling match between Kennedy and the generals to get control of our nuclear arsenal that Presidents Truman and Eisenhower had relinquished unwittingly to the military caused a great deal of friction between the White House and the Pentagon. In addition, McNamara's dogged efforts to bring competency and efficiency to our military budgets and policy prompted General LeMay to ask an Air Force colleague, "I ask you. Would things be much worse if Khrushchev were the Secretary of Defense?"[94]

This preemptive war plan was presented to Kennedy in 1961 and 1963. As stated above, the plan devised by **SAC** consisted of bombing hundreds of Soviet and Chinese cities with nuclear weapons. They had estimated that 15 to 30 million Americans would be killed and this according to their assessment was acceptable collateral damage.[95] The military brass argued that war with the communists was inevitable, and it was to our advantage to preemptively strike the enemy when they least expected it. Kennedy was so appalled that he exited the meeting early. As he left the room, he turned to his Secretary of State Dean Rusk and said "and we call ourselves the human race."[96]

The second meeting when this doomsday scenario was discussed with the President occurred in the fall of 1963. He was told that the window of opportunity was closing. By late that year, the U.S. nuclear arsenal would be large enough to assure victory. They argued that in 1964 and beyond Soviet strength would grow rapidly. It was estimated that 300 to 400 million would die. This time Kennedy remained to expose the insanity of their plan to guarantee it was abandoned and would never be resurrected.[97]

Kennedy had initially believed in a missile gap that had been originally presented to the public in the **Gaither Report** of 1957, as well as estimates projected by the Air Force.[98] The successful launch of **Sputnik** that same year appeared to reaffirm fears of Soviet dominance in space and rocket technology. This assessment was perpetuated by the **RAND Corporation** up through the 1960 election. Kennedy because of these estimates was deeply concerned that the failure of the Eisenhower administration to at least maintain parity with the Soviets threatened the peace. He believed that our nuclear force had to be of a sufficient strength to deter Soviet or even Chinese aggression. This mythology was dispelled in the **Missile Gap Study** of September 1961 which verified that the Soviets had only 4 ICBMs.[99] The U.S. clearly held an overwhelming nuclear advantage over our **Cold War** adversary. As his military pressed for a "preventive war fought over a pretext", he became more concerned with restraining our military's aggressive impulses rather than focusing on the exaggerated Soviet threat to peace.[100] The public and the media were completely oblivious to the perilous course senior military advisors had pressed upon our young president until these documents were released pursuant to the **JFK Records Act**.

The guidance he received from his military advisors was disturbing. He told an aid "The first advice I'm going to give my successor is to watch the generals and to avoid feeling that just because they are military men their opinion on military matters were worth a damn."[101] If this was not in itself bad enough, there were the nefarious and treasonous actions of the CIA to sabotage Kennedy's vision for peace to contend with as well.[102]

A peaceful solution to Southeast Asia would thwart their huge drug trafficking operation, and a peaceful resolution to the **Cold War** could result in their eventual demise just as the end of World War II had terminated the need for the Office of Strategic Services. Consequently, the leaders in Langley and many in the field were unwilling to idly stand by while Kennedy reduced their influence and power. Although this power struggle Kennedy was engaged in with his national security state, and more particularly the CIA, was frequently hidden from the public the media was aware to a limited degree of the treachery and power of the CIA. In an article written by Journalist Richard Starnes for the Washington Daily News, dated October 2, 1963, he quoted a high ranking U.S. American official as stating "The CIA growth was 'likened to a malignancy' which the 'very high official was not sure even the White House could control...any longer'. If the United States ever experiences an attempt at a coup to overthrow the government, it will come from the CIA and not the Pentagon." The agency "represents a tremendous power and total unaccountability to anyone." The statement as quoted should cause a chill to run down your spine considering what transpired that November.

Starnes concluded; "The story of the Central Intelligence Agency in South Vietnam is a dismal chronicle of bureaucratic arrogance, obstinate disregard of orders, and unrestrained thirst for power." Kennedy had read the article and was so concerned about the disclosures that he discussed it in a National Security Council meeting that October. As Dallas loomed, Kennedy had commissioned another major enquiry into the CIA's treasonous activities.[103]

Kennedy's policy goals for his second term as described by Bundy were to reduce East-West tensions; a reduction in nuclear weapons; to negotiate strict arms control accords; and to normalize relations with China.[104] I would add that he was seeking rapprochement with Castro's Cuba and was intending to visit the Soviet Union, China and Indonesia. His ultimate objective was to end the **Cold War** and to improve the quality of life for many in the Third World by continuing his **Alliance for Progress,** the **Peace Corp** and by assisting those nations seeking to liberate themselves from the bondage of colonialism as he was doing in the Democratic Republic of the Congo.

Kennedy eloquently set forth his strategic vision in his commencement address at American University on June 10, 1963.

In that address, often referred to as the peace speech, he declared that America will never start a war. He added that Americans have had enough of war and that is why, "… I have, therefore, chosen this time and place to discuss a topic on which ignorance too often abounds and the truth too rarely perceived. And that is the most important topic on earth: Peace, what kind of peace do I mean and what kind of peace do we seek? Not a Pax Americana enforced on the world by American weapons of war. Not the peace of the grave or the security of the slave. I am talking about genuine peace, the kind of peace that makes life on earth worth living, and the kind that enables men and nations to grow, and to hope, and build a better life for their children — not merely peace for Americans but peace for all men and women, not merely peace in our time but peace in all time." He declared we had to re-evaluate our attitude towards peace just as much as our adversaries did.

He also accepted that we may not be able to agree on all issues. He said "So let us not be blind to our differences but let us also direct our attention to our common interests and the means by which those differences can be resolved. And if we cannot now end our differences at least we can make the world safe for diversity. For in the final analysis, our most basic common link is that we all inhabit this small planet. We all breathe the same air. We all cherish our children's futures. And we are all mortal."

He concluded by announcing that negotiations with the Soviet Union to achieve a **Comprehensive Test Ban Treaty** would be initiated in Moscow. The long term goal he reported had already begun in Geneva which was to attain arms control accords with the ultimate objective of complete disarmament. In addition, as a gesture to demonstrate his good faith, he stated that the U.S. would unilaterally suspend all nuclear bomb testing and would not resume its development program unless the Soviets breached the moratorium. This statement of his intent to end the **Cold War** was clearly at odds with the hawks at the Pentagon, the CIA and the state department. This was probably the reason the content of the speech was only known by a few trusted advisors before he delivered it at American University.[105] This oration, however, inspired a young man in Russia who was unaware of the historical events he would not only participate in, but initiate. This man was Mikhail Gorbachev.

Daniel Ellsberg once asked Robert Kennedy what he thought his brother would have done in Vietnam if he had lived. He replied that he would never have sent troops. Ellsberg asked, "What made him so smart?" Robert slammed his hand on the table, causing Ellsberg to jump. He then exclaimed "Because we were there!" A reference to their trip to Vietnam in 1951.[106] It was not only the President's brother or inner circle that were aware of his future plans for Vietnam. General Vo Nguyen Giap's youngest son disclosed to journalist Mani S. Kang that his father through intelligence sources knew Kennedy was withdrawing in late 1963.[107] Their hope to avoid a war with the goliath of North America faded as Dallas approached.

The shockwave from Dallas shattered what was known as French Indochina and transformed it into another manmade holocaust. Once Kennedy had been removed, the Johnson administration immediately took action to Americanize the war. The first combat troops arrived in early 1965. Their numbers continued to grow until late 1968 when the American force consisted of 538,000. The bombing campaign codenamed **Operation Rolling Thunder** attempted to save the country by destroying it. By the time the Nixon administration had negotiated a ceasefire in 1973, more bombs had been dropped on North Vietnam than in any war in the history of mankind. The suffering of the Vietnamese people as bombs and chemicals such as Agent Orange and napalm fell on their villages, farms and cities was horrific. The consequence was that two million perished while tens of thousands remained sick and disabled. In addition, the CIA tortured and murdered another 26,000 as part of their **Phoenix Program**. In Cambodia and Laos, the casualties mounted to well over 500,000. The destruction in Cambodia eventually opened the door to the rise of Pol Pot and the Khmer Rouge in the late 1970s that murdered another one million of its citizens. This tragedy was dramatically revealed to the American public by the academy award winning film **The Killing Fields**.

Ho Chi Minh responded to a message from President Johnson on February 15, 1967. He replied "Vietnam is thousands of miles away from the United States. The Vietnamese people have never done any harm to the United States. But contrary to the pledges made by its representatives at the 1954 **Geneva Conference**, the U.S. has ceaselessly intervened in Vietnam, it has unleashed and intensified the war of aggression in North Vietnam with a view to prolonging the partition of Vietnam and turning South Vietnam into a neocolonial and a military base of the United States." He continued that "The U.S. government has committed war crimes, crimes against peace and against mankind. In South Vietnam, half a million U.S. and satellite troops have resorted to the most inhuman weapons and most barbarous methods of warfare, such as napalm, toxic chemicals and gases, to massacre our compatriots, destroy crops, and raze villages to the ground. In North Vietnam, thousands of U.S. aircraft have dropped hundreds of thousands of tons of bombs, destroying towns, villages, factories, schools. In your message, you apparently deplore the suffering and destruction in Vietnam. May I ask you: Who has perpetrated these monstrous crimes?" Minh answered his own question. "It is the United States and satellite troops. The U.S. government is entirely responsible for the extremely serious situation in Vietnam." He added that the Vietnamese people "deeply love independence, freedom and peace." There could be no rational response by Johnson to dismiss the charges articulated in Minh's correspondence. Minh had spoken the truth.

The war cost the United States hundreds of billions of dollars and 58,000 lives by the time it ended. Many soldiers returned with post-traumatic stress disorder (PTSD) as a consequence of their combat experience and many others developed neurological and other physical pathologies because of their exposure to Agent Orange and napalm. Toxic chemicals that the military had assured them were safe. Thousands more came home with severe heroin dependency because of all the raw opium the CIA had transported in their fleet of planes into South Vietnam. The war significantly damaged our nation's reputation and credibility throughout the globe that lingered for decades. The resources for Johnson's **Great Society** were significantly diverted to the war effort, eroding the effectiveness of many of the programs. By the end of the decade, the nation had entered another recession; two more prominent visionaries were assassinated; thousands marched in the streets across the nation demanding not only an end to the war but also social and economic justice; and when the fog of events cleared, Nixon was in the White House.

Nixon and Kissinger on a peace with honor platform dropped more bombs on North Vietnam than Nixon's predecessor and illegally expanded the war into Laos and Cambodia. The scandal of **Watergate** in the early 1970s humiliated our nation as congressional investigative committees uncovered the chicanery and criminal activity within his administration that necessitated his resignation in 1974.

The Sukarno government in Indonesia that Kennedy had planned to visit after the election was overthrown in 1965 by General Suharto and his cohorts who were backed by the CIA. The CIA provided the new regime with thousands of names of potential threats to the new government. As the death squads that were formed murdered those on the list, the CIA placed a check next to their name. This eventually evolved into a bloodbath that caused over 500,000 Indonesians to lose their lives. In the Congo, Kennedy had supported the United Nation's policy to unify the nation and to end the colonial control of

Belgium. This policy was abandoned by Johnson, causing thousands to die as the war continued. The negotiations with the Soviets and the Cubans also ceased after Dallas.

The Johnson administration did reinitiate a dialogue with the Soviets in an attempt to revitalize his legacy that was slowly being eroded by his policy in Vietnam that was increasingly occupying more and more of his time. These negotiations resulted in the signing of the **Outer Space Treaty** of 1967 which demilitarized space and the **Nuclear Non-Proliferation Treaty** of 1968. Both accords could be partially attributed to the road that had been paved by Kennedy in the final year of his life. In spite of these agreements, the optimism in 1963 that had been ignited by Kennedy's peace speech, and encouraged by the initiation of arms control discussions and the signing of the **Partial Test Ban Treaty** faded into the mist of memory. Although Nixon achieved a short lived period of détente with the Soviets, his achievement appeared primarily motivated by a Machiavellian political strategy based on power rather than an urgent plea for peace that embraced diversity that Kennedy had envisioned in 1963. The hope inspired by Kennedy and Khrushchev that fall appeared vanquished by Dallas. Khrushchev ironically was removed from power in October of 1964 by a non-violent coup prompted by hawks in the politburo that were led by Leonid Brezhnev. He was banished to his oasis on the Black Sea where he eventually completed his memoir which was smuggled out of Russia and published in the West. Fortunately for mankind, the **Cold War** ended in 1991 predominantly because of the courage of Soviet Premier Mikhail Gorbachev whose unilateral efforts to disarm had convinced Reagan to join his quest for peace.

The assassination in Dallas was not only a seminal moment in American history, but had unleashed solemn shock waves around the globe. The gunfire of Dallas did not just result in the death of a man, but his vision of hope for a more just and peaceful world. Kennedy clearly was a prime example that one man with courage can make a difference. Consequently, after his death, Kennedy was commemorated on stamps throughout the world for his support of their yearning to be independent and free.

Nobel Prize laureate Arthur Schlesinger, Jr. refuted the revisionists' account of Kennedy's policies and the character of the man in an article he wrote for Cigar Aficionado in December 1998 entitled "The Truth as I see it." He described Kennedy as "...one of the most unfailingly courteous and considerate men I have ever known. He was easy, accessible, witty, candid, enjoying the clash of ideas and the ripples of gossip... He was in his own self-description, an 'idealist without illusions.' He was the best of my generation. It is good for the country that he remains so vivid a presence in our minds and hearts."

This assessment of him was not only held by a majority of the public or those that considered him a friend or had worked in his administration. 65 American historians, composed of liberals and conservatives, in a 2009 poll concluded that Kennedy was the sixth in overall presidential performance just ahead of Thomas Jefferson. He continues to be the only one-term president that is consistently ranked in the top ten.[108]

Norman Cousins, who was the editor of the Saturday Review and an emissary of Kennedy when he met with Khrushchev in the spring of 1963 to reinitiate the test ban negotiations, told his daughters that Kennedy feared that the U.S. military might position itself in such a way to "undermine his executive power." It, therefore, was crucial to initiate a dialogue between our nations that would allow us to resolve our differences and end the **Cold War**. Andrea Cousins stated that Kennedy should be remembered for his courage "to go against a group that was powerful and speak up even though he was alone." Her sister Candis added that the nuclear threat is still prevalent today and the need to disarm and live in peace is as important now as it was then. She stated to "take a stand against it, as we know from

Kennedy, is not just difficult but it is a dangerous thing, but it must be done anyway."[109]

Nikita Khrushchev while contrasting Eisenhower and Kennedy in his memoir wrote, "The comparison would not be in Eisenhower's favor...It quickly became clear that Kennedy understood better than Eisenhower that an improvement in relations was the only rational course."[110]

The mythology that has been implanted since his death of who Kennedy really was and what he stood for is drastically different than the realities that were understood at the time by those who knew him. The declassified documents have allowed his true legacy as a peacemaker to rise above the pile of deception that was intentionally placed in the public realm to obscure the threat he posed to our national security state. He clearly was not a cold warrior determined to prove his manhood as proposed by critics and that is why he was perceived as a **Cold War** liability by the Pentagon and the CIA. As he told Ben Bradlee, the famed Washington Post Editor during **Watergate,** that the epitaph he wanted inscribed on his stone was, "He kept the peace." In a more radical statement, at least as perceived by the hawks, Kennedy told his good friend William Walton, "I am the peace at any price President."[111]

The reason for this is that Kennedy had served his country in the Pacific during **World War II** and had witnessed the carnage that occurred in that war. The death of his older brother, brother-in-law, friends and colleagues continued to haunt him for the rest of his life. There was an op-ed written in the Hartford Courant in November 2013 by Ken Fuchsman the Director of General Studies at the University of Connecticut, regarding a 1946 Harvard Grant Study. This study had consisted of 272 undergraduates from 1939 through 1944. The purpose of the study was to assess the trauma sustained as a consequence of their combat experiences. This study was resurrected and re-evaluated in 1995 by Dr. George Vaillant and his colleagues. The

JFK Library apparently has Kennedy's responses to the original survey. Because this study was confidential, the scholars that reviewed Vaillant's work concluded based on circumstantial evidence that, "One of the men most troubled by traumatic memories of war became president of the United States."

Hugh Sidey, a journalist and a friend, wrote that JFK's leadership was guided by a "total revulsion" of war.[112]

Chapter 3

JFK Assassination

"He who controls the past controls the future. He who controls the present controls the past."
George Orwell

"Instead of running down the men who killed John Kennedy, the U.S. government simply ratified the execution and moved on to more important matters. With regard to the men who actually killed him, because of their displeasure with his foreign policy, the assassination has been treated not as an offense but as a mandate for change."
James Garrison

"It is hard to understand today how heretical JFK's proposal for coexistence with the Soviets sounded to America's right wing. It was a Cold War boilerplate that any objective short of complete destruction was cowardice or treachery."
Robert F. Kennedy, Jr.

When discussing his version of the Bay of Pigs with a young writer, Dulles unexpectedly and without any warning said in a cold tone. "That little Kennedy...he thought he was a god."
Allen Dulles

"He looked far ahead and he wanted to change a great deal. Perhaps it is this that is the key to the mystery of death of President John F. Kennedy."
Mikhail Gorbachev

"Of course, there are some CIA documents we'll never see.

When the Warren Commission asked to see a secret CIA memo on Oswald's activities in Russia...word came back that the Agency was terribly sorry, but the secret memo had been destroyed while being photocopied. This unfortunate accident took place on November 23, 1963, a day on which there must have occurred a great deal of spontaneous combustion around Washington."
James Garrison

Dr. McClelland of Parkland Hospital stated "the cause of death was due to massive head and brain injury from a gunshot wound of the left temple (when facing Kennedy)."
Dr. Robert McClelland

Bob Tanenbaum who was one of the original prosecutors described the CIA's cooperation with the House Select Committee to investigate the assassination. He sarcastically remarked "When they (investigators) look at documents and they talk about this great sensitivity that exists, that redaction Eddie Lopez talked about. You know what that's like? You have a document here and it says, 'The investigation,' and down at the bottom it says 'Lee Harvey Oswald.' Everything else is black."
Bob Tanenbaum, Esq.

"Truth never envelops itself in mystery, and the mystery in which it is enveloped is the work of the antagonist, and never of itself."
Thomas Paine

"A nation can survive its fools, and even the ambitious. But it cannot survive treason from within. An enemy at the gates is less formidable, for he is known and carries his banner openly. But the traitor moves amongst those within the gates freely,

his sly whispers rustling through all the alleys, heard in the very halls of government itself. For the traitor appears not a traitor, he speaks in accents familiar to his victims, and he wears their face and their arguments, he appeals to the baseness that lies deep in the hearts of all men. He rots the soul of a nation, he works secretly and unknown in the night to undermine the pillars of the city, he infects the body politic so that it can no longer resist. A murderer is less to fear. The traitor is the plague."
Marcus Tullius Cicero

Katzenbach wrote in his infamous memorandum that "The public must be satisfied that Oswald was the assassin; that he did not have confederates who are still at large; and that the evidence was such that he would have been convicted at trial. ... We need something to head off public speculation or Congressional hearing of the wrong sort."
Nicholas Katzenbach

A few days prior to Jack Ruby's death Deputy Sheriff Maddox visited him. "Then one day when I started to leave, Ruby shook hands with me and I could feel a piece of paper in his palm... [in his note] he wrote it was a conspiracy and he said, 'If you will keep your eyes open and your mouth shut you're gonna learn a lot.' And that was the last time I saw him." Maddox later divulged in a 1966 TV interview that, "Ruby's motive in killing the alleged presidential assassin was not patriotism, but rather to silence Oswald."
Deputy Sheriff Maddox

"Everything pertaining to what's happening has never come to the surface. The world will never know the true facts, of what occurred, my motives. The people had, that had so much to gain and had such an ulterior motive for putting me

in the position I'm in, will never let the true facts come above board to the world."
Jack Ruby (formerly Rubenstein)

"New opinions often appear first as jokes and fancies, then as blasphemies and treason, then as questions open to discussion, and finally as established truth."
George Bernard Shaw

William Walton a close friend of the Kennedy family in a trip to Moscow in December of 1963 hand delivered a note written by Robert and Jacqueline Kennedy to Georgi Bolshakov, reassuring Khrushchev that the family did not believe that the President's death was the result of a communist conspiracy. "...despite Oswald's connections to the communist world... there was a large political conspiracy behind Oswald's rifle...the President was felled by domestic opponents...the victim of a right-wing conspiracy."
Robert F. Kennedy and Jacqueline Kennedy

An Expert Examines the Forensic Evidence in the Kennedy Assassination
Enemy of the Truth (2012) by Sherry Fiester

I enthusiastically awaited the delivery of **Enemy of the Truth** by forensic expert Sherry Fiester which was published in 2012. After reading this cathartic and methodical analysis of the crime of the century, I was not disappointed.

I normally do not provide a short biography of an author's professional background but in this case it is important to be familiar with her training and experience to appreciate the magnitude of her conclusions. She is a retired Certified Senior Crime Scene Investigator and law enforcement instructor whose career spanned three decades. She has testified in federal and state court as a certified expert in crime scene reconstruction and investigation, as well as blood stain pattern analysis. She has authored articles in numerous professional publications and has delivered presentations at state, regional and national conferences. In terms of the issues she confronts in this book, she has presented her findings at the annual Coalition of Political Assassination Conference and at the conference held in Dallas each November sponsored by JFK Lancer of which she has been a guest lecturer since 1996. Fiester has also won awards for her contribution to the ongoing research in the Kennedy assassination. Her tome has been endorsed by many researchers and fellow practitioners, including Certified Forensic Crime Scene Investigator William LeBlanc and Cyril Wecht, MD, JD who participated in the House Select Committee on Assassinations in the late 1970s.

The reason she decided to apply her expertise to this case was primarily influenced by her sister, Debra Conway, who is the co-founder of the JFK Lancer website. For many years, she was apprised of her sister's important research on the CIA's attempts to assassinate Fidel Castro, and the evidence she had discovered that related to the assassination of the President. So in 1995 with her sister by her side, they began interviewing witnesses to the crime or individuals who knew Lee Harvey Oswald (hereinafter Oswald) such as Marina Oswald. Fiester's investigation culminated in her writing and publishing this book that astonishingly was for the most part ignored by the mainstream media (MSM). The ultimate goal of her work was to apply twenty-first century forensic procedures and techniques to dispel myths that have been debated for decades in search of the truth.

Her first task was to assess the performance of the Dallas Police Department (DPD) by comparing the techniques and procedures they utilized while investigating the assassination of the President with the national standards that existed in 1963, regarding crime scene investigation, as well as collection and preservation of evidence. She determined after a thorough review of how the DPD conducted its investigation that the claims that their department had complied with the local and national standards of the time was a myth. In numerous instances, the evidence was contaminated and the chain of custody was not properly documented. For example, detectives at the alleged sniper's nest on the sixth floor of the Texas School Book Depository (TSBD) picked up the shell casings found near the southeast corner window with their bare hands and moved said evidence before it was photographed and the crime scene was sketched by an artist. In addition, the DPD did not secure the sixth floor, or any portion of Dealey Plaza, which allowed the media, the public and other law enforcement to walk through the crime scene. It was so bad that when photographers did arrive the officers in charge had to recreate the scene based on their memory. In addition, they did not meticulously document in their reports where the evidence had been located or adequately describe the items that were collected.

The first rifle that was discovered was a 7.65 Mauser. The FBI wrote a report that sufficiently described the rifle so that it could be properly identified at a later date. Once the 6.5 Mannlicher Carcano short rifle was found behind some boxes on the sixth floor, the Mauser magically disappeared from the public record.

Because of their poor investigative performance, most of the evidence could have been excluded or at least its authenticity placed in doubt at trial by a good defense attorney.

The most important chapters in the book evaluate the evidence of the head shot that killed the President, and the single bullet theory proffered by the **Warren Commission** (WC). The section of the **Zapruder film** where Kennedy is hit in the head is frame 313. His head after being struck by a high velocity bullet traveling at approximately 2000 feet per second moved forward by 2.25 inches and then his head and upper torso abruptly recoiled "back and to the left." When the bullet struck Kennedy's forehead and began to penetrate his skull, blood was forced out the front of his head and then vanished such that it was not visible in the next frame. As the bullet fragmented and traversed through Kennedy's brain, the right front side of Kennedy's skull partially fractured. The bullet than exited the occipital region of the skull which caused blood, brain matter and bone, such as the **Harper fragment** found after the shooting, to be expelled all over the trunk of the car and a Dallas Police Officer operating a motorcycle just behind and to the left of the President's limousine.

Jackie Kennedy in an attempt to retrieve a piece of her husband's brain climbed out of her seat onto the trunk of the vehicle. She was returning to the backseat when Special Agent Clint Hill of the Secret Service was able to climb onto the trunk. It was at this moment that Hill observed a large hole in the rear of Kennedy's head which was consistent with what the doctors and nurses at Parkland Hospital in Dallas reported to the investigating authorities and the press.

Fiester's review of the medical testimony from the doctors at Parkland Hospital and Bethesda Naval Hospital, as well as the x-rays, photographs and diagrams of Kennedy's injuries to his skull determined that the bullet entered the upper right front quadrant of his forehead just below the hairline. Based on her examination of the available forensic evidence, the bullet struck the skull and immediately transferred its energy to brain matter in the cranial cavity, causing blood and brain tissue to exit the entrance wound as back spatter. As the bullet penetrated the skull, it caused radial fractures that extended out from the wound. The bullet fragmented as it traversed through the cranial cavity, exerting enormous pressure on Kennedy's skull which caused concentric or heaving fractures. The concentric fractures are essentially perpendicular to the radial fractures which create an appearance similar to a spider's web. She explained that current research indicates that fracturing patterns of this type correspond with an entry wound located in the front of the head. She explained "The direction of force is determined by examination of radial fractures." She added that current forensic studies demonstrate that beveling, which was what the autopsy doctors primarily relied upon, is not as accurate when trying to ascertain the direction of a bullet penetrating a human skull.

The main portion of the bullet exited the occipital or lower right rear of the skull leaving a hole the size of a baseball. As the bullet exited, it caused large amounts of blood, brain tissue and bone to jet out the back as forward spatter. Essentially, she determined that the lethal bullet had emanated from a rifle that was in front of the limousine not from the rear as stated in the **Warren Commission** or in the **House Select Committee on Assassinations'** reports.

The head's slight movement forward as depicted in the **Zapruder film** caused critics of the **WC** to speculate that the film had been altered by the federal government to support the proposition that Kennedy was hit by a bullet that was discharged from the sixth floor of the TSBD. Fiester indicated that the initial transfer of kinetic energy caused the target to move slightly forward into the force and against the line of fire just prior to movement with the force of the bullet. She wrote, "the greater the transfer of energy the more pronounced the forward movement." She concluded that the movement as depicted in the film was predictable because it was consistent with Newtonian physics and contemporary forensic research. She determined that the alterations of the film, at least those portions involving the head shot, was a myth. She also addressed and dismissed claims that Kennedy was hit simultaneously by two bullets that were fired from the rear and the front.

The supporters of the lone nut theory were also confronted with movement that contradicted their premise that the head shot was the result of a bullet that originated from behind the President. The President's movement "back and to the left" caused experts, as well as investigators, to proffer theories such as the jet effect and muscle spasms to explain this movement. Fiester reviews and analyzes these theories quite extensively and dispels both as myths. In effect, she decimated the **WC's** conclusion that the fatal shot had been fired from behind the President.

She further determined using modern trajectory techniques that the fatal shot had emanated from a position to the left of Kennedy "near the south end of the triple overpass or the parking lot adjacent to that portion of the overpass." She wrote that a shot from the grassy knoll would be perpendicular to the President because his head at the moment of impact was turned 20 degrees to his left. This meant that a grassy knoll shot would have caused significant damage to the left hemisphere of his brain which we know did not happen. All of the damage that the President's brain sustained was on the top and to the right hemisphere. She does not dismiss the possibility that a shooter was located on the grassy knoll, but disputes that was the location of the fatal head shot. Her conclusions do not contradict but rather corroborate the findings of an expert panel assembled by the HSCA that examined the acoustic evidence. This panel had determined that one of the gunshots was fired from the grassy knoll as witnesses had stated but added that this shot had missed its target. By proving this, she has established a conspiracy because Oswald, if he was one of the assassins, was located in the TSBD to the rear of the presidential limousine.

She also concluded using trajectory analysis that the seven remaining wounds in Kennedy and Connally were not caused by a single bullet. The wound that a bullet inflicted in Kennedy's back was located approximately 5.6 inches below his right shoulder and had entered the body at an angle of 38.84 degrees. The wound in the throat of Kennedy was calculated to be 0 degrees, and the entrance wound to Connally's lower right back was determined to be 22 degrees. Because of the conflicted testimony and trajectories used by prior investigations, she could not with any assurance conclude that the wound in Kennedy's throat was an entrance wound as suggested by the doctors who examined it at Parkland Hospital. It is clear, however, that the trajectories proposed by the **WC** to support their single bullet theory do not line up.

She further concluded that the calculations used in documentaries such as the one done by the Discovery Channel omitted important information that misled their viewers in their attempt to verify the **WC's** theory. She wrote, "The Discovery Channel documentary did not correctly apply forensic investigative techniques to discover the truth. They manufactured evidence and manipulated experts to guarantee an inevitable outcome." The single bullet theory based on her calculations is a myth.

It is important to understand the shooting sequence, and the time frame that was captured by Zapruder's film that caused the **WC** to adopt the single bullet theory to avoid any doubt that Oswald acted alone. The establishment of another assassin would be empirical proof of a conspiracy which was what the government was determined to circumvent as clearly articulated in the **Katzenbach Memorandum**.

The FBI's original report indicated that all three shots fired by Oswald from the sixth floor sniper's nest hit Kennedy and Connally. The FBI surmised that the first and third shots hit Kennedy, and the second shot caused all of Governor Connally's injuries. The **WC** was willing to accept this shooting sequence until it was discovered that a bullet had hit a curb near Main Street, causing a fragment of the cement to strike a bystander named James Tague in the cheek. The damage to the curb was photographed and examined by the DPD to ascertain if it had been caused by a bullet.

This created a serious problem primarily because of a citizen with an 8mm movie camera named Abraham Zapruder. His film not only documented the tragic event, but it also captured the time frame of the shooting. According to the film, the assassination lasted for 5.6 seconds. The FBI had already calculated that an assassin using a Mannlicher Carcano bolt action rifle would need 2.3 seconds for each shot. Therefore, the most shots that Oswald could have fired within that allotted time sequence was three. Tague was hit by a bullet that had missed the President by approximately 200 feet. This clearly established that one shot had completely missed the target which meant that Oswald, or any assassin, based on the above scenario only had two shots to cause the nine wounds in Kennedy and Connally. This is what prompted Arlen Specter, an investigator and attorney for the **WC** who would later become a U.S. Senator from Pennsylvania, to propose the single bullet theory which has become infamous and was immediately attacked by the original **WC** critics as impossible.

When Gerald Posner wrote his tome **Case Closed**, the MSM applauded its conclusions that the **WC** was right and that anyone who doubted it was a conspiracy nut that could not face the fact that a nobody could assassinate someone as powerful and admired as President Kennedy. This also occurred when famed prosecutor Vincent Bugilosi published his specious book entitled **Reclaiming History**. It is curious if not incredulous that Fiester's book was hardly mentioned or reviewed by the MSM. You would have thought her expertise and experience in examining and reconstructing crime scenes for thirty years, and the conclusions that she had made would have been newsworthy. Their silence was deafening to say the least.

It is clear that the MSM would rather believe in myths that are safe and reaffirm the reality they wish to promote. A reality that exonerates their failure to question and confront the ridiculous propositions of our government such as the single bullet theory that was a desperate attempt to evade any notion that the President may have been assassinated as a result of a conspiracy. Instead, they left the questioning and investigating to a small band of citizens to unravel the fabrications and obfuscations of the facts by their government to ascertain what really happened in Dealey Plaza and to determine why the President was murdered. President Kennedy stated, **"The great enemy of the truth is very often not the lie, deliberate, contrived and dishonest; but the myth, persistent, persuasive and unrealistic."**

The President was not assassinated by a lone nut using an antiquated Italian rifle with a defective scope while performing at a level that experts were unable to duplicate in their simulations of the shooting sequence. And Oswald was not murdered by a misguided patriot that simply wanted to spare his nation and the Kennedys a long trial, causing everyone to relive that emotionally disturbing and tragic moment. And NO – Newtonian physics were not suspended that day. It was a conspiracy! It is time the MSM emerge from its baseless denial of the forensic evidence and direct its vast resources to assist in our search for the truth.

The Patsy
(A walk through the "wilderness of mirrors")

Jim Garrison, the former DA of New Orleans, and the only person to indict an individual for the murder of our President in his 1967 Playboy interview stated "I hesitate to use the words 'second Oswald', because they tend to lend an additional fictional quality to a case that already makes 'Dr. No' and 'Goldfinger' look like auditors' reports." It is true nevertheless that someone in the fall of 1963 was impersonating Oswald on numerous occasions in ways that would make an indelible impression upon the person that witnessed the event or interacted with him. For instance, a man walked into the Lincoln/Mercury auto-dealership in Dallas near Dealey Plaza and indicated to the salesman, Albert Guy Bogard, that he wanted to purchase a vehicle and pointed to a

Mercury Comet. Bogard asked him if he wanted to test drive the vehicle. The man accepted Bogard's offer, and they both got into the Comet. The man then accelerated the vehicle to 80 mph while explaining to the salesman, who probably was expecting to die at any moment, that he was anticipating the receipt of a lot of money in two or three weeks. After the test drive, he told Bogard that his name was "Lee Oswald." When Bogard checked his credit, he found that Oswald had none and promptly reported this to him. He became agitated and retorted that he would have to purchase a vehicle in the Soviet Union.

The problem with this scenario is that the real Oswald did not have a motor vehicle license and according to the **Warren Commission Report** (WCR) did not know how to drive. He also had an alibi that day. He was with his wife and daughter at Ruth Paine's home. After the assassination, the salesman came forward to report to the FBI his encounter with the alleged assassin. He posed additional difficulties for the authorities when he did not identify the real Oswald as the man he interacted with that day. He was subsequently almost beaten to death by unknown assailants. He feared for his life and fled Dallas. A year later he was found dead. It was officially declared a suicide by the coroner. As you research the assassination, it becomes apparent that a significant number of witnesses would commit suicide, be murdered, have heart attacks or were involved in lethal accidents.

Another example was a man who was shooting at a local firing range in Dallas that was named the Sports Dome Rifle Range. There were four reported incidents that occurred at that facility. The first occurred in late September when a man asked Malcolm Price Jr. if he could assist him with his scope. Price indicated that it was getting dark and that he had to turn his headlights on so that they could see the targets. Once the scope was adjusted, the man fired three shots that hit the target dead center. The same man was seen practicing in late October and on

November 10, 1963. In another encounter, this man not only shot at his target but also the target of the man next to him. When confronted by Garland Slack, the man gave him "a look he would never forget." Slack said that the man looked like Oswald. This incident occurred just before the assassination around November 17th. The witnesses claimed that he appeared to be training for something.

The real Oswald had an alibi to some of the incidents. For example, he was with his family at the Paine's home in Erving when the November 10th event occurred. The first incident in September posed problems for the **Warren Commission** (WC) because Oswald was supposed to be in Mexico City at this time. These events appeared to have several purposes. The first was to ensure that Oswald was identified as the one who was practicing with a rifle with a scope, and secondly, was to impress the witnesses with his expertise as a rifleman. Lastly, it was clear that the imposter wanted to leave the impression that he was emotionally unstable. I would presume if these sightings were of the real Oswald he would have been more discrete while preparing to commit the crime of the century.

The next mysterious encounter was reported by Ralph Yates who indicated on the morning of November 20th he picked up a hitch hiker with a 4-foot brown package. The hitch hiker kept the package on his lap. Yates asked what was in the package and the passenger replied that "it was curtain rods." Yates then introduced himself and the passenger responded that his name was "Lee Oswald." As they drove into downtown Dallas, Yates mentioned that the President was scheduled to be in town that Friday. The man responded by asking him if he knew the motorcade route. Yates reported that it was in the papers. The man then asked him if he thought the President could be killed by a rifle from a tall building. Yates indicated that he supposed it was possible. The man then pulled out a picture of him holding a rifle and inquired if he thought it could be done with that particular weapon. Yates began to get nervous and was relieved to let the hitchhiker out at his destination on Houston just before the Texas School Book Depository (TSBD). He told a friend at work about this strange encounter and later that day he repeated it to his wife. Yates was subsequently admitted to a psychiatric hospital by his wife who had been convinced by the FBI after her husband had passed his polygraph examination that he was delusional and a threat to himself.[113]

The problem the WC had with the above occurrence was that the real Oswald was at work when this event took place. As Jim Garrison pointed out in the above mentioned interview, "The Warren Commission recognized that the individual involved in all these activities could not be Lee Oswald; but they never took the next step and inquired why these incidents of impersonation occurred so systematically prior to the assassination." A second Oswald would not only support his claim that he was a "patsy" but would establish a conspiracy. In addition, his expectation of receiving large sums of money and returning to the Soviet Union were also indicative of a conspiracy not a lone nut scenario. These witness encounters were more emblematic of an intelligence operation trying to frame Oswald rather than a lone nut preparing for the assassination. For those reasons and others, the WC had to discredit and dismiss these eyewitness encounters. The most revealing impersonation of Oswald would occur in Mexico City in early October which I will discuss later.

Robert Blakey, the former special prosecutor for the **House Select Committee on Assassinations** (HSCA), stated on Frontline in 1993 "Any attempt to explain what happened in Dallas must explain Lee Harvey Oswald...He is not, to put it in simple words, an easy man to explain." Especially difficult if you are trying to prove he was a lone nut whose primary motive was to avenge the duplicitous policies against Castro while imprinting his name in the annals of history. His actions and associations become much more apparent if he is viewed as a low level intelligence agent, a pawn being manipulated and moved on the chessboard of the Cold War, and an informant for the FBI.

Lee Harvey Oswald was born in New Orleans in October 1939. He was the child of Robert and Marguerite Oswald. His father died of a heart attack two months prior to his birth. He thus was raised by a single parent. He had two brothers. His older brother was named after his father Robert and would later join the United States Marine Corp (Marines). He resided in Fort Worth Texas and New York City as a child before moving back to New Orleans. In 1955, he joined a local Civil Air Patrol unit under the command of David Ferrie. Ferrie was known for encouraging his men to join the military services. Ferrie was a CIA pilot who also flew for mob boss Carlos Marcello. He would later get involved in training the anti-Castro Cubans who would eventually land on the shore at the **Bay of Pigs**. There are several pictures that have surfaced that show Ferrie and Oswald together while working for the Civil Air Patrol.

Ferrie was found dead in February 1967 with two typed unsigned suicide notes in his apartment. After his name appeared in a local paper on the front page as a potential suspect in the Garrison probe, he contacted Garrison's office and spoke with Lou Ivon who was Garrison's chief investigator in the Kennedy murder. According to Ivon, he was very agitated and nervous. He agreed to meet with him and pay for a room at a local motel. Ivon indicated further that Ferrie was very excited and was pacing back and forth. He admitted to Ivon that he, Oswald, Bannister and Shaw (aka Clay Bertrand) were working for the CIA. He indicated that Oswald was chosen to be the "patsy." His responsibility was to fly the mechanics out, but the plane had apparently crashed en route to Dallas. He further exclaimed that he was a "dead man" now that his name was associated with Garrison's investigation of the President's death. The night before his death he telephoned his ex-roommate in San

Francisco and told him that he was fearful for his life. The official cause of death was a brain aneurism.

Oswald attempted to join the Marines by forging his mother's signature on an affidavit indicating that he was older than he was. When this failed, he got a job at Gerald Tujague's Shipping Company. Tujague was Vice President of the **Friends of Democratic Cuba** which was an anti-Castro organization whose members were staunch anti-communists. It is important to note that the former head of FBI's Security Division in Chicago and a former officer in the Office of Naval Intelligence (ONI) in **World War II**, Guy Bannister, was also a member of the same committee.

There are two important incidents that come out of this part of Oswald's life as an agent provocateur in New Orleans in the summer of 1963, posing as a member of the **Fair Play for Cuba Committee** which was headquartered in New York City. This particular committee was the focus of two intelligence operations involving the Counter Intelligence Department of the CIA chaired by infamous James Jesus Angleton, and J. Edgar Hoover's secrete domestic intelligence operation named COINTELPRO (Counter Intelligence Program). The purpose of both operations were to infiltrate and discredit the committee that had significant influence and support in Latin and South America.

The first event was called the "Bolton Ford Incident." Members of the Friends of Democratic Cuba wanted to purchase vehicles to be sent to Cuba to assist those who were attempting to encourage opposition to Castro. The person that was present with several others falsely identified himself as "Lee Oswald." The real Oswald was in Russia at this time. The second incident occurred after the assassination during a press conference that was being held by DA Henry Wade. He stated to the press that Oswald was a member of the "Friends for a Democratic Cuba." It was Jack Ruby who corrected him by exclaiming that Oswald was a member of the "Fair Play for Cuba Committee."

Ruby was the owner of a strip joint called the Carousel Club in Dallas. He was a low level hood that had organize crime contacts and connections. He was also involved in anti-Castro activities running guns to Florida where they would be shipped to Cuba. These activities caused him to come in contact with intelligence assets and agents. He also had an unwritten agreement with many of the Dallas Police Officers that he would provide them free drinks and access to his girls if they did not interfere with his other illegal activities or his anti-Castro operations.

A former dancer from his club, Rose Cheramie, would tell Lieutenant Francis Fruge of the Louisiana State Police after the assassination that Oswald and Ruby knew each other. Prior to the assassination during his first encounter with her, she indicated that she was traveling with two Cubans from Miami to Dallas to pick up a drug shipment in Houston when they had an argument, and she was left behind at a bar off of US Highway 190 near Eunice called the Silver Slipper Lounge. The argument got so heated that Mac Manual, the bartender, and the two Cubans physically threw her out into the parking lot. As she was hitchhiking along Route 190, she was accidentally hit by a motorist that brought her to Moosa Memorial Hospital which was a private facility. The administrator of the hospital had contacted the State Police to report Cheramie's accident and that she appeared to be suffering from withdrawal symptoms. Lieutenant Fruge of the narcotics unit was sent to assess Cheramie's situation. Because Cheramie did not have medical insurance or an ability to compensate the hospital for services rendered, the administrator asked Officer Fruge if he could arrange her transfer to a state facility. He transported her to the Eunice City Jail and contacted a local physician that not only prescribed her a sedative but requested an ambulance that would transport her to a charitable hospital in Lafayette. While in the ambulance, Cheramie told Officer Fruge that the two Cubans had discussed in her presence that the President was going to be assassinated in Dallas. She also provided names and addresses regarding the drug transaction to the officer who was able to verify her story. As to Kennedy, he thought her story was dubious at best so he wrote up a report and filed it without further action taken.

After the events in Dallas, he and his supervisor divulged his conversations with Cheramie to the Dallas Police Department (DPD) and the FBI. Both departments were not interested. After all, they had already solved the case.

Lieutenant Fruge then forgot all about Cheramie until DA Garrison had him transferred to his unit in 1967 to assist in his investigation of the Kennedy assassination. Garrison was intrigued with the Cheramie story and requested that Officer Fruge try to locate her. He would eventually find Cheramie's sister who told him that her sister Rose had died in 1965. She added that her body was found on a remote highway between Tyler and Daywood, Texas. Her death remains a mystery to this day. When Officer Fruge reported this to Garrison, he gave him photographs of Cubans who were potential suspects and asked him to locate the bartender at the Silver Slipper Lounge. Officer Fruge then met with Mac Manual and asked him if he could identify the two Cubans who were with Rose Cheramie that day. Manual looked at the photographs and pointed to the pictures of Sergio Arcacha Smith and Emilio Santana.

Oswald finally joined the Marines in 1956. His boot camp was in San Diego. He served in several south-eastern states, California and eventually in Asia until he received his hardship discharge in September 1959. He was trained as a radar operator. His training included basic radar theory, map reading and air traffic control assignments, as well as radio communications, avionics and electronics. Oswald graduated seventh out of a class of 30 and was given a "Certificate for Aviation Electronics Operator." He received his first security clearance when he completed his training. It is important to note that although he was reading communist literature at this time his fellow Marines never considered him a communist sympathizer. He was also required to take a Russian examination. He got 50 percent of the questions right. Jim Garrison thought this was "remarkable." He was involved in military service for over two decades and never once was he asked to take a Russian examination. If he had, he would not have been able to get one of the questions right never mind 50 percent.

Oswald would later be assigned to the Atsugi Naval Base in Japan which was 20 miles west of Tokyo. This essentially was a major base of operations for the CIA's top secret U2 program. There were only three units in the world that flew this secret high flying reconnaissance jet that was manufactured by Lockheed Aircraft for the CIA and equipped with highly advanced cameras. Before the advent of satellites, these jets were the primary mechanism to obtain information on Soviet military bases and the number and location of their nuclear ICBMs. These jets routinely flew over Russia and China while Oswald was stationed there as a radar operator. As a radar operator, he frequently communicated with the pilots of the secret jets. He eventually was granted "crypto clearance" which was higher than top secret. Some of Oswald's other duties involved guarding the hangars where the U2s were kept.

While in Japan, Oswald continued to read communist literature, listen to Russian records and often spoke in Russian to his fellow Marines. His nick name was "Oswaldskovich." None of them thought he was a communist. If they had, one of his colleagues pointed out that Oswald's experience in the Marines would have been very difficult. They also reported that his shooting capabilities were an ongoing joke among his unit. Oswald ultimately was reassigned state side to attend The Monterey School of Languages for the Army where he became fluent in the Russian language.

Oswald was granted a hardship discharge from the Marines in the fall of 1959 because a candy jar had fallen on his mother's nose. It is amazing how easy it is to be discharged from the Marines. His claim was that he had to go home and care for his mother. While he was in Russia, the Secretary of the Navy changed his status to a "dishonorable discharge." I believe this was done to enhance his profile as a communist.

Seven days before his discharge he applied to an obscure college in Switzerland high in the Swiss Alps that was called Albert Schweitzer College. There were only 30 students enrolled in the college during this time. His admission date was set for April 1960. He also received a passport during this period. He stopped by and only stayed a few days with his mother before allegedly departing to attend college. His mother became worried when he did not respond to her letters. She wrote to the FBI for assistance in helping locate her son. No one at the FBI had ever heard of the college and had to contact their counterpart in Switzerland who spent two months searching for this school. Once it was located, they were unable to find Oswald. The question is how did Oswald become familiar with such an obscure college? In my opinion, his application and admission to this college was used as a cover for the actual reason he was travelling to Europe. As an aside, it was later learned that this school was significantly funded by the CIA and was closed down after the Kennedy assassination.

Meanwhile, Oswald was in Helsinki, Finland in October 1959 trying to obtain a visa to the Soviet Union. While Oswald was in Helsinki, he stayed at the Torni Hotel which was the finest hotel in the city. Oswald before departing for Europe only had $203 in his bank account. After spending one night at the Torni, he transferred to the Klaus Kurki Hotel which was a 4-star hotel. How could Oswald afford such luxurious accommodations? He also purchased 10 tourist vouchers at $30 apiece. He was either selling drugs or someone with a deep pocket was funding his trip.

Once he applied for a visa to Russia, it was granted within 24 hours. The Russian Embassy in Helsinki is the only one in Europe that an officer was allowed to issue a visa in a matter of hours. Most embassies would take days if not weeks to issue the visa. How did Oswald know this?

The CIA clearly knew this was the most efficacious way to get a visa to Russia. This is the route that many used in their **False Defector Program** which I believe Oswald was a part of. This program was administered by James Jesus Angleton's Counter Intelligence Department. Our country was for the most part an open society and as a result there were hundreds of KGB agents in the United States. The Soviet Union in contrast was a very closed society with significant security barriers which made it very difficult for the CIA to get intelligence operatives in the country. This false defector program which operated in the late 1950s and early 1960s often used young soldiers who allegedly became disillusioned with their country and as a result decided to defect to the Soviet Union. Many of these soldiers had access to classified matters that were used to entice the Soviets to let them into their security networks and use them as double agents or simply as a means of obtaining the desired intelligence. The ONI and other military intelligence were aware of the CIA program and provided support when needed. This in my opinion is why Oswald received his hardship, or what is also referred to as a dependency discharge, for such a minor matter.

The KGB quickly caught on to this program and were highly suspicious of these so called defectors. They had them under constant surveillance. Oswald as part of this program got to the U.S. Embassy in Moscow and met with Richard Snyder – a former CIA employee who now worked for the embassy. Oswald told him he wanted to defect to the Soviet Union and renounce his citizenship. According to Snyder, he also claimed that he had top secret classified information which we know involved the U2 program and radar technology. Snyder said that he had spoken as though he had memorized what he was going to say and that the message was not meant necessarily for him. Everyone in the embassy knew it was bugged and under 24-hour surveillance by the Soviets just as we were doing to their embassies around the world, including Mexico City which will become very important in the framing of Oswald as a communist agent.

Snyder convinced Oswald not to rescind his citizenship at least not until he reflected on the consequences of such an action. Oswald never came back to fill out the paperwork. Snyder promptly reported his encounter with Oswald to the State Department, FBI, ONI and the CIA. He did not detain him or have him arrested for threatening to disclose classified information to the enemy. If it were you or I, we probably would have been shot in the embassy. After all, this was the height of the Cold War. These matters were not taken lightly as was demonstrated in the cases of Julius and Ethel Rosenberg who were sentenced to death, and Alger Hiss whose career with the State Department, as well as his reputation was ruined. The response each agency had to Snyder's provocative report regarding Oswald's defection was predictable with exception to the CIA.

The FBI immediately placed a "flash order" on his file, dated, November 2, 1959, and the ONI took similar action. The State Department referred it to its intelligence department. Hugh Cummings, the Director of State Department's Intelligence and Research Bureau, sent a memo to Assistant Director of Covert Operations of the CIA, Richard Bissell, requesting information on 18 defectors of which Lee Harvey Oswald was #8. He had become suspicious because prior to these rash of defectors in 1958 through 1959 there had not been any reported cases. In any event, Bissell sent the inquiry to none other than Angleton to respond to Cummings' request. Someone working for Angleton provided the information to Bissell who promptly forwarded it to Cummings' office. Although information was provided on some of the alleged defectors, next to Oswald's name was written "classified – secret." They did add, however, that he had renounced his citizenship which was not true as pointed out above.

At the CIA, Snyder's letter goes into a black hole and then magically appears on December 6, 1959, in Counter Intelligence/Special Investigative Group (CI/SIG) which is part of Angleton's unit. The question posed by John Newman, a former military intelligence officer for 20 years, was where was the letter for 30 days and why did it not appear in the Soviet Russian Division of the CIA where it would normally be deposited? In addition, there is no evidence that there was a comprehensive security investigation that should have been immediately triggered to assess the potential damage to the U2 program, as well as other classified information such as "height finding radar technology." The CIA did not even open a 201 file on Oswald for over a year. This is a common file that is opened on anyone of interest to CIA and/or an employee under suspicion. When Richard Helms, the former CIA Director, was asked during the **Church Committee Hearings** why it took one year to open a 201 file, he appeared dumbfounded and added that he could not explain it.

What is even more incredulous is that Francis Gary Powers' piloted U2 was shot down over the Soviet Union in May 1960 just six months after Oswald's defection. This was the first time the Soviets were able to bring down a U2. He was convicted of espionage against the Soviet Union and sentenced to three years of incarceration and seven years of hard labor. Oswald would attend his trial. The Kennedy administration was able in February 1962 to consummate a spy swap that allowed Powers to return to the United States. Powers did not believe that it was a coincidence and has always suspected foul play. For example, he noted that the top secret cameras on his jet were replaced with older models which he thought was strange.

The shooting down of his plane was not a minor event. This incident resulted in the disruption of a conference in Paris to discuss a possible **Comprehensive Test Ban Treaty** between the two super powers that was to culminate in a visit by President Eisenhower to Moscow which was cancelled by Khrushchev. Some historians and researchers have speculated, based on circumstantial evidence, that Eisenhower was assured by Dulles that he did not have to suspend U2 flights prior to the summit because the reconnaissance jet would be invulnerable to Soviet weapons. He added that even if a Soviet missile struck the plane it would disintegrate before it hit the ground. Eisenhower was furious when Power's U2 was not only shot down but the pilot and the plane were paraded in front of the international media embarrassing the administration. For it was after the shooting down of Powers' plane and the cancelled summit that provoked Eisenhower to confront the Director of the CIA and accuse Dulles of handing him a "legacy of ashes" to leave for his successor. This incident may also have contributed to the President's decision to include in his farewell address in January 1961 the warning to the nation about the growing influence of the "military industrial complex" and its corporate sponsors.

The CIA was against the summit, and Dulles may have intentionally misled the President. Hence, the sacrifice of the plane may have been deliberate. The U2 was soon to be replaced by a faster jet that was capable of flying at Mach 3 and at altitudes of 85,000 feet called the SR 71 Black Bird. Only a few of them were manufactured by Lockheed because of the introduction of satellite technology. Therefore, the U2 information that Oswald threatened to disclose to the Soviets at the U.S. Embassy in Moscow, and the U2 captured by them when Powers' jet was shot down was old technology that was expendable. This is why the CIA in my opinion never conducted a security investigation because this technology obtained by the Soviets was going to be replaced and was now obsolete.

While in the Soviet Union, Oswald was employed in an electronics factory in Minsk. It is there that he meets and marries his wife, Marina. The declassified KGB documents indicate that Oswald's movements and contacts were closely monitored. In early 1962, Oswald requested permission to come home. Believe it or not, this individual who should have been treated as a traitor was not only granted a return visa within 24 hours, but he also received a loan from the State Department to cover his travel expenses. When he arrived by ship in New York City, he was greeted by a staunch anti-communist who worked for the State Department.

He quickly relocated in Dallas after being debriefed by the FBI and CIA. It must be noted that the CIA has always denied that they debriefed Oswald for their standard narrative is that they had no interest in him and that they had little knowledge of him prior to the assassination. The truth of the matter was that he was debriefed by Ellen Reid of the Soviet Russian Division of the CIA.

When Oswald arrived in Dallas, the CIA quickly appointed "babysitters" to watch over him and introduce him to other assets in the community. George De Mohrenschildt (hereinafter George) was an intelligence asset who did favors for the CIA in exchange for "profitable business connections" facilitated overseas by the Agency. George admitted in 1977 while the HSCA's investigation was pending that he was asked by J. Walton Moore who was the CIA Domestic Contacts Service Chief in Dallas to watch over Oswald and his Russian wife. Otherwise as George pointed out, he would never have associated with people like the Oswalds because of their communist background. He was a rich baron who was part of the White Russian community in the Dallas area whose relatives were part of the elite Russian ruling class before the Bolshevik Revolution of 1917. Their purpose and hope was to retake their country much like the anti-Castro Cuban community who resided primarily in southern Florida had hopes of overthrowing the Castro regime. After he fulfilled his duties, he introduced the Oswalds to Michael and Ruth Paine. But just before he exited Oswald's life, he helped him acquire employment at Jaggars-Chiles Stovall which was a commercial advertising photography firm that had contracts with the U.S. Army Map Service. It naturally was classified work that required a security clearance. One might wonder how a communist that defected to the Soviet Union and threatened to divulge top secret information to the enemy was approved for such a job.

Several years later George and his wife Jeanne confided to Jim Garrison that they believed that "Oswald was a scape goat in the assassination." George was rewarded for his work with Oswald by the U.S. Embassy in Haiti when they were able to convince Papa Doc Duvalier, a CIA puppet, for an oil exploration deal. As an aside, when Gaeton Fonzi an investigator for the HSCA located him in southern Florida to question him further, he found George dead. The cause of death was a shotgun blast to the head. It was officially ruled as a suicide. His wife said he was fearful for his life but was not suicidal.

Michael and Ruth Paine were also not your average citizens. Ruth's sister was employed by the CIA and her father was also involved in intelligence. Michael was a high ranking executive with security clearances for Bell Helicopter who would reap huge profits during the Vietnam War as the famed Huey Helicopter quickly became the work horse in our war effort. Both had relatives who were part of the elites of Wall Street. Why would such a couple befriend the Oswalds? Ruth provided the lame excuse that she wanted to learn Russian from Marina. After the assassination, most of the alleged evidence that supposedly would have convicted Oswald came from his so called friend Ruth such as the infamous backyard photo.

This photo was astonishing if you reflect on what it is depicting. In one photograph, the prosecution can establish Oswald was a communist because of the literature he is holding in one hand and that he owned the pistol and the rifle that allegedly killed Dallas Police Officer J.D. Tippit and the President. The central question of course was was this photograph real? Over time, two other photos would be discovered. Each one was slightly different than the other. However, each photo had the exact same face.

She also failed to advise him in late 1963 after his return from New Orleans that one of the managers of a high paying job he had applied to called to schedule an interview. Instead, she apprised him of a potential employment opportunity at the TSBD that paid much less than the other job. He now was employed at a business that was conveniently located at the most vulnerable location of what would become the motorcade route for the President on November 22.

Lee and Marina with their daughter moved to New Orleans in April 1963. He quickly got a job at the Reilley Coffee Company. Because the job was not very eventful, Oswald spent most of his time next door at a garage that only serviced the intelligence community. It was not open to the public. By July 1963, he was the only member for the local chapter of the **Fair Play for Cuba Committee**. He was seen, photographed and even made the local television newscast that showed him handing out leaflets for the committee. At one point, the leaflets had stamped on them the address of 544 Camp Street near the heart of the intelligence community in New Orleans. Lee had made a rookie mistake by placing the address of Guy Bannister's Private Detective Agency on the pro-Castro literature.

Bannister was a rabid anti-communist who had allowed Oswald to have office space in his agency while operating as an agent provocateur attempting to embarrass the committee. As Jim Garrison stated, he was sure Bannister and his associates probably all had "heart attacks" when they saw their address stamped on communist leaflets and fliers. Needless to say, the address was quickly changed to an address around the corner of

Bannister's office. Bannister at that time was not operating a private detective agency. This agency was a front for his intelligence work. He was working for the CIA running guns and supplies to Cuba. He was also, along with his associates David Ferrie, Clay Shaw, Sergio Arcacha Smith among others, managing a facility at Lake Pontchartrain north of New Orleans for the CIA. This operation was training Cubans to assassinate Castro and to reinvade the island even though the President had made a pledge that the U.S. would not invade Cuba as part of the accord that peacefully ended the **Cuban Missile Crisis** in October 1962. This camp was eventually raided in the fall of 1963 by the FBI, enforcing President Kennedy's policy that all anti-Castro operations were to be shut down in the United States. A whole building of supplies and weapons were confiscated.

The President at this time was secretly seeking rapprochement with Castro and attempting to settle the Cuban matter peacefully. The CIA closely monitored these negotiations and may have even leaked some of the communications to the anti-Castro Cuban community.

During this period, Leon Oswald was at a meeting with David Ferrie, Clay Shaw, Sergio Arcacha Smith and other anti-Castro Cubans. Smith was the head of the Cuban Revolutionary Counsel which was organized by E. Howard Hunt and David Atlee Phillips of the CIA. This was observed by the prominent witness for Garrison, Perry Russo. Russo was a local insurance agent that attended a party and inadvertently became part of a discussion that involved the murder of the President with high powered rifles. They wanted to get the President in a crossfire once he hit the kill zone. Regrettably for Garrison's investigation, Ferrie and Bannister (died of heart attack in 1964) were dead, and Texas refused to honor his subpoena for Sergio Arcacha Smith. Oswald, however, was also seen by numerous witnesses with David Ferrie and Clay Shaw in the townships of Clinton and Jackson just north of New Orleans.

Clay Shaw was a respected businessman in New Orleans who was the CEO of the International Trade Mart. In the 1950s, he was a CIA asset and contact who did favors for the agency and was compensated for his services. A document discovered in the National Archives by Peter Veer in 1994 which was attached to a listing of Shaw's multiple contacts with the Domestic Contact Service of the CIA indicated that he was an active covert operator for the CIA during the period of Garrison's investigation. In addition, he had security clearances for project QKENCHANT. Shaw did not need a security clearance for the Domestic Contact Service, but he would need one if he was involved in the Domestic Operations Division which was the most secret unit within the clandestine services of the CIA.

While in Italy, he was associated with a company named Permindex whose connections to an assassination attempt on President Charles De Gaulle of France in 1962 was reported by a journalist employed by an Italian newspaper. The press got so bad that Clay Shaw and others (who were probably CIA) were told to leave Italy by the Italian Government. In fact, Permindex moved to South Africa.

Permindex was incorporated in 1956. The financial backing originally was provided by J. Henry Schroder Banking Corporation. Schroder was closely associated with Allen Dulles ever since the 1930s when Dulles was employed as a senior partner at the law firm of Sullivan and Cromwell. At one point, Dulles was the general manager of the bank. After Dulles was appointed by President Eisenhower to become the CIA Director in 1953, Schroder provided a $50 million contingency fund that was controlled by Dulles. The Bank benefitted immensely from CIA operations such as the overthrow of the democratically elected governments in Iran and Guatemala.

The Board of Directors of Permindex all had significant contacts with fascist governments and associations that reverted back to Nazi Germany. This corporation was clearly a strange creation. Journalists in Italy for example were unable to ascertain the origins of its funding or determine what it did. In fact, one paper proposed that "Permindex may have been a creature of the CIA...Set up as a cover for transfer of CIA... funds in Italy for illegal political espionage activities." The paper also alleged that it may have been involved in assassination projects such as the attempt on President De Gaulle. It must be noted that the motive to assassinate De Gaulle was his policy to allow Algeria to become an independent sovereign nation. Just as the motive to kill President Kennedy may have been related to his policy to normalize relations with Cuba and withdraw from Vietnam among others. Permindex was clearly not what it purported to be and just like Oswald's communist affiliations was another example of the "wilderness of mirrors."

In September, Ruth Paine picked up Marina and her daughter and brought them back to Dallas. Lee stayed in New Orleans a little longer to finish his work. It was at this time Oswald's role began to take shape for the conspirators and the part that he would play in the assassination.

Sylvia Odio and her sister were visited at her home outside Dallas by two Cubans and a white male whose name was "Leon Oswald." She claimed that this incident occurred on September 26 or the 27, 1963. The two Cubans did all the talking and claimed they had heard of her father and his efforts against Castro. They were hoping that she could help. She declined primarily because she did not know or trust them. She wrote her father who was in a prison in Cuba. He responded that he did not know them as well and advised against her offering any assistance. She then received a mysterious phone call from one of the Cubans asking for help. She again refused. He then asked her what she thought of "Leon." She indicated that she had no opinion as to him. The Cuban then volunteered that Leon had stated that the President should have been assassinated after the Bay of Pigs. He then hung up.

The WC had three major problems with what is commonly referred to as the "Odio Incident" by researchers. First, Oswald was supposed to be traveling to Mexico City at this time, and secondly, what was he doing hanging around anti-Castro Cubans? The third issue is that these instances were destroying their lone nut theory. Rather than confront these issues, they concluded that she was mistaken when this took place and that "Leon" was not Oswald even though she perfectly described Oswald's physical characteristics. In fact, she recognized Oswald as the individual who had visited her apartment when she observed pictures of him after his arrest. They never investigated the matter to ascertain who the two Cubans might have been.

Before I discuss the implications of Oswald's activities or should I say his impersonator's actions in Mexico, I need to provide some contextual background to present a cogent explanation on what was being done to Oswald's files within the CIA and the FBI and how they related to the framing of Oswald in the assassination just prior, during and after his visit to Mexico City.

The FBI had a "flash order" on Oswald's file ever since they received news of his defection from Snyder. On October 9, 1963, just 24 hours before U.S. intelligence agencies were apprised of Oswald's meeting and telephone conference with a Russian agent in charge of their assassination unit, Marvin Gheesling, a senior intelligence agent for the FBI, would inexplicably remove his flash order which in affect took him off of the FBI's Security Index which was a listing of all known communists. When Hoover found out after the assassination what Gheesling had done, he was furious. We know this from an FBI document that said that Hoover wanted to demote him and send him to "Siberia." I guess Siberia for Hoover was the FBI's Detroit Office because that is where he was sent. This information was never provided to the WC or the HSCA. In fact, Gheesling was never interviewed and no document has surfaced to date that would illuminate on whose authority he implemented the removal of the flash order.

He took this secret to his grave.

At the CIA during this period, Oswald was removed from the "watch list" that was the impetus for the CIA to intercept and read his mail without his knowledge. Even though, he was no longer on the watch list, according to the documents reviewed by John Newman, they were still secretly reading his mail.

These actions had two significant consequences for the security alarms that protected the President and for the plan to set up the patsy. The first result was to lower Oswald's profile at a time when it should have been raised. The events described should have triggered drastic action within the intelligence community to assess the implications of Oswald's meeting and conference with a KGB assassination expert. Instead, the reports were received by Angleton's unit and held dormant until they were released after the assassination. Once this information was disclosed, it caused panic in many of the agencies when they realized they had filed similar information in their data collection files which caused some to immediately go into CYA mode. At the CIA, witnesses said that the atmosphere was "electric" when Oswald's name was announced after his arrest.

The other consequence was that when the Secret Service requested information from their Protective Research Section (PRS) prior to the President's visit in Dallas seeking individuals that might pose a threat to the President Oswald's name was not on the list. How did this assist the conspiracy? This allowed Oswald to work at a location along the motorcade route without notice. After all, if the authorities were monitoring him, you would have numerous professional witnesses that would eliminate him as a patsy by providing him an alibi during the shooting.

There are a number of theories regarding what Oswald did or did not do in Mexico City. In fact, the research community are divided on this issue. Some believe he never went to Mexico and others speculate he was only there for several days (September

27 – October 2). Jim Garrison when commenting on the mystery of these events to Lou Ivon observed that "All information regarding Lee Harvey Oswald in Mexico City is clouded in a mist, as if it were something that happened about the time of the Druids. This place is the thing wherein we'll catch the conscience of the Queen Bee." In essence, the Mexico City events say more about the CIA and the plot to kill the President than they do about Oswald. This is probably why the Agency backtracked on the tape recordings and the photographs allegedly of Oswald which I will describe below.

This is the Government scenario adopted by the WC. He went to Mexico seeking an in-transit visa through Cuba with his ultimate destination to return to the Soviet Union. He did this even though he already had a visa that would allow him to return to Russia the same way he went in 1959. In any event, the Cuban embassy refused to grant him one, and he decided to return to Dallas. The WC essentially opined that the Mexico City events were unrelated to the assassination. In their view, Oswald's decision to kill Kennedy was planned only a few days before the President's announced visit to Dallas. The only relevance the events in Mexico had for the WC was to enhance Oswald's profile as a communist.

Their scenario was founded on inaccurate and insufficient information. The CIA was monitoring the Cuban and Russian Embassies around the clock every day. They had bugged and wire tapped the buildings and had multiple cameras taking pictures of everyone entering and leaving the embassies. David Atlee Phillips was the head of the western hemisphere for the CIA and Win Scott was the Chief Operating Officer in their Mexico City office.

Lee Oswald or his imposter went into the Cuban Embassy and Russian Embassy over a period of several days. He allegedly, with the help of a secretary in the Cuban Embassy named Silvia Duran, made several phone calls to the Russian Embassy and spoke with a man named Valery Kostikov who was the head of the KGB's Department 13 which directed all sabotage and assassination programs in the western hemisphere. The CIA provided two photographs of a man they reported was Lee Harvey Oswald. One was taken on October 1, 1963, and the other was taken on October 15, 1963. Both were of a blonde haired man who was heavy set. Oswald had brown hair that was receding. He was 5 foot 9 inches tall and weighed 135 pounds. The man that was photographed was not Oswald. This man was not identified until investigators from the HSCA were able to determine that he was an employee of the Soviet Embassy. The CIA personnel in the Mexico City office knew who this man was in 1963 and yet they still sent the pictures to the FBI and to Langley. If Oswald was there, the CIA would have provided pictures of the real Oswald. Of course, their final excuse for not being able to produce a picture of Oswald was that the cameras were not functioning properly during this period which we know was false.

The other issue revolved around the tape recording of Oswald's alleged telephone conference with the head of the KGB's assassination unit. The significance of this connection was only known by a select few within the CIA and FBI who were familiar with a highly sensitive joint agency operation against Kostikov that was known as project "TUMBLEWEED." As we know today because of declassified documents from the CIA, Oswald's 201 file was manipulated and restricted in such a manner that incoming intelligence from Mexico City regarding his alleged Cuban and Soviet contacts would not be fully understood by those whose responsibility was to respond to this information. Since they did not recognize Kostikov, and more importantly his position within the KGB, they simply filed the reports into the CIA archives without recommending further action. This would partially explain the bizarre behavior of the CIA after the plotters within the Agency divulged the true identity of Kostikov after Oswald's arrest. At first, the CIA said they had tapes. The story quickly changed to they were mistaken and that all the tapes were destroyed as part of their normal recycle procedure. All of this was not true.

Unbeknownst to the CIA, two FBI agents who were observing the interrogation of Oswald by the Dallas Police Department after his arrest on November 22 had obtained the tape of Oswald allegedly speaking to Kostikov. They listened to it and reported to Hoover that the voice on the tape was not Oswald. In addition, Silvia Duran reported that one of the tapes was allegedly done with her on a Saturday. She stated that the Cuban Embassy is always closed on Saturday and that she never made that call on behalf of Oswald. In fact, many years later when Dan Hardway and Eddie Lopez went to Mexico City on behalf of the HSCA, they brought pictures of the real Oswald to present to Silvia Duran and three other employees at the Cuban Embassy that allegedly had contact with him. Silvia along with two of her colleagues indicated that the person they interacted with in 1963 was not Oswald. The only person that thought it was Oswald only saw him at a distance. Duran, however, was the only employee that had sustained and direct contact with the person who claimed to be Oswald.

The evidence clearly demonstrates that an imposter was impersonating Oswald with the apparent objective to incontrovertibly link him to a Soviet KGB assassin and the Cubans. This is disturbingly similar with an assassination memorandum that was prepared by CIA Agent William Harvey who was the supervising officer of ZR/RIFLE and Task Force W which were both assassination programs that were implicated in the attempts to assassinate Fidel Castro. In that memo, Harvey wrote that a "false 201 file" should be created to construct the legend or profile of the "patsy." The patsy should be set up as a communist so that the "Czechs and the Soviets" could be assigned blame for the assassination.

In a debate between Mark Lane and David Atlee Phillips (he was retired at this time) at the University of Southern California, a student from the audience asked "What really happened in Mexico City?" Phillips surprisingly gave a very candid answer although he was careful not to disclose too much. He answered "...when the record comes out, we will find that there never was a photograph taken of Lee Harvey Oswald in Mexico City." He added "Second, there is no evidence to show that Lee Harvey Oswald ever visited the Soviet Embassy." He could not admit that Oswald was never in Mexico City. For as John Newman pointed out, there cannot be a benign reason for someone impersonating Oswald while connecting him to a KGB assassination expert just six weeks before Dallas.

At first, President Johnson was worried that the Cubans and the Russians were behind Oswald's gun and that if this became known it would cause a third world war that would kill 40 million Americans. It was this scenario that President Johnson used to bully Chief Justice Earl Warren to become the head of a commission that was to investigate the assassination. There instructions were to satisfy the public that Oswald committed the crime alone as clearly stated in the **Katzenbach Memorandum**. After Hoover in a telephone conference explained the CIA deceit and chicanery in Mexico City to the President, the motive to cover up the crime for Johnson and Hoover was no longer to prevent a world war but to avoid the humiliation of the American government from looking like another "banana republic." This new evidence was never shared with the commission. The fodder and propaganda this would offer our enemies could affect our relations with countries all around the world and would also tarnish our reputation with our allies. The cover up became a matter of national security and everyone, including the media, had to do their patriotic duty.

I now turn to the evidence. As one writer, David Josephs, wrote "the evidence is the conspiracy." After Oswald moved back to Dallas, Ruth Paine told him there was a job opening at the TSBD in Dealey Plaza. He applied and was hired. He worked 40 hours a week at $1.50 per hour. He worked Monday through Friday from 8:00am until 4:30pm.

After his return, he was seen meeting with "Maurice Bishop" in Dallas by an anti-Castro Cuban named Antonio Veciana whose contact was Bishop while working with an aggressive anti-Castro group called Alpha 66. Fonzi an investigator for the HSCA spent a decade investigating this matter which culminated in a book entitled **The Last Investigation**. He concluded that "Maurice Bishop" was a pseudonym used by the case officer for Alpha 66 and the CIA's chief of all operations in the western hemisphere named David Atlee Phillips. Veciana signed an affidavit in 2014 finally acknowledging that Phillips (aka Bishop) was the one meeting with Oswald in Dallas just two months prior to the assassination.

Phillip's brother had always suspected that his brother David was involved in the tragedy in Dallas to the point that he terminated their relationship. Just before Phillips died, he telephoned his brother to say goodbye in an attempt to mend fences. Once his brother was on the phone, he demanded to know if David was in Dallas on November 22. His brother David began to cry and reluctantly said "yes." Upon hearing this, David's brother hung up. Phillips was also involved in the lies regarding the tapes and the photographs that were obtained in Mexico City. After his testimony, the HSCA recommended to the Department of Justice that he should be charged with perjury. The charge was never filed. Lastly, he was the field agent in charge of the operation to discredit the Fair Play for Cuba Committee. In my opinion, he was one of Oswald's controllers for the CIA.

We return to November 21, 1963, to trace Oswald's actions through the eyes of the witnesses that he interacted with or was observed by right up to the moment of the first shot heard in Dealey Plaza at 12:30pm the following day. On the afternoon of the 21st, Oswald asked Wesley Frazier, a fellow employee, if he could drive him to Ruth's home to see his wife and daughter after work. Marina and his daughters resided with Ruth Paine while Oswald paid for a room in a boarding house in Dallas close to the TSBD where he was employed. His routine was to visit his family every weekend.

Ruth came home after shopping to find Oswald sitting on her front lawn. She did not expect him until that Friday evening. He spent the evening with his family and went to bed at 9:00pm. Everyone else stayed up to 11:00pm watching television. According to the WC, the rifle was stored in a blanket in Ruth's garage. No one that evening saw Oswald go into the garage and retrieve a rifle. When he left for work, Marina and Ruth indicated that he was not carrying a package. He was picked up by Frazier who indicated that Oswald was carrying a large brown bag the size of a grocery bag. This would not have been large enough to store the rifle he had allegedly purchased in March. The 40-inch rifle when broken down had a part that was 34 inches long. All the metal parts weighed 7.5 pounds and would have made metallic sounds as they rubbed each other when the package was carried. None of this was reported by Frazier and his wife. In fact, Frazier indicated that Oswald told him there were "curtain rods" in the bag. Some of the researchers do not find his testimony very credible in that none of the other witnesses corroborated his story. When Frazier dropped Oswald off at work just before 8:00am, he was observed coming into the TSBD by Edward Shields and Jack Dougherty. Both testified to the WC that he did not have anything in his hands.

Oswald worked on all the floors of the TSBD but primarily was assigned to the first floor. On the morning of the 22nd, he worked on the sixth floor where the sniper's nest was located. Charles Givens was also on the sixth floor. He testified that he left at 11:30am and took the elevator to the fifth floor. The elevator was a slow freight type that was primarily used for the top floors. He then stated that Oswald yelled down to him to send the elevator back up. The next time Givens saw Oswald was in the "Domino Room" on the first floor around 11:50am reading a newspaper.

Eddie Piper also saw Oswald on the first floor at 12:00pm. Bill Shelly testified that he too saw Oswald in the Domino Room at 11:50am. Junior Jarman and Herald Norman were with Eddie Piper and saw Oswald eating his lunch around 12:00pm. This is curious behavior for someone who is about to murder the President. And it is extremely baffling when the original time line for the Presidential motorcade to pass by the TSBD was between 11:55am and 12:10pm. Fortunately for Oswald or maybe the WC, Air Force 1 landed at Love Field in Dallas at 11:45am not at 11:30am as originally scheduled.

The motorcade was approximately 45 minutes away from the Trade Mart where the President was supposed to give a brief speech before eating his lunch. The VIP invitations indicated that the luncheon was to begin at 12:00pm. It is important to note that Oswald according to the WC had a broken down rifle hidden somewhere in the building that needed to be reassembled and a sniper's nest that had to be prepared to hide his location as he took aim at the President. The sniper's nest would have required a lot of work. 40 boxes that weighed 20 pounds each were moved to obscure the view of others on the sixth floor. I do not think even James Bond would have been so cool and calm before committing the crime of the century.

Carolyn Arnold testified that she saw Oswald around 12:25pm on the lower floors. The WC changed her testimony without her permission to 12:15pm. Meanwhile Bonnie Ray Williams took his lunch to the sixth floor at 12:00pm and ate it to approximately 12:15pm. He saw no one else while he was there. However, Arnold Rowland reported seeing a man with a rifle on the sixth floor at 12:15pm. This shooter knew when to expect the motorcade unlike Oswald. Another witness corroborated

Rowland. He indicated that there were two of them and that one of the men was holding a rifle. One of the men was described as Caucasian, and the other reportedly had a darker complexion. Both were observed looking out the windows.

The motorcade arrived in Dealey Plaza at 12:29pm when the large Lincoln took a 90 degree turn onto Houston from Main. The gunfire began at 12:30pm. It is important to remember that the original motorcade route had the President continuing on Main Street through the center of Dealey Plaza which would have allowed the limousine to maintain the requisite speed of 35 mph. By the time this large vehicle made the 120 degree turn onto Elm in front of the TSBD, it was travelling at 18 mph. In fact, it would slow down to as low as 9 mph before taking off under the triple underpass after the shots were fired. The President was essentially a sitting duck for professional killers. This change in route was requested by the Secret Service in late November and approved by Mayor Cabell, the brother of General Charles Cabell, who was fired by President Kennedy after the Bay of Pigs.

Between 11:50am and 12:20pm, there are employees on the elevator and stairs either coming down for lunch, retrieving cigarettes or going up to eat their lunch as Williams did. They were also getting in position to view the motorcade whether it was from a window in the upper floors or meeting friends outside the building. No one reports seeing Oswald going up to the sixth floor never mind with a 34-inch package.

The shots are fired mortally wounding the President and seriously injuring Governor Connally. Vickie Adams and Sandra Styles were on the fourth floor watching the motorcade as the tragedy played out. They immediately left the window after the last shot travelling 60 feet to the fourth floor stair landing. They began their descent to get out of the building. They both stated that it took them 15 to 20 seconds to get to the stairs. They also avowed that they saw no one running down the stairs or heard anyone on the stairs ahead of them. They both reached the first floor, and this was verified by Carolyn Arnold. Both statements were also corroborated by their supervisor Dorothy Garner. She was with them on the fourth floor and followed them to the stairs. She stayed there long enough to observe a police officer and Roy Truly (Depository Superintendent) running up the stairs. Since Styles and Adams did not observe Mr. Truly or the officer on the stairs, they had to have exited the building before they had entered the first floor.

Dallas Police Officer Marion Baker ran into the TSBD approximately 75 to 90 seconds after the shooting. He met up with Mr. Truly, and they immediately began running up the stairs where they encountered Oswald in a second floor hallway. The officer was about to pull his gun when Truly stated that "he is an employee." The officer testified that Oswald turned around and acknowledged them. He was holding a bottle of coke. They then proceeded to the upper floors where they passed Dorothy Garner on the fourth floor. There were also several witnesses on the fifth floor who reported hearing shots above them and that they ran to the fifth floor landing outside the elevator and did not see or hear anyone on the stairs.

Since the assassination, the Dallas Police Department have asserted that there were no notes taken during their interrogation of Oswald. In the 1990s, Dallas Police Captain Will Fritz's notes were found by researchers. His notes reveal that Oswald's account of his whereabouts before and after the shooting are consistent with the other witnesses. He told Fritz that he did not own a rifle and that he was on the first floor eating his lunch. He indicated that two other employees could vouch for him. One of them was named "Junior." After eating his lunch, he went out with Bill Shelley to watch the motorcade. There is a picture of someone who appears to be Oswald in the front door entrance of the TSBD watching the motorcade. He further added that while he was on the first floor shortly after the shooting two men that had badges asked him where the nearest phone was located. These two men turned out to be journalists. Both verified Oswald's statement. He then indicated he went to the second floor to get a coke when he was confronted by a Dallas Police Officer. Furthermore, as written in Captain Fritz's report, Oswald stated that he did not bring curtain rods to work that day. He indicated that the only bag he had contained his lunch. At no time was Oswald a suspect after the shooting that is until the DPD received an anonymous tip. This individual has never been identified. Oswald was arrested at a movie theater at 1:50pm.

There were multiple rifles observed that day in Dealey Plaza. Two of them were found in the TSBD. A witness observed a man running from the building shortly after the shooting carrying a 30 caliber weapon. Several witnesses observed a man with a rifle behind the fence on the grassy knoll.

The third rifle was found on the sixth floor by Deputy Sheriff Eugene Boone and fellow officer Roger Craig which was identified as a 7.65 Mauser. Craig affirmed that he was no more than eight inches from the weapon and could read "7.65 Mauser" stamped onto the barrel of the gun by the manufacturer. This weapon was not mounted with a telescopic lens. However, it was considered a top quality weapon used by hunters and snipers. This rifle would magically disappear from the record until documents that described the gun were declassified. Another interesting piece of evidence was discovered in the 1990s which was an FBI evidence envelope from Dallas, dated, December 12, 1963. The envelope was empty, but the cover indicated that it had contained a 7.65 mm rifle shell found in Dealey Plaza after the shooting. There was also a witness, Mr. Evans, who reported that he observed a rifle sticking out of that sixth floor window in the TSBD about 14 inches to 15 inches. He claimed he could see 70 percent to 85 percent of the rifle. He stated "I did not observe a scope." Could this have been a Mauser?

The fourth weapon was also located on the sixth floor at

1:22pm. It was identified as a 6.5 Mannlicher Carcano (MC) that was an antiquated Italian rifle that was nicknamed by the Italian infantry as the "humane weapon" in that it was difficult to hit what you were aiming at. This rifle had a telescopic lens that was not properly aligned with the barrel of the gun. If you went by the site without adjusting or accounting for the misalignment, your shot would miss to the left of the target. Before you go admiring Oswald's marksmanship considering the rifle he allegedly used and the defective scope he had to account for, one must review his military record.

The military has three tiers to determine the competency of a shooter. The lowest tier is marksman followed by sharp shooter, and the highest is designated as an expert. The Marines in his unit were classified as sharp shooters, and some were experts. Oswald while being trained every day in boot camp on how to care for and use his weapon never attained expert status. In his first test, he barely made sharp shooter and in his final test he passed as a marksman by only two points. The testimony of his fellow Marines with exception to one whose background included work for intelligence said that Oswald was a lousy shot who really had no interest in guns which was unusual for a Marine. And yet, Oswald accomplished in Dealey Plaza what experts from the FBI and military could not achieve in their simulated tests trying to duplicate what he had allegedly done.

There is a video on **YouTube** of Jesse Ventura, a former Governor of Minnesota and member of the Navy Seals, trying to replicate what Oswald had done on November 22, 1963. He stood in a tower that was set at the same height as the sixth floor of the TSBD with a vehicle with figures in it that represented the President's 1961 Lincoln. He was using the same weapon Oswald was supposed to have used when he mortally wounded the President. The goal of the simulation was to hit the target two out of three times in 5.6 seconds. Ventura was classified as an expert while in the military and when he was tested again during his time as Governor his scores were still in the expert category. The first thing he did with another expert rifleman was to get familiar with the archaic bolt action rifle. His first comment after trying to get used to the bolt action mechanisms of the rifle was "This is a piece of shit." In the demonstration, targeting a stationary target with none of the stress that would be present when shooting a President, Ventura was only able to get one head shot but was never able to get three rounds off in 5.6 seconds. After the simulation was over, he turned to the camera and said, "Oswald shot the President with this weapon...THAT IS BULLSHIT!"

Most assume that Oswald owned the above rifle even though they might concede he had accomplices. They most likely have come to this conclusion by two dubious pieces of evidence which are the backyard photos depicting Oswald holding the rifle in one hand and communist literature in the other, and the money order he allegedly mailed to purchase the rifle.

When you examine the photographs, it becomes apparent as described by many experts that the face in each picture is the same, but the bodies are different. Oswald worked for a commercial photographic company and learned many tricks of the trade. When asked about the photos during his interrogation, he indicated that the face was his but that the bodies were of someone else. He added that in time he would show the officers how the photographs were made. In support of his statement, a box was located in the 1990s at the Dallas Police Department that was given to the National Archives. There were photographs contained in the box that had a figure cut out of one of the pictures which was later determined to be of Oswald in addition to multiple copies of the above mentioned photograph. There was also a picture of DP Officer Bobby Brown in a similar pose as Oswald.[114] James DiEugenio posed this question. Could this be evidence of the DPD using a matte insertion technique to create a composite that eventually became the infamous "backyard photos"?

I now turn to the acquisition of the rifle. According to the WC, Oswald ordered the 6.5 MC rifle on March 12, 1963, while he was in Dallas. He allegedly ordered the rifle through an ad he found in "American Rifleman" and sent a money order of $21.45 made payable to Klein's Sporting Goods Store located in Chicago. In this order, he used his alias A. Hidell.[115] This sounds reasonable until you examine the purchase and wade through the weeds.

This order travelled 700 miles and was received and deposited all in one day, and this was done without the assistance of computer technology.[116] Klein's "microfilmed the mailing envelope and the order coupon but not the money order."[117] In addition, the bank deposit slip, the extra copy provided by the bank at time of transit, is dated February 15 not March 13. If the February date is accurate than the serial number (C 2766) cannot be correct as stated in the WCR.[118]

There are also problems with the money order itself. The order deposited by Klein's at First National Bank of Chicago does not contain the requisite financial endorsements that it should according to Vice President Robert Wilmouth of First National Bank. He stated that the endorsements should have included, in addition to First National Bank of Chicago, the Federal Reserve Bank of Chicago and/or the Federal Postal Money Order Center in Kansas City.[119] Because this money order was not properly endorsed, there is significant reason to surmise that the money order was never paid to Klein's. This conclusion is bolstered by the fact that the FBI was unable to locate in Klein's records proof of payment. In addition, the FBI reported that Oswald's prints were not found on the order.[120] In fact, the rifle that was allegedly sent to Oswald's Post Office Box was not the rifle he allegedly ordered. He ordered a 6.5 MC carbine which is 36 inches long. The rifle in the National Archives is a 40.2 inch 6.5 MC short rifle. Klein's indicated that they only mounted scopes on the 36 inch not the 40.2 inch.[121]

The other issues arise out of the regulations pertaining to mail orders. In order to ship a firearm, the seller had to include form 2162 which the FBI and the U.S. Postal Service could not locate. This form could have helped prove their case so it was not a minor matter. The other postal regulation that was violated in this alleged mail transaction had to do with regulation #355.111. This requires that "mail addressed to a person not authorized to receive mail" will be returned to sender as "addressee unknown." Klein sent the rifle to A. Hidell who was not authorized to receive mail at Lee Harvey Oswald's P.O. Box. The Post Office indicated further that no 3-foot-long package was received never mind picked up.[122] The WC and the FBI knew they had serious problems in their purchase of the weapon and attempted to obfuscate the issue by fudging the evidence and not mentioning the postal regulations in the Warren Report. This type of chicanery only worked when you have a dead defendant. In a real trial, a good defense lawyer would have easily dismantled the prosecution's case regarding the purchase of the rifle. In any event, why would Oswald mail order a weapon leaving a paper trail when he could have walked into any gun shop in Texas and purchased a gun without any documentation?

Lastly, the FBI did locate a witness named Dale Ryder who was employed at a local gun shop with a repair ticket with Oswald's name on it. There were two serious problems that this witness posed for the FBI. He did not identify the real Oswald and the repair order was for an Argentinean gun which of course would be a Mauser not a Mannlicher Carcano. Another case of someone impersonating Oswald. Of course, the FBI never followed up on this lead.[123]

There are also problems with the paper that Oswald allegedly wrapped the gun in, and the blanket it was supposed to be enfolded in while stored in Ruth Paine's garage for two months. The individual who dispensed the brown paper used at the TSBD, Troy West, never left his desk on November 21, 1963. In fact, he stated that he ate his lunch at his desk.[124] Oswald, therefore, had no opportunity to take some of the paper without permission that day before leaving to visit his family that Thursday evening. In addition, the paper in the archives is not the same as the one that was found on the sixth floor of the building. It also had no oils on it as would be expected if it had been used to wrap a gun. The gun in the archives was covered in a lubricant called Cosmoline that was used by the manufacturer to prevent corrosion while being transported overseas.[125] The blanket also did not contain oils that would be consistent with this rifle. Lastly, there were no fibers found on the gun or the paper that were consistent with the blanket from the Paine's Garage. The investigative authorities did find fibers that were similar but were not identical.

I now turn to the sniper's nest on the sixth floor at the southeast window of the TSBD. Oswald allegedly moved 40 boxes and left no finger prints. The only finger prints that were identified were Dallas Police Officers and one unidentified set of prints that one author attributes to Malcolm Wallace who was an associate of Lyndon Johnson. The experts are divided if there is a match or not. In addition, there were no prints found by the DPD or the FBI on the weapon originally. When the weapon was sent back to Dallas from the FBI lab, a mysterious palm print that matched Oswald was discovered by a Dallas Police technician on the barrel of the gun. Paul Groody of the Miller Funeral Home who prepared Oswald's body for his burial testified that men in suits (he thought were FBI agents) came into the funeral home demanding to see Oswald's body. He pointed them to Oswald's casket. They opened it and printed his fingers and palms. When asked how he knew this, he indicated that he had a difficult task getting the ink off after they left.[126]

There were also problems with the shell casings found at the sniper's nest. The forensic pathologist, Forrest Chapman, that examined CE 543 (the dented shell) indicated that this shell was probably "dry loaded." The FBI tested his theory and the results were consistent with the markings on CE 543. The experts concluded that CE 543 could not have been fired by a bolt action rifle that day. This means that it was placed there which only left two casings.[127]

CE 544 is the only shell casing that was ejected from a bolt action rifle on the day of the assassination. When the shell casings were originally found, they were so close together that it appeared they had been placed not shot out of the mechanism of a bolt action rifle.[128] It was reported that Captain Fritz, before the scene was photographed, picked up the three casings and dropped them.

The question then becomes whether the DPD was part of the conspiracy. The short answer is no. The more complex answer is that some of them were corrupt, others were incompetent and then some were following orders from the federal government that they had to establish Oswald did it alone because of matters of national security. This implicated them in the cover up but not the planning and execution of the crime. As clearly set out in Fiester's book **Enemy of the Truth**, the DPD did not follow their own protocol and procedures when investigating the murder – never mind satisfying the national standards for law enforcement at the time.

It was reported that 50 percent to 70 percent of the DPD were members of the local KKK in 1963. President Kennedy's civil rights bill being debated in Congress to say the least did not endear him to most of the members of the department. Journalist and author Joseph McBride observed while interviewing Detective Leavelle of the DPD for his book **Into the Nightmare** that the recordings of the police after the shooting of the President appeared to be "relatively calm and a matter-of-fact in comparison to the sound of their voices when it is reported that a police officer was also shot." Leavelle did not dispute the observation. McBride then asked "What was the department's reaction to the shooting of the President?" The detective smiled and said, "As the old saying goes back then, 'it wasn't no different than a South Dallas nigger killin' ... It was just another murder to me."

I must also point out that the reputation of the District Attorney's office was not much better. After DA Henry Wade retired there were numerous convictions that were reversed because of exculpatory evidence located in the files that were never provided to the defense, as well as evidence that was fabricated by the DPD. In addition, some of the convictions were overturned because of the advent of DNA technology. As former ADA Bill Alexander from that office once remarked, "It takes a good prosecutor to convict a guilty man. It takes a great prosecutor to convict an innocent man."[129] They were not concerned with justice but were primarily focused on obtaining convictions.

There were, however, officers who conducted themselves with honor and courage such as DP Officer Joseph Smith and Sheriff Deputy Roger Craig. As an aside, Roger Craig while investigating matters in the late 1960s in Dallas for Garrison was hospitalized for two months after his car inexplicably exploded. Once he recovered from his injuries, he continued investigating leads. He also, through serendipity, avoided an attempt on his life when a bullet just missed him when stepping off of a curb in Dallas. He stated in an interview that he had been set up by a gentleman he was meeting with that day. During his interview, he described the bizarre circumstances of a motor vehicle accident that caused him to be partially disabled. He clearly was a broken man by the time of his interview in 1973. In 1975, he was found dead in his apartment as a result of a rifle shot in the chest. It was ruled a suicide. Friends and family had reported that he was at the time of his unexpected death writing a book on the investigation of the President's murder and his participation in the Garrison probe.

I will not spend much time on CE 399 which is commonly

referred to as the "magic bullet." It suffices to say that the bullet had no tissue or blood on it when examined by forensic experts at the FBI and the DPD even though it had smashed bones and caused seven wounds in Kennedy and Connally. In addition, there were more fragments located in Governor Connally's right wrist than were missing from this pristine bullet.

Sherry Fiester, a crime scene investigator and reconstruction expert, in her book **Enemy of the Truth** destroys this myth, as well as dismantles the WC's claim that all the shots were fired from behind the President. She clearly demonstrated using blood spatter analysis, Newtonian physics and trajectory calculations that the fatal head shot emanated from the front. In addition, a dicta belt recording obtained from an open microphone on a motorcycle of an officer for the DPD during the motorcade was examined by a panel of experts for the HSCA. The panel determined that five shots not three could be identified on that recording. One of the shots the panel deduced had come from the "grassy knoll." Special Prosecutor Blakey, however, determined that the acoustic evidence for one of the gunshots was weak, and he recognized that the panel's assertion that one shot had emanated from the grassy knoll had already placed him in a difficult position. This finding would obviously have serious political repercussions in Washington and potentially could expose his committee to significant criticism. The decision to announce that four shots could be surmised from the acoustic evidence was based on political considerations not on scientific grounds.

At the conference in September 2014 sponsored by the National Archives and Research Center, Dr. Donald Thomas, the author of **Hear no Evil**, gave a presentation entitled the "Acoustic evidence in the Kennedy assassination." He concluded after reviewing the above study, and others that were critical of the HSCA's acoustic conclusions, that the dicta belt recording of the DPD was "contemporaneous with the Kennedy assassination." He further determined that five impulsive sounds that have the "acoustic waveform" consistent with gunfire in Dealey Plaza could be detected on that recording. He stated that one of the sounds match the echo pattern of a test shot fired from the grassy knoll that was conducted in 1978.

The HSCA study concluded that the echo patterns indicated that three shots were fired from behind the motorcade and one emanated from the grassy knoll. The location of the fifth shot has not been determined. This shot could have emanated from the triple overpass where Fiester had surmised was the origin of the fatal shot that killed President Kennedy as shown in Zapruder frame 313.

Oswald was also subjected to a paraffin test which is used to determine if there are traceable nitrates on a person's hands and/or face that would be consistent with the discharge of a firearm. At separate press conferences, DA Wade and Dallas Police Chief Curry misled the press when they reported that the test was positive. The truth is that the test did not detect any nitrates on Oswald's face as you would have expected if he had fired a rifle that day. They did find nitrates on his palms but not on the back of his hands which you would normally detect if someone had fired a pistol. The nitrates on his palms could be explained by the defense as being deposited there while reading a newspaper or by materials he handled frequently while performing his duties at the TSBD. Furthermore, the FBI conducted tests with the rifle which clearly demonstrated that if someone had fired that weapon they would have nitrates all over their face and hands. Hoover was dismayed by the results that were indicia of Oswald's innocence not guilt and as a consequence never reported them to the WC. The paraffin test was not supportive of the prosecution's case.[130]

There are also serious evidentiary problems with Officer J.D. Tippit's murder, as well as the attempted murder of General Edwin Walker. The witness for the Walker case said he saw two men outside of Walker's residence just before the shooting. After the shot, they ran to a vehicle that was parked nearby. Both descriptions did not match Oswald. In addition, the bullet found was originally reported as a shell from a 30 caliber weapon not a 6.5 MC rifle. The police investigated this attempted murder for eight months, and Oswald was never listed as a suspect until after the assassination. The evidence began to mysteriously change which was common place in this case.[131]

As to the murder of Dallas Police Officer J. D. Tippit, there were eye witness identification and ballistic problems with that as well. For instance, there were four shells found at the scene. Two were Winchesters and two were manufactured by Remington. The bullets, however, that were removed from Tippit's body were three Winchesters and one Remington. Also, the FBI could not match the bullets with Oswald's pistol. The timeline as in the President's murder is very problematic as well. At the time when Tippit was shot, Oswald was at a location that made it highly improbable for him to have been able to get to where Tippit was and commit the murder in the timeframe as allotted in that case. In fact, witnesses at the theater where he was arrested stated that he was in their building at the time of the Tippit murder.

The importance of these two cases from WC's perspective is that if he did A and B he must have done C. If you wish to learn more about the Tippit murder and the Walker incident, I would refer you to **Reclaiming Parkland** by James DiEugenio and **Into the Nightmare** by Joseph McBride.

I also did not present much of the evidence that Oswald was an FBI informant. When a document surfaced during the WC inquiry, the commission asked J. Edgar Hoover if Oswald was an FBI informant. As expected, he said "no." This was the extent of their investigation. The evidence that contradicts Director Hoover is mounting and will continue to grow. For example, Oswald had FBI Agent James Hosty's address and telephone number in his address book. There is also evidence that Oswald was reporting on the plot to the FBI. In Chicago, a plot to kill the President was disrupted by an anonymous tip by a man named "Lee."

Douglass, author of **JFK and the Unspeakable**, opined from the evidence that Oswald may have been a "CIA dissenter in the plot" and was attempting to "blow the whistle on the CIA to the FBI." This is why he was chosen to be the patsy. As Douglass concluded "Dallas eliminated two Cold War security risks, Kennedy and Oswald, in the same weekend, blaming the second for the murder of the first." In addition, there were family members and other witnesses that reported that Oswald agreed with the President's policies and admired the man. I refer you to Douglass' book for more information on the Chicago plot and Oswald's perceptions of the President.

While Oswald was in custody, the press and the public did get to hear brief comments from the alleged assassin on several occasions. These brief encounters were not to allow the public or the press to learn more about Oswald but rather to prove he was not being mistreated while in custody. When the press asked him "Did you kill the President?" Oswald calmly responded that "I have not been charged with that." He had been apparently arraigned earlier that evening on the Tippit murder but had not been formally charged with the murder of the President. When the press reported that he would be soon, Oswald looked down and grimaced as though the severity of his situation had just become apparent to him. Oswald then requested that someone come forward to assist in his defense. In one encounter, he exclaimed "I have shot no one", and just before he was shoved into another room he stated "I am just a patsy." These are strange comments for someone whose primary motive in killing the President was to implant his name in the history books.

During his last visit with his older brother Robert on November 23, 1963, he told him "Don't believe the so called evidence." His brother Robert would later tell the press after Oswald had been silenced that his brother was an innocent man.

Before Oswald was shot by Ruby in the basement of the DPD, the FBI and DPD received several phone calls the prior night, warning them that Oswald was to be killed. In one call, a DP Officer recognized the voice as Jack Ruby. None of these warnings were adhered to by DPD.

In my opinion, the above witness testimonials and physical evidence, or lack thereof, would have compelled a jury to find Oswald not guilty either because they believed he was innocent as I do, or because they determined that there was reasonable doubt he committed the murders of Officer Tippit and the President.

There were no witnesses that saw the real Oswald target practicing, carrying or cleaning a rifle. He was a poor marksman in the Marines, and there is no evidence that his competency improved after his military service ended. The proof that Oswald owned the weapon that allegedly was used in the shooting is also suspect. The money order was not properly endorsed and at least two federal mail regulations would have been violated in order for the mail transaction to have been completed. In addition, none of the postal employees remember the delivery of the rifle never mind Oswald picking up the weapon. Also, the FBI never did locate any additional bullets, empty boxes or gun cleaning accessories at the Paine garage or his room in Dallas. What is even more perplexing, there was only one shell casing found at the sniper's nest that experts determined had been fired from a bolt action rifle on November 22, 1963. The other two casings had been placed there by someone who wanted it to appear as though three shots had been fired from that location. And more significantly, the paraffin test did not support the prosecution's premise that he had fired a rifle or a pistol that day.

I would also submit that the motive offered by the WC was weak for a multitude of reasons. For example, he was not a social isolate, or a loner and was evaluated by the Marine Corp as psychologically fit for duty with no mental pathology recorded. His known associates, other than those he worked with and family members, were either rabid anti-communists, anti-Castro Cubans, fellow Marines, individuals with intelligence connections or members of the CIA and FBI. It is amazing how open minded these individuals were to befriend and associate with not only a communist but an alleged traitor. In addition, Oswald never had money and yet he was constantly traveling and funding operations, as well as staying at the most luxurious hotels. There was testimony before the **Church Committee** by CIA accountant James Wilcott, who worked at the Atsugi Base in Japan, that Oswald was a paid employee of the Agency. He vaguely remembered checks being paid to "Oswald" or the "Oswald Project." It is clear to me that someone was funding his travels and activities. The evidence as it stands is pathetic as to means and motive.

This leaves opportunity. He of course was employed in a tall building at the most vulnerable spot of the presidential motorcade. Unfortunately for the WC, all the witnesses have him reading a newspaper or eating lunch when the President's limousine was originally scheduled to pass the TSBD. Oswald did not seem worried that he might miss his opportunity for fame and glory. Luckily for the WC, the motorcade did not arrive in Dealey Plaza until 12:29pm. Even then, a witness saw Oswald on the lower floors as late as 12:25pm. Also, there were a multitude of witnesses on the elevator and the stairs before and after the assassination and not one of them observed Oswald going up the stairs, never mind with a package, to the sniper's nest. There were also no witnesses that observed him running down the stairs to the second floor landing where he got thirsty and decided to purchase a coke just before Mr. Truly and Officer Baker confronted him. Neither by the way reported that he was sweating or out of breath. This man must have been bionic. In fact, the DPD Chief Jesse Curry admitted in a 1977 interview with Professor Peter Dale Scott that "They were never able to place Oswald on the sixth floor with a rifle."

The last two points I will make as to the evidence is that all snipers, hunters or trained military personnel know that it is much easier to hit a target coming at you then one that is moving away from your location. The best shot that Oswald or anyone had from that sixth floor window would have been when the limousine made that right turn onto Houston and was traveling towards the sniper's position. It would have been insane to wait for the vehicle to pass the TSBD on Elm and then try to shoot through a tree at a target that was descending as it moved away from the shooter. This was a very difficult shot. The only reason I believe that would rationally explain the actions of the shooter is that a "kill zone" on Elm had been predetermined by professional mechanics that were waiting for that moment when the President was in a "cross fire" position where multiple gun teams could ensure the termination of the target. Also, if Oswald was a lone nut, why was so much of the evidence classified? Most of the documents were not scheduled to be released until 2039. Apparently, this lone nut was a matter of national security.

After the echo of the last shot in Dealey Plaza was heard and before the shock of what had just transpired before their eyes could take hold, many of the witnesses that included law enforcement rushed up a grassy hill to locate the assassins. 51 witnesses said they heard shots, saw smoke or felt bullets pass by them from that infamous hill that Jean Hill had referred to as the "grassy knoll" in an interview with a reporter. She was standing next to Mary Ann Moorman who took a picture that many claim caught one of the assassins on film who's referred to as the "badge man" in that it looks like he is wearing a police uniform.

One of the witnesses who climbed the hill was Dallas Police Officer Joe Smith who was accompanied by a young deputy from the Sheriff's Department. As they got to the top of the hill and went behind the fence, they encountered a man in a suit standing by a vehicle parked in the lot. Officer Smith without thinking went for his gun believing he may be confronting one of the assassins. The man quickly pulled out a Secret Service Badge that Officer Smith immediately recognized and placed his gun back in his holster. They both continued to search the parking lot.[132]

Unknown to Officer Smith, a deaf mute named Ed Hoffman had witnessed his encounter from the triple overpass. The only difference is that he knew based on what he had observed just prior to Officer Smith getting behind the fence was that the officer's original instincts were correct. Ed, with a sign interpreter, years later described what happened just before the officer's encounter. As the President's limousine was traveling towards him on Elm, he noticed a flash of light and then smoke rise above the bushes behind the fence on the grassy knoll. He quickly turned in time to observe a man toss a rifle to another man who was wearing railroad apparel. The second man broke down the rifle and placed it in a bag and ran down the tracks. It was at this time Officer Smith got behind the fence.[133]

Another witness, Lee Bowers, Jr., who was a railroad employee that was working in one of their switch towers adjacent to the parking lot behind the fence, partially verified the above when he stated to the authorities that he saw two men standing next to the fence smoking cigarettes while occasionally peering over at Elm just before the motorcade arrived in Dealey Plaza. He then got distracted until he saw smoke rise above the bushes where the men had been earlier.[134] The police would find cigarette butts and footprints near where Bowers had said the men were standing. It has been reported by friends of Bowers that he witnessed more than he was willing to acknowledge. According to John Barbour's video, Bowers was warned by investigators to keep quiet. In fact, he died in August 1966 after his car inexplicably drifted off of a North Texas road and struck a concrete abutment. The circumstances were suspicious, but the official report listed his death as a result of injuries sustained in an accident.[135]

As Officer Smith reflected on the event, he remembered that the man he had confronted had dirty finger nails just like an auto-mechanic. He initially dismissed these minute details but over time these observations embedded in his memory would haunt him for years.

There were others that were confronted by men in suits that identified themselves as Secret Service agents. Some of them confiscated cameras and other evidence from witnesses. There were also men in suits observed behind the TSBD with guns that were never identified. The Secret Service has always maintained that all the agents that were in Dallas went with the motorcade to Parkland Hospital or had been previously assigned to the Trade Mart.

Shortly after the assassination, the department that made the badges which was under the auspices of the CIA was quietly transferred to the Department of the Treasury in January 1964 just two months after the assassination. We know this because of a document written by Stanley Gottlieb, Chief of the CIA's Technical Services Division (TSD), that was declassified in 2007. It was TSD that furnished the Secret Service with their gate passes, security passes, passes for Presidential campaigns, emblems for presidential vehicles and their security ID badges prior to the assassination.[136] With this capability, it gave them the means and opportunity to kill the President and escape without suspicion or interference from other law enforcement agencies.

Many of the agents protecting the President believe shots came from the front and subscribe to the theory that the President was killed by a conspiracy. I would refer you to Vincent Palamara's book entitled **Survivors Guilt** that not only discusses the agents' views on the assassination but also reveals the security measures that were not taken to protect the

President in Dallas and for a counterview I would read **The Kennedy Detail** by Gerald Blaine.

One of the major problems, among many, regarding the claims that the CIA had no interest in Oswald is the fact that Oswald was one of three hundred U.S. citizens in a nation of over 180 million in 1963 that the CIA was intercepting and reading his mail pursuant to a program called HT/LINGUAL which was supervised by Angleton. This was the program that was discovered during the **Church Committee Hearings** that caused his resignation in 1975. In addition, the CIA said all of Oswald's files were classified as "confidential" which is another blatant fabrication. Most of his files were classified as "top secret" especially those controlled by the CI/SIG within Angleton's division. As Senator Richard Schweiker stated, "We know Oswald had intelligence connections. Everywhere you look with him, there are fingerprints of intelligence."

Ann Egerter, a former CIA employee, reluctantly admitted to John Newman in an interview that he included in his ground breaking book **Oswald and the CIA** that the 201 file on Oswald was indicative of a significant intelligence interest in Oswald and that he was being "carefully watched."

It is important now to remember Angleton's testimony to the **Church Committee** that intelligence was a "wilderness of mirrors" and that nothing could be accepted on face value. It was a world in which "Black is white and white is black." In essence, they were the "Ministry of Truth" as described in George Orwell's dystopian novel **1984**. The CIA and all its dark alliances, especially in the covert operation sector, was constantly rewriting the past to reflect the reality it wanted history to record. Those that challenged its version of reality were either discredited, destroyed or murdered. Oliver Stone, the controversial director of **JFK**, once remarked, "I've always regarded the CIA as a criminal organization."

In terms of the plot to kill our president, the debate continues as to who in the CIA was involved and what roles did they play. John Newman in his epic book surmised from the evidence that the plot had the imprint of a diabolical genius that he suspected was James Jesus Angleton. He was the ultimate "spook." He was the one who created the "legend of Oswald" and was probably in charge of turning off the security alarms that protected the President and implanting the virus that caused the government to cover up the crime as a matter of national security. As Jim Garrison speculated, there were approximately 32 or more who were on a need to know position in the plot. But none of them were privy to all the details. The rest were pawns, like Oswald, who had limited knowledge, if any, on what was going to happen in Dallas. He further speculated that there were three levels of conspirators. There were the sponsors, such as Angleton, Dulles and Helms, and then there were the facilitators and controllers who manipulated and watched Oswald such as Bannister, Shaw, Ferrie and Phillips. At the bottom were the mechanics, the professional killers that waited for the President to enter the kill zone.

When Angleton was being compelled to resign in early 1975, he uttered his famous self-exculpatory statement that "A mansion has many rooms, and I was not privy to who struck John." This is not the quote that anyone would have expected from the man who was the CIA liaison to the WC. I thought he believed that Lee Harvey Oswald killed the President. What did he mean by the statement he made? When he referred to a mansion has many rooms, I suspect that he was referring to the compartmentalization of the CIA. Each room represented a separate department or division within the Agency. The second half of the answer is vintage Angleton. His responsibilities in the plot did not involve the mechanics. He did not need to know who they were and probably preferred it that way so that he could plausibly deny their identities. James DiEugenio, author and co-founder of the website **Citizens for the Truth about the**

Kennedy Assassination (CTKA), presumed that he was firing a warning shot across the bow of the CIA. If the HSCA, that was just beginning its probe was able to expose the plot, he was not intending to take the "rap" alone. I am surprised this statement is rarely analyzed for I believe it offers a tantalizing glimpse into the "wilderness of mirrors." Years later when he was gravely ill he contacted his friend Dick Cheney and told him he had important things to tell him before he died. He died before the meeting took place.

The other issue I wanted to address is that the conspiracy that involved the plan to kill the President was composed of different individuals than the cover up of the assassination after the fact. There was of course some that were involved in both such as Angleton and Phillips. I do not, however, believe that Chief Justice Earl Warren, or any of WC members, with the exception of Dulles, ever knew what really happened in Dallas. Warren was simply doing his duty to prevent a war that would kill 40 million Americans. Many of those implicated in the cover up were innocently, if not naïvely, doing what they perceived to be their patriotic duty. For others, the motivation was to protect the integrity and reputation of their agencies such as J. Edgar Hoover.

The impersonations of Oswald in Mexico City was only known by a few individuals in Washington. This would change over time. The education of many was enhanced by the **Church Committee Hearings** and the HSCA's investigation in the late 1970s. This is important to understand when assessing the WC apologists' efforts to portray the critics as "conspiracy nuts." They buttress their allegations by falsely claiming that the critics of the WC are implicating the whole federal government in the plot to kill the President which is not an accurate or fair depiction of their view. This is not true at least for those researchers that are carefully presenting their case for a conspiracy based on the facts and the evidence.

It also must be pointed out that there was not a consensus by the members of the Commission regarding the "magic bullet" or that Oswald acted alone. I must also underscore the fact that many high ranking officials and officers within the federal government either suspected or believed that President Kennedy was killed as a result of a conspiracy, including Attorney General Robert F. Kennedy and First Lady Jacqueline Kennedy. This list included foreign leaders as well. When President Charles De Gaulle of France was apprised of the lone nut theory by a reporter, he responded "You're kidding me. Cowboys and Indians."

Max Holland, an author, journalist and editor of the Washington Decoder which is an online newsletter, has written extensively on LBJ's views on Dallas and based on his research the President was haunted by the assassination as much as he was plagued by Vietnam. In fact, President Johnson told many of his associates, as well as CBS anchor Walter Cronkite, that he believed the President's death was the result of a conspiracy. Of course, he would usually in public accuse the Cubans but in private it was the CIA.

In an internal FBI memo from Agent DeLoach to Agent Tolson, dated, April 4, 1967, of which the subject was the "Assassination of President Kennedy", DeLoach apprised Tolson of a meeting between columnist Jack Anderson and DA Garrison. It was reported that Anderson discussed Garrison's case against Clay Shaw at length and much to his surprise he thought Garrison's claims were very convincing. Anderson had also reported the jest of this conversation to the White House. In fact, DeLoach added that he was contacted by Marvin Watson of the White House seeking further information. Watson explained that President Johnson had confided to him that "he (the President) was now convinced that there was a plot in connection with the assassination." DeLoach continued that Watson stated further that the President had concluded that the "CIA had had something to do with the plot."[137]

When FBI Director Hoover was asked by Billy Byars' (Texas oilman) teenage son, Billy, Jr., at Del Charro resort in California in the summer of 1964 "Do you think Lee Harvey Oswald did it?", Hoover was reportedly silent for a few moments when he finally said "If I told you what I really know, it would be very dangerous to this country. Our whole political system could be disrupted."[138] How could a lone nut be that dangerous?

The WC was not the last word of the government on the assassination. The HSCA in 1979 did conclude that the assassinations of Martin Luther King, Jr. and President John F. Kennedy were "probably" the result of a conspiracy and not the actions of a couple of lone nuts. Their final recommendation was that the Justice Department should initiate a criminal investigation into the murders which was never done.

Oswald never did get his day in court thanks to Jack Ruby whose primary job for the plotters was to silence him. He was deemed guilty by the media who accepted the WC's findings without question even when their conclusions were improbable or even contradictory. To this day, the corporate media defends the WC's conclusions as though their integrity and future are dependent upon its fiction remaining the accepted history of the assassination. As Mark Lane the author of the best seller **Rush to Judgment** stated, "The only way you can believe the Warren Report is not to have read it." Allen Dulles cynically remarked "that the American people don't read."

Jim Garrison, who not only read the 900-page Warren Report, but also memorized the 26 volumes of evidence that allegedly supported the government's position that Oswald acted alone caustically remarked, "To show you how cosmically irrelevant the Warren Report is for the most part...one of the exhibits is classified in the front as 'A Study of the Teeth of Jack Ruby's Mother'. Even if Jack Ruby had intended to bite Oswald to death, that still would not have been relevant." He further elaborated in his closing argument in the Shaw trial, "This is not to say that the government has not shown concern for the people's right to know. For those citizens who are curious about how and why their President was killed, the Ministry of Truth has made available the dental charts of Jack Ruby, photographs of Russian scenery, grammar school records of Oswald and Ruby, a careful analysis of Oswald's pubic hairs, irrelevant letters, irrelevant telegrams, picture post cards showing bull fights, a copy of the proceedings in an unrelated divorce case, a list of traffic citations received by Jack Ruby and an excellent photograph of an unidentified man."

The only member that lobbied to be on the commission through third parties was former CIA Director, Allen Dulles, who was fired by President Kennedy after the Bay of Pigs. As the old CIA adage goes, it does not matter how well the plan was executed as long as you control the investigation after the fact. Republican Richard Schweiker, a former **Church Committee** member, speaking on **Face the Nation** in 1976 concluded, "I think the Warren Report, to those who have studied it closely, has collapsed like a house of cards…the fatal mistake the Warren Commission made was not to use its own investigators, but instead relied on the CIA and FBI personnel, which played directly into the hands of senior intelligence officers who directed the cover-up."

Although the public suspects that something was rotten in Dallas, they choose to remain ignorant of the facts and the mounting evidence of a domestic conspiracy that haunts those that have dared to look into the abyss and face what Thomas Merton called "the unspeakable." Why would a nation do this? The answer I suppose is that to be suspicious does not oblige one to act because there is always the possibility it is untrue, but to know that something is true imposes an obligation to act – to right the wrong. Or maybe, it is the perception that the assassination is part of the past and is no longer relevant to their present reality. Their lack of interest could also reflect their sense of powerlessness to do anything about it. This is the frustration we all have as was described by one of Garrison's ADA's during their investigation of the President's murder.

He remembered one evening when they were all working late into the night when "Jim" went into one of his "tirades that the CIA killed our President." He indicated that he was tired and just wanted to go home. He finally out of frustration exclaimed "If the CIA killed our President, there is nothing a chicken-shit ADA can do about it." The room became silent, and he expected to be fired. Instead, Garrison laughed and said, "There is probably nothing this chicken-shit DA can do about it either."

As John Barbour emotionally stated in his documentary on the assassination entitled **The Last Word**, "Until people care more about who killed their President than who gets killed in the Super Bowl" those involved, as well as their successors, will continue to dishonor our nation. In the final analysis if the people do not demand the truth, there will be no justice for Oswald and his family, or President Kennedy and his vision for America, and sadly, there will be no justice for our nation. For what is justice really but a search for the truth.

A Contagion Infects the Nation
(More than just a murder, it was the plague)

Mark Lane died on May 10, 2016, at the age of 89. His rendezvous with death was mourned by family and friends, and a few researchers that were inspired by his courage to seek the truth and to confront a government that was consumed with its censored history as it subtly manipulated the narrative that was emanating from Dallas. This narrative that was hijacked by the CIA and FBI only 40 minutes after the President was mortally wounded. Prior to taking control, the media interviewed witnesses and openly discussed the fact that gunshots had originated from the front, as well as behind the motorcade.

He stepped into the fray oblivious of how omnipotent and menacing the adversaries he was fomenting each step he made towards the truth. A truth that could have torn the nation asunder as each stubborn fact that remained amongst the obfuscation was revealed to an unsuspecting public that genuinely believed in their government. Consequently, the conspirators were inadvertently concealed by the immense wave of patriotism that justified the whitewash as a matter of national security. Those that developed the plan had anticipated this predictable reaction and had even made it more likely by incorporating a virus that compelled this response. If the patsy was a communist that was supported by Havana and possibly Moscow, the public and the media would have demanded retribution that risked dragging us into a nuclear war. A war that Defense Secretary McNamara had estimated would cause 40 million Americans to die within an hour. And even if the government, as the leadership eventually did, suspected a domestic plot that eliminated Kennedy over policy disputes, those that designed the plan knew the authorities would cover it up to avoid the humiliation of resembling another "banana republic." It, therefore, was imperative from the civilian leadership's perspective, whether it was the former or latter scenario, to establish to the public's satisfaction that Lee Harvey Oswald was a lone wolf without any other accomplices who were still lurking about potentially seeking more targets.

When the Warren Commission had completed its incompetent investigation and submitted its 900-page report to President Johnson on September 24, 1964, Lane quickly began to read the report that the New York Times and CBS News had endorsed before they even had an opportunity to review it. The report was accompanied by 26 volumes of evidence that allegedly proved Oswald's guilt beyond any reasonable doubt that would have taken days not hours to examine meticulously.

As Lane waded into the report and its supporting testimony and documentation, he recognized as an accomplished lawyer in New York that the case against Oswald and the sequence of events as proposed by the Commission were not only not compelling, but were highly improbable.

He decided to go to Dallas and interview the witnesses and examine the scene of the crime. Each witness he spoke with contradicted, or at a minimum placed into question, the conclusions of the government's inquiry. He found numerous witnesses for instance that were never interviewed by the Commission who had seen smoke, heard shots or felt bullets pass over their shoulder from that hill that became known as the grassy knoll. The importance of this is quite self-evident in that the fence that ran along this small hill was to the right-front of the President's limousine. Oswald had allegedly fired all three shots from the southeast corner window of the Texas School Book Depository (TSBD) located on the sixth floor which at the time of the shooting was behind the President.

Many of his interviews can be viewed on YouTube. In any event, this investigation culminated in his groundbreaking book **Rush to Judgment**. None of the New York publishers were interested in publishing his book. Undaunted by their dismissal of his work, he printed and sold his tome quite successfully in Europe. The response was so positive that it became a best seller. It was only then that his book was picked up by a domestic publishing firm and sold in the United States. The sales catapulted his work onto the New York Times bestseller list as well.

His investigation was immediately followed up by Sylvia Meagher's book **Accessories after the Fact**, **Whitewash** by Epstein, **Six Seconds in Dallas** by Josiah Thompson and the prolific writings of dissident attorney Vincent Salandria. Nevertheless, Lane's death for the most part was shamefully ignored by the corporate media, which to some degree was expected, but also was overlooked by Democracy Now which was disappointing.

The CIA immediately allocated resources to discredit Lane and this small band of WC critics that were beginning to awaken a public that for the most part was initially in shock after the assassination and then as the government asserted that it was back in control went back to sleep. This was strange, if not peculiar, for an agency that professed no interest or knowledge of the lone nut prior to Dallas. The echelon of this powerful Agency proclaimed that they only became aware of this disgruntled citizen, who allegedly had communist affiliations, after he was arrested by the Dallas Police Department (DPD).

In the defense of the WC, they coerced and intimidated witnesses. Many of these witnesses committed suicide while others allegedly died by natural causes and accidents. Most of these deaths occurred at the most inopportune time and the circumstances of their deaths are considered suspicious. The Agency also destroyed top secret documents, sabotaged official investigations, omitted important information in their communications with the Commission, committed obstruction of justice and perjury. And while the nation watched in horror, cohorts of organized crime silenced the patsy. This was all done to maintain the fiction that President Kennedy was felled by a loner. An event that was simply a random act of violence completely void of any relevance to anything they or some rogue elements within the Agency might have been involved in. The question that must be asked is why an Agency that was charged with obtaining and interpreting foreign intelligence was meddling, if not taking the lead, on a domestic matter that was primarily the domain of the FBI and the Justice Department. A state crime that occurred within the jurisdiction of the city of Dallas.

The CIA partially answered that question in a document it disseminated to its media allies and assets around the country. In that document designated 1035-960, the CIA confronted the concern the Agency had regarding the mounting criticism of the

Warren Report. They indicated that a poll in 1964 had revealed that 46 percent of the American public did not believe that Oswald acted alone. They wrote "This trend of opinion is a matter of concern to the U.S. government, including our organization...Innuendo of such seriousness affects not only the individual concerned, but also the whole reputation of the American government...Conspiracy theories have frequently thrown suspicion on our organization, for example by falsely alleging that Lee Harvey Oswald worked for us."

The purpose of the memorandum was "to provide material countering and discrediting the claims of the conspiracy theorists..." The Agency listed several strategies on how to achieve their stated mission. They encouraged publications by "friendly elite contacts", such as editors and politicians, buttressing the position that the Warren Commission was an exhaustive examination that investigated every aspect of the assassination. The CIA wrote further that it should be emphasized that "... parts of the conspiracy talk appear to be deliberately generated by communist propagandists."

The Agency further specified that propaganda assets should be employed to attack the critics. This could be achieved by book reviews and articles that discredit pro-conspiracy publications. The CIA asserted it will provide background information to assist in accomplishing this objective. They also pointed out that these publications should make it clear that no "new evidence has emerged which the Commission did not consider."

The memo goes on to proclaim that a conspiracy of this scale could never be done by the government, and if Oswald had accomplices they most likely were a "...group of wealthy conspirators..." that were more capable of arranging such a secretive operation. They proffered this incredulous claim while they were secretly murdering foreign leaders and overthrowing governments that were all hidden from the American public for decades. I also would be interested to know what group of "wealthy conspirators" were capable of altering the President's motorcade route, turning off the internal alarms that protect our chief executive, reducing the security measures in Dallas in violation of Secret Service's protocol and procedures as outlined in their manual, and effectuating a cover-up that implicated the most powerful officers and agencies within our government. This would be some extraordinary group to achieve all that and still remain a ghost that even several decades later cannot be clearly identified or proven to even exist except within the imagination of the CIA.

They concluded by pointing out that Oswald "would not have been any sensible choice for a co-conspirator. He was a 'loner', mixed up, of questionable reliability and an unknown quantity to any professional service." The death of multiple witnesses can also be explained as the result of "natural causes" and other reasonable grounds.

This is an extraordinary document that bootstraps the CIA with specific positions that we know are untrue or are very controversial based on all the evidence we possess today. First of all, the CIA held thousands of pages of documents on Oswald prior to the assassination. Pursuant to a program administered by the Counter Intelligence Department whose chief was the CIA's liaison to the WC, they were closely monitoring his mail and maintaining close tabs on his location. Some of the files on him were designated top secret. Furthermore, we know that Oswald was not a social isolate and was quite competent and intelligent. We even have discovered evidence that he admired the President.

We also know that the Commission failed to interview witnesses or follow any evidentiary trail they surmised would undermine their thesis that Oswald was a lone nut with communist sympathies. Even Robert F. Kennedy, Jr. conceded in an interview with Charlie Rose that his father thought the report was a "shoddy piece of craftsmanship." He added that "the evidence at this point is very, very convincing that it was not a lone gunman." When asked by Rose who he thought was involved, he replied that in his opinion members of organized crime, anti-Castro militants and "rogue" CIA agents conspired to murder his uncle.

Doug Horne of the Assassination Records Review Board has asserted that in his opinion there are several documents that he classifies as "smoking guns" that were discovered in the declassified medical evidence. He determined that these documents when combined with all the testimony that the ARRB recorded establishes that Kennedy's wounds were altered and that the official autopsy, which by the way is the third draft, cannot be trusted. The first and second drafts of the autopsy conducted at Bethesda Naval Hospital have disappeared. In fact, Dr. James J. Humes reluctantly admitted to the ARRB that he burned all his notes after the autopsy. Therefore, their conclusion that it was a comprehensive investigation and that there was not any new evidence being discovered by these audacious researchers we know is false. In fact, the Agency deliberately failed to apprise the Commission of numerous facts and relevant documents that they possessed in their archives. And finally, this document is unequivocal proof that the Agency was actively engaged with their media assets in discrediting the publications of the critics while attempting to impugn their integrity and their credibility.

Consequently, the CIA since Dallas has not been a passive observer of each government investigation that was formed to examine what happened in Dealey Plaza, or any film or book that has galvanized public interest and support for the proposition that Kennedy's assassination was the result of a domestic conspiracy. In each case, whether it be James Garrison's investigation of Claw Shaw or the House Select Committee on Assassinations, they were actively involved in obstruction of justice and perjury, among other nefarious activities. They even joined a crusade led by the mainstream media to discredit Oliver

Stone's film **JFK.** Why would an agency do this if Kennedy was felled by some alienated lone wolf who got extremely lucky when he fired three shots from an antiquated Italian rifle with a defective scope? A random act of violence just like the act that resulted in his death by Jack Ruby in the basement of the DPD. If this were the case, why devote so much time and resources in discrediting theories that have no basis in reality? Maybe the answer is in an analysis of the scene of the crime and the chain of events as we know them today.

Kennedy was visiting several cities in Texas to mend fences within the state's Democratic party and to begin to generate support for his bid to be re-elected in 1964. He knew that Texas was an important state to hold since he anticipated the defection of many southern states to the Republicans as a consequence of his submission of a controversial civil rights bill that was being scrutinized by Congress. On November 22, 1963, he was visiting the city of Dallas which was the last leg of his whirlwind Texas trip. He was scheduled to give a brief speech at a luncheon at the Trade Mart. His plane arrived at Love Field 30 minutes late. Other than that, everything appeared to be going well. He and his wife got off the plane and walked over to greet a large crowd that had gathered behind a small fence. The couple appeared in good spirits as they got into the blue convertible Lincoln and started their tour of Dallas. All the way to Dealey Plaza that was named after George B. Dealey, a local businessman and publisher for many years of the Dallas Morning News, enormous crowds, sometimes five or more rows deep, waved flags and cheered as the presidential vehicle passed them. The reports that this could be a turbulent visit seemed inane as the motorcade travelled further into the city.

Just outside of Dealey Plaza, a bizarre event occurred 20 minutes prior to the motorcade's arrival. An ambulance was dispatched to attend to a man who was allegedly having seizures at the corner of Main Street and Houston. He was placed into the only ambulance assigned to that area of the city and taken to Parkland Hospital. Upon their arrival, the man got out of the vehicle and disappeared before staff could admit him to the ER. This Caucasian male has never been identified. This in my opinion, in addition to the patsy, was another diversion set up by the conspirators.

The lead car that held the Chief of the DPD Jesses Curry, and the President's 1961 Lincoln that followed directly behind, entered Dealey Plaza on Main Street at approximately 12:29pm. The crowds began to position themselves to get the best view of the young couple. They pulled out their cameras and double-checked their settings as the motorcade took a right turn onto Houston. Governor John Connally's wife Nellie, while observing the enthusiasm of the large crowds along the motorcade route, remarked "You can't deny Dallas loves you Mr. President."

The large Lincoln then approached the TSBD which allegedly had the lone gunman waiting for an opportunity to make his mark on history. As the presidential vehicle began to navigate the 120 degree turn onto Elm just in front of that infamous building, Abraham Zapruder was filming what ex-CIA Agent E. Howard Hunt had confessed to his son, Saint John, many years later was called "the big event" by the plotters.

The large vehicle slowed to approximately 18 mph while passing the TSBD as it approached what was called the triple underpass by the natives. Dealey plaza had three major roads that travelled through the large park as tall buildings outlined three sides of the green. If facing the railroad bridge, Commerce Street was to your left while Main Street went through the center of the plaza. Elm was located to the far right which ran next to the grassy knoll. All three roads converged at the base of the plaza as they went under the bridge.

The sequence of the shooting continues to be debated. This is my interpretation of what transpired that day. The first shot was fired at 12:30pm.

The first shot emanated from the sniper's nest on the sixth floor of the TSBD that missed its target by approximately 200 feet, hitting a curb on Main Street which caused a small piece of cement to hit a bystander named James Tague in his right cheek. Many of the witnesses, including those in the motorcade, mistook this shot for a firecracker. This is the only shot fired by the 6.5 Mannlicher Carcano that the Commission alleged Oswald used to kill Kennedy. The primary purpose of this shot was to grab the attention of the crowd below to the window of the patsy. The second shot also emanated from the sixth floor, but at a different window, hitting the President in the back at a 38-degree angle. The third shot originated from the far end of the grassy knoll at a lower elevation that hit Kennedy in the throat at 0 degrees. The next shot fired almost simultaneously originated from the Dal-Tex Building from a second floor window which hit Governor Connally in the lower right back at 22 degrees, causing all his injuries. The fifth shot fired from the grassy knoll hit the Stemmons freeway sign. This sign was inexplicably removed shortly after the assassination. As Kennedy pulled up his arms and leaned forward as a result of the bullet that hit him in his throat, the agent operating his vehicle slowed the Lincoln to approximately 9 mph as he glanced over his right shoulder to ascertain what was happening. It was at this moment that a mechanic fired the fatal shot from a location on the triple overpass between Main Street and Commerce that hit the President in the upper right portion of his forehead just below his hairline. The kinetic energy that was released out of the entrance wound caused him to slightly move forward. As the bullet traversed through the skull and exited the lower occipital area of his head, causing a wound the size of a baseball, Kennedy then fell "back and to the left."

The motorcade then sped off to Parkland Hospital where doctors quite familiar with gunshot wounds attended to his injuries, attempting to save his life. 23 out of 24 medical personnel and observers concluded that Kennedy had been hit twice in the front. They surmised after examining his wounds that his throat and forehead were entrance wounds.

Jack Ruby, the owner of a local strip joint called the Carousel Club in Dallas who was a known mob asset, had two primary duties for the plotters. His first task as speculated by researchers was to plant what became known as the magic bullet on a stretcher that had been used by Governor Connally. He was seen by two local reporters at the hospital just prior to authorities discovering the bullet. One of the reporters even conversed with him briefly. As amazing as it may sound, the WC believed Ruby's denial that he had been there over the testimony of the two journalists. His second task was to silence the patsy.

Once Kennedy had hit the kill zone, professional mechanics fired at the President from what was a triangular formation; a standard practice by experts. Some of the assassins were provided with official Secret Service identification with fictitious names that had been prepared by the Technical Service Division of the CIA. This enabled them to confiscate evidence and exit the scene of the heinous crime without interference by other law enforcement agencies. The second part of the plan was to get control over Kennedy's body and begin the cover up. They also had to get the cover story out before the public had formed an opinion regarding the event.

There were two cover stories that were available to the plotters, depending on the reaction of other key elements within the government. The first one was to link Oswald's actions with Castro and the KGB in the hope that this might prompt an invasion of Cuba and the perpetuation of the Cold War. When the civilian leadership balked at the prospect of a nuclear war that could result from any aggressive action against Cuba, the CIA planners changed their cover story to the lone nut scenario that was eventually adopted by the WC. Oswald's alleged communist affiliations were no longer used to implicate Cuba or the Soviets, but rather to suggest a plausible motive for his killing of the President. Once they had chosen their cover story, they had to revise history and promote the fiction that Kennedy was a traditional cold warrior whose policies were similar to his predecessor if not more belligerent. By establishing this mythology, it made his death appear less necessary, as well as obscured the primary motive that compelled the conspirators to act. It also made it easier for President Johnson to pursue a more aggressive policy in Vietnam and other hot spots while claiming he was fulfilling the objectives of the martyred President. They very cleverly used the President's own words to reinforce this image.

Without rehashing the details presented in my article **The Patsy**, this is the conspiracy in a nutshell. The events in Dallas as described above and as supported by the forensic evidence were unequivocally not the actions of a lone nut and accordingly was not a random act of violence as outlined in their memorandum. The death of Kennedy was clearly the result of a sophisticated plot that was consistent with the modus operandi of an intelligence operation. Because this operation was compartmentalized and information was only shared on a need to know basis, the conspirators were able to get many to assist in the execution of the plan, and its cover up. Government employees or assets were assigned tasks that were so vague they had no clue what they were contributing to. Those who figured it out after the fact or were privy to matters that clearly contradicted the official version were intimidated, coerced, blackmailed or murdered. Most of the murders were made to look like a suicide or death by natural causes. Those that were clearly executed by traditional methods were done primarily by organized crime gangsters, such as the deaths of Johnny Rosselli and Sam Giancana.

The motive attributed to Oswald by the WC was pathetic. If he had killed the President to make his mark on history, why claim he was a "patsy" that was not involved in the crime? Furthermore, his word choice to describe his predicament has always bothered me. Most people in his position would have claimed that they were "framed" or that they were left "holding the bag." I heard these phrases quite frequently when I was a defense attorney. The use of the word "patsy" was primarily a term of art for intelligence. This was another piece of evidence that hints that he was not the person he was portrayed as by the government.

In retrospect, as pointed out by Garrison, it is not a mystery why certain rogue agents of the CIA, including Allen Dulles who at the time of the assassination was retired, had joined organized crime bosses and vitriolic anti-Castro Cubans to perpetrate the crime of the century. Their motives are blatantly obvious once you become familiar with Kennedy's actual policies that threatened the Cold War orthodoxy that the covert sector of the CIA and the Pentagon zealously believed in. Essentially, there actions amounted to a coup as it was called by Colonel Fletcher Prouty.

There were also those that had been tactfully approached by Allen Dulles, as surmised by the circumstantial evidence exposed in Talbot's **The Devil's Chessboard**, that did not object to the proposal and as a consequence had foreknowledge of the operation. In my opinion, powerful members of the military brass and Wall Street were among those who knew a plan was being developed. They intentionally were not provided any specific details on how and when it was to occur to maintain plausible deniability. They were confident that the "old man" would take care of it.

Since Kennedy's death, the word "conspiracy" has been transformed into some mysterious and remote occurrence that is an aberration in civilian and government social structures. And those who invoke it as an explanation for an event or a policy are quickly dismissed as paranoid or attributed with some sinister motivation for making their allegations. This has become so pervasive in our society that even obvious conspiracies are dismissed by our corporate media and cynical public. Whereas in Europe, they do not discard conspiracy theories so easily. For instance, the situation in Brazil was initially reported by the Brazilian and American corporate press as a corruption scandal that involved the President, Dilma Rousseff. The alternative media outlets more disposed at seeking the truth immediately recognized that the opposing party's leadership, many of which were under investigation for corruption, were taking advantage of an opportunity fomented by the weakened Brazilian economy to achieve what they could not in prior elections. They basically initiated a bogus impeachment process to disguise what was essentially a coup. Once they took power, they introduced severe austerity measures that had been opposed by Rousseff and began dismantling the agencies that were primarily responsible for the corruption probe. After the President was forced to step down until the trial in the Senate can determine if her accounting maneuvers amounted to "high crimes and misdemeanors", a transcript of a discussion between Senator Romero Juca and oil executive Sergio Machado just prior to the impeachment vote acknowledged that the best way to terminate the corruption probe was to oust President Rousseff. A clear indication that Rousseff was the victim of a conspiracy to usurp her authority.

Even highly educated individuals cringe whenever they hear the word used in a sentence. One of my close friends declared to me "that everything is not a conspiracy, Rick." He in one sense was right. Everything is not the result of two or more persons conspiring to achieve a common sinister or selfish objective. However, his broader implication which is that conspiracies are rare is clearly false. Most policies and programs developed in our government or in Wall Street are the result of conspiracies. Many of these conspirators are not necessarily seeking nefarious objectives but some clearly are.

In my opinion, there are soft and hard conspiracies. A soft conspiracy is when two or more individuals or organizations are

The Paradox of our National Security Complex

aware of their common interests and the methodology being utilized to achieve their objective. They, however, are not coordinating their efforts through direct communication. A hard conspiracy is two or more persons or organizations that directly communicate to develop their plan of attack and the methods to be employed for its success. We see this type in the criminal courts all the time.

The other absurd assertion is that our government is not capable of such a heinous act. We are more committed to the principles of democracy than other nations who remove leaders as a result of a coup quite regularly. Of course, most of those coups were directly and indirectly instigated by the CIA, but I digress. If you review our turbulent history dispassionately, the above thesis begins to unravel quite precipitously.

The original sin of slavery was a brutal institution that justified its offense against humanity by relegating the oppressed as nothing more than assets of an estate or as written in our Constitution as three fifths of a human being for census purposes. Even then it was not an attempt to acknowledge their humanity but to enhance the South's power in Congress. This view of slaves as nothing more than property was affirmed by Chief Justice Roger B. Taney in his infamous majority opinion in the **Scott v. Sanford** case of 1857. This decision is generally referred to as the Dred Scott case.

Dred Scott was a slave that had been acquired by U.S. Army surgeon John Emerson from the Blow family in 1831 who were residents of St. Louis. Emerson travelled with Scott into slave and free states for 12 years. When he died, Scott attempted to purchase his freedom from Emerson's widow. When she refused to accept his offer, he filed his first case in federal court in 1846. Scott's lawyer argued that Dr. Emerson had in prior years brought him to the state of Illinois that prohibited slavery and to the territory of Wisconsin where federal law banned its establishment as part of the **Missouri Compromise** of 1820. His

230

attorney argued that his physical presence in jurisdictions that did not recognize slavery as a legitimate and legal institution should be reason enough for the court to grant his just request to be designated a free man. He lost his first trial and amazingly won his second only to have it overturned by the Missouri State Supreme Court.

He then filed suit with the assistance of abolitionists that supported his bid for freedom against Fred Sanford who was the brother of Emerson's wife in federal court. When the court ruled in favor of the defendant, Scott appealed to the U.S. Supreme Court.

President-elect Buchanan was hoping the case would be resolved by the date of his inauguration which was set for March 1857. He sided with the justices from the South that he antici-pated were going to vote against the emancipation of Scott. He knew if the decision was purely made along sectional lines that this could cause a great deal of difficulty for his new adminis-tration as abolitionist groups ratcheted up anti-slavery senti-ments that had significant support throughout the North. With this concern, he intruded inappropriately on the independence of the court when he pressured Justice Robert Cooper Grier, a northerner, to vote alongside the southern majority.

Chief Justice Taney wrote the majority opinion for the court that denied Scott's claim by a seven to two decision. He pontifi-cated that a negro whose ancestors were brought into the United States and sold as slaves, whether they be enslaved or free, were not citizens and as a consequence had no standing to file a lawsuit in federal court. He added that the federal government had no authority to regulate, never mind prohibit, slavery in federal territories that were acquired after the founding of the nation. He concluded "...They (negroes) had for more than a century before been regarded as beings of an inferior order, and altogether unfit to associate with the white race, either in social or political relations; and so far inferior, that they had no rights which the white man was bound to respect; and that the negro might justly and lawfully be reduced to slavery for his benefit."

Abraham Lincoln as a candidate for the senate in 1858 denounced the decision and used it as the inspiration for his "House Divided" speech in which he declared "A house divided against itself cannot stand." He argued that by necessity we will all be free, or we will all be slave states. At some point, these two opposing forces would clash to resolve this crisis. Although he had accurately forecast the crisis that lurked just beyond the horizon, he could not have anticipated the extent of that calamity that would befall an unsuspecting nation. And much more than this, he could not have known the pivotal role he would play in that resolution.

When that crisis arose, 600,000 died in a bloody war to finally end the division so that this nation could stand and begin to purge the stain of injustice that soiled our national spirit from the beginning.

Another prominent example was our despicable treatment of Native Americans that culminated in the Indian wars from 1860 through to 1890. We deluded ourselves with this concept of **Manifest Destiny** that we were ordained by God to possess all the land from sea to shining sea. In fulfillment of that quest, we attempted to eradicate the indigenous peoples who had lived on this continent long before we ever discovered it. We senselessly killed millions of buffalo which we had discerned were a major source of food and clothes for the tribes that lived on the Great Plains. As the war lingered, the military became embittered. They were informed by the newspapers that Civil War hero General Sheridan had exclaimed, "The only good Indians are dead Indians." In this ominous environment, we committed many atrocities, but none more depraved than the naked savagery of Sand Creek and Wounded Knee. We essentially mutilated and massacred unarmed elderly men, women and children.

Black Elk described what Wounded Knee had meant to his

people when he said, "I did not know then how much was ended. When I look back now from this high hill of old age, I can see the butchered women and children lying heaped and scattered all along the crooked gulch as plain as when I saw them with eyes still young. And I can see that something else died there in the bloody mud, and was buried in the blizzard. A people's dream died there. It was a beautiful dream…the nation's hoop is broken and scattered. There is no center any longer, and the sacred tree is dead."[139]

In their yearning for wealth, the white settlers and prospectors combed the hills and valleys, hoping to discover valuable minerals that included gold. Infected by this fever, we promised everything to cheat the Indians out of their land. And when it was over, their culture and heritage were buried beneath the onslaught of white settlers that considered their way of life as savage and uncivilized. Over time, it became apparent to even the most obstinate resistors that they were outnumbered and outgunned. And as the wilderness dwindled, leaving them with no space to hide, their people were relegated to desolate parcels of land that were called reservations. As Chief Red Cloud recounted in old age, "They made us many promises, more than I can remember, but they never kept but one; they promised to take our land, and they took it."[140]

There lies in the dark recesses of our history another ingrained cultural dimension that was intertwined with our racist social constructs that taints our innocent image. The **Eugenics Movement** of the late nineteenth and early twentieth centuries have long been forgotten by our historically illiterate generation. It nevertheless was a significant part of our history and culture prior to World War II. The primary purpose of the movement was to purify and improve the genetic development of human beings. It was believed that those who lived in poverty, especially young women of ill repute, were considered inferior and were prime candidates for sterilization which was an offshoot of the movement. This also applied to those who were mentally retarded and as such were placed in large psychiatric institutions hidden from society. At the time, family members were embarrassed by this perceived genetic abnormality that compelled their removal from public scrutiny.

This ideology intensified during the massive emigration of Eastern Europeans to the United States in the 1920s. The mixing of inferior races as opined by many stimulated the growth of racist organizations such as the Ku Klux Klan. It also enhanced the practice of sterilization programs being implemented around the country. In 1927, the U.S. Supreme Court in **Buck v. Bell** constitutionally upheld the Virginia Sterilization Act of 1924.[140]

Carrie Buck was a psychiatric patient that was contesting the validity of this act. Justice Oliver Wendell Holmes, Jr., a celebrated jurist from Harvard, composed the majority opinion. He wrote "It is better for all the world, if instead of waiting to execute degenerate offspring for crime or let them starve for their imbecility, society can prevent those who are manifestly unfit from continuing their kind...Three generations of imbeciles are enough." It was considered in the interest of society to permit her sterilization. Although this practice of forced sterilization is now considered a violation of an individual's human rights, this abhorrent case has never been overturned. In fact, 70,000 U.S. citizens suffered this indignity up through the 1970s.[142]

The program did not escape the awareness of German scientists in the 1930s. Their knowledge was significantly enhanced by California eugenicists that produced literature that promoted this philosophy, as well as sterilization, and sent it overseas to German scientists and medical professionals. The forced sterilization program by the Nazis was instituted shortly thereafter. Their program was initially supported and applauded by their American counterparts until it morphed into an extermination project that eventually murdered millions that were considered inferior to the Aryan specimen that represented the future of the

Third Reich. Prior to this development, institutions such as the Rockefeller Foundation funded Nazi eugenic programs, including the barbaric research of Dr. Josef Mengele before he arrived at Auschwitz.

It is also important to recognize the amoral principles internalized by those that founded the CIA and the despicable policies they promoted to achieve their dubious objectives in the name of national security. The MK ULTRA program experimented with the use of powerful drugs, hypnosis and other reprehensible tests on unsuspecting patients that received care in psychiatric wards and hospitals around the country and in Canada in the 1950s and 1960s. The primary goal of the project was to create a Manchurian candidate that they could control and manipulate into position to assassinate selected targets. Although this program was dismissed as unsuccessful by Helms and others within the CIA who were compelled to answer questions before Church's committee, its methods may have been used to place Sirhan Bishara Sirhan into a hypnotic trance when he fired at Senator Robert Kennedy in the pantry of the Ambassador Hotel. This was the conclusion by experts who examined him on several occasions prior to and subsequent to his trial. In essence, Sirhan was another patsy that diverted the attention of most of the witnesses while a second gunman fired the shot that mortally wounded the senator. This scenario was corroborated by the conclusion of the Chief Medical Examiner of Los Angeles, Dr. Thomas Noguchi, who conducted the autopsy of Senator Kennedy. He determined that the bullet that ended Bobby's quixotic campaign had emanated from a gun that was 1.5 inches from his lower right ear. The second gunman must have been standing just behind and to the right of Kennedy. Sirhan, according to the witnesses, was standing two to four feet in front of the senator.

There is a memorial in Montreal that attests to this abhorrent program while remembering the suffering of those who were subjected without their consent to these horrific experiments that permanently diminished the quality of their lives.

It is also imperative to examine the capacity of those within the hierarchy of the Agency to appreciate what they were capable of as individual human beings. There is one example, among many, for instance that I believe captures the essence of the evil that Allen Dulles was quite capable of when he deemed it in his interests or that of his offspring, the CIA. He was a spy for the United States in World War I and was stationed in the beautiful city of Bern. On many occasions, his contacts caused him to wander into the remote villages surrounded by the majestic mountains of Switzerland when he became involved with a beautiful young woman of Czech descent. They had become acquainted while working together at the American legation offices. Their relationship quickly became very intimate. When it was brought to his attention by British intelligence that she was a German spy, he casually, as they had done many times before, took her to dinner. After they had finished their meal, he walked with her on the streets of cobblestone that had become quite familiar to both of them to a designated location that had been prearranged by his British counterparts and immediately trans-ferred her to their custody.[143] Her life was taken, as had 20 million in that war, and was quickly forgotten as collateral damage. Dulles resumed his duties the following day with little regret of what had been done that prior evening to another human being that he had shared dinner and a bed with on many occasions.

Based on the above, I submit that powerful elements within our government unfortunately are quite capable of assassinating a president over significant policy disputes that implicate the division of power in our society. This capacity is tremendously enhanced when rogue agents within our government cloaked by national security can act with impunity protected by a wall of secrecy that rarely is breached.

Those that were complicit with the murder of our President

walked amongst us, talked like us and spoke the same language. They, however, were not democrats or true proponents of the republic founded by revolutionaries, seeking independence and liberty. Their philosophy was quite opposed to government that represents and responds to the needs of the people as eloquently affirmed in Lincoln's iconic speech at Gettysburg. Many of the cabal that directed our secret government were neo-fascists, elitists and corporatists that vehemently believed that the interest of the nation was too important to be left to the ignorant masses that they so easily manipulated. Thus, the citizenry needed their sagacious guidance to protect them from their naïve understanding of global intrigue and the intricate machinations of power. Their primary objective of advancing our ordained prosperity and the sustained growth of our empire could only be achieved by supplementing the interests of the ruling class and their corporate manifestations. Their insidious philosophy infected the secret government and spread throughout our institutions like an epidemic. The successful murder of our chief executive emboldened them to assassinate Martin Luther King. Jr., Malcolm X and Senator Robert F. Kennedy. They were in essence traitors who hid amongst us quietly subverting every principle that made us proud to be Americans. As Cicero so pungently pointed out, we have less to fear from a murderer than a traitor that infects the instruments of power like the plague. A contagion that is unseen but nevertheless continues to contaminate the spirit of our nation to this very day.

Chapter 4

The Dissenters

"There are laws to protect the freedom of the press's speech, but none that are worth anything to protect the people from the press."
 Mark Twain

"It is dangerous to be right when the government is wrong."
Voltaire

"The issue today is the same as it has been throughout history, whether man shall be allowed to govern himself or be ruled by a small elite."
Thomas Jefferson

"Few are willing to brave disapproval of their fellows, the censure of their colleagues, the wrath of their society. Moral courage is a rarer commodity than bravery in battle or great intelligence. Yet it is the one essential, vital quality for those who seek to change the world that yields most painfully to change. Each time a person stands up for an ideal, or acts to improve the lot of others, or strikes out against injustice, he sends forth a tiny ripple of hope, and crossing each other from a million different centers of energy and daring, those ripples build a current that can sweep down the mightiest walls of oppression and resistance."
Robert F. Kennedy

"...witnesses in this case (JFK assassination) do have a habit of dying at the most inconvenient times."
James Garrison

"The name of the game is not truth it is power."
James Garrison

"Dissent is the highest form of patriotism."
Howard Zinn

"The very concept of objective truth is fading out of the world. Lies will pass into history."
George Orwell

"TV pollutes our minds and dulls our senses. It is a babysitter that molests our children. And yet those who are on the television scream 'first amendment' and 'freedom of speech'. How is corporate control freedom of speech? And what rights did our forefathers grant corporations, anyway?"
James Rozoff

"What progress we are making. In the Middle Ages they would have burned me. Now they are content with burning my books."
Sigmund Freud

"Unpopular ideas can be silenced, and inconvenient facts kept dark, without the need for any official ban...The British press is extremely centralized, and most of it is owned by wealthy men who have every motive to be dishonest on certain important topics. But the same kind of veiled censorship also operates in books and periodicals, as well as in plays, films and radio. At any given moment there is an orthodoxy, a body of ideas which it is assumed that all right-thinking people will accept without question...Anyone who challenges the prevailing orthodoxy finds himself silenced with surprising effectiveness. A genuinely unfashionable opinion is almost never given a fair hearing, either in the

popular press or in the highbrow periodicals."
George Orwell

"The freedom of the press is one of the great bulwarks of liberty, and can never be restrained but by a despotic government."
Thomas Jefferson

"Freedom of the press is not an end in itself but a means to the end of achieving a free society."
Felix Frankfurter

"Blind belief in authority is the greatest enemy of truth."
Albert Einstein

"Once a government is committed to the principle of silencing the voice of opposition, it has only one way to go, and that is down the path of increasing repressive measures, until it becomes a source of terror to all its citizens and creates a country where everyone lives in fear (His statement in opposition to the 1950 Internal Security Act)."
Harry S. Truman

"Power concedes nothing without a demand. It never did and it never will."
Frederick Douglass

"Animal Farm is not a book about how pigs—animals—when bestowed with power start to behave like men. It is a book about how men, when given power over other men, start to behave like pigs."
George Orwell

"When the people fear their government, there is tyranny;

When the government fears the people, there is liberty."
Thomas Jefferson

When reacting to the nefarious conduct of the CIA, Bernie Sanders in 1974 called the Agency, "a dangerous institution that has got to go...right-wing lunatics who use it to prop up fascist dictatorships."
Bernie Sanders

The Dissenters

The foundation of our republic is based primarily on our concept of liberty. In the Declaration of Independence, Thomas Jefferson wrote "...that they (the people) are endowed by their creator with certain unalienable rights and that among these are life, liberty and the pursuit of happiness." It is liberty, however, that nourishes and provides for the others. For it can be argued that life, as long as you were of the preferred genetic code, and the pursuit of happiness were components of daily existence even in Nazi Germany. It is the lack of or abundance of liberty, however, that determines the quality of that life, and the happiness that can be obtained within the acceptable social construct of any given time. So the question that must be posed is what is liberty and how is it defined in a true republic?

The founding fathers astutely observed that to maintain a moral government that emulates the will of the people will not only require internal structures that balance and limit power, but also must provide an instrument for which the people are fully informed on how that government is serving the welfare of the governed. This is why the only business afforded protection in the Constitution is the fourth estate. The founders opined that one of the primary guardians of liberty was a free and independent press. The media would not only apprise the public on government proposed policy but would also hold it accountable by unveiling deceit and corruption.

It is the responsibility of each citizen to avail themselves of that knowledge that will enable them to prudently contribute to the public debate inherent in a democratic republic and to intelligently choose those who will sensibly represent their interests in their town, state and federal governments. As Thomas Jefferson wrote, "If a nation expects to be ignorant and free...it expects what never was and never will be." Therefore, true liberty is realized in a society that promotes and protects freedom of speech, freedom of thought and freedom of the press.

To determine the health of our republic, it is necessary to measure the vigor in which we defend our liberty. It is also important to evaluate the qualitative knowledge of our citizens, not only on current affairs, but our national history and the ideals that exulted our heritage and our growth as a people. One of the barometers that can be used to make this determination is how our media monitors and reports on the power centers of our society and to what extent is the press that we rely on maintaining its independence and objectivity. I think when we examine this aspect of liberty we can clearly identify serious flaws that have incrementally evolved over time, eroding the independence of our mainstream media (MSM).

Since President Reagan repealed the Fairness Doctrine and President Clinton removed the restrictions on how many media outlets one corporation or an individual can own, we have seen the growth of ideologically driven radio and television stations that promote propaganda not knowledge. Their purpose is no longer to serve the public interests.

The other more disturbing development has been the purchase of our media outlets by a few large corporations that have constricted the content of the news we are allowed to read, see or listen to. It has become so prevalent that most refer to our national news outlets as corporate media. Clearly, this is a conflict of interest that is inhibiting and distorting the primary purpose of the media as intended by our founders.

Any journalist that reports on issues outside the box is immediately reprimanded, censored or worse fired by their employer. Two major examples of this was Ed Schultz and Cenk Uygur on MSNBC which is considered a liberal progressive network. Those that do not prescribe to this conventional and myopic view are discredited or labeled "conspiracy nuts." Because of this lack of independence, the corporate media ignore issues that normally would be exposed such as government encroachment on our liberty, or the passage of legislation that does not benefit the people but rather the wealthy and the powerful. The most egregious example in modern times was the lack of critical reporting regarding the Bush administration's justification for invading Iraq in 2002 and 2003.

The last dramatic infringement on the media's objectivity is the alliance it has formed with the government that it is supposed to be monitoring as the people's eyes and ears. The CIA, for example, ever since the implementation of Operation Mockingbird in the 1950s has infiltrated and exploited our media, in many cases with their consent, to advance its agenda and obfuscate its nefarious conduct while allegedly enhancing our national security. This unholy alliance between Wall Street, the MSM and government not only threatens our concept of a free press, but is also transforming our republic to what most would define as an oligarchy.

Another way we can ascertain the health of our republic is to assess how those that dissent in our society are treated by the media and our government. For example, the disclosure of documents that were collected by whistle blower, Edward Snowden, who exposed programs administered by the National Security Agency (NSA) that were infringing on our freedom of thought and our privacy without judicial authorization was not generally applauded by our national media. He was significantly criticized and in some media outlets was labeled a traitor. Our government responded in a similar fashion such that he has had to seek asylum in Russia. The assault on Snowden's reputation and character, however, is mild compared to those who have dared to speak out on abuses of power and misconduct particularly when this is directed at the Pentagon or the CIA.

The individuals that I intend to discuss in this series were completely discredited and in some cases were physically destroyed. Most of our citizens are oblivious to these transgressions and abuses of power because they are preoccupied with their smart phones, their video games and the vast wasteland of reality television. These individuals will defend their indifference to politics and the policies of our leaders by asserting that they can pursue a plethora of entertainment options and can purchase whatever they can afford. They define liberty as the freedom to choose whether they eat at McDonalds or Burger King or shop at Target or Walmart. Their primary concerns are connected to their freedom of choice and their pursuit of material wealth. This focus induces them to concentrate on government regulations and policies that enable federal agencies to police our commercial markets while ignoring other policies that threaten liberties that truly enhance their lives. As a result, they are less concerned with their privacy, their freedom of thought and their freedom of speech which motivated Snowden to risk everything he had, including his own liberty.

They further rationalize that it does not matter who we elect for president or Congress. They would add that their friends can be critical of our government or Wall Street, and yet suffer no discernible consequences no matter which party is in power. As one comedian sarcastically remarked, "I do not care if the government knows which porn sites I prefer."

The fallacy of their argument is that they do not pose a threat to the power structure within our society. If that comedian had an opportunity to run for Congress, he then would care if the government agencies knew which porn sites he preferred and what they potentially would do with that information. This would also be true for a journalist, a politician, a civil rights activist or an individual citizen that had access to forums that potentially could disseminate their ideas that challenged the status quo to a large audience. This is when the infringement of our privacy and our thoughts becomes important, and it is at this point that we recognize that our liberty has been diminished and that our republic is in jeopardy.

George Washington warned "If the freedom of speech is taken away then dumb and silent we may be led, like sheep to the slaughter."

In addition, we must appreciate that government encroachment on our liberty will not be as dramatic as it was done in Nazi Germany or Stalinist Russia. As Jim Garrison pointed out in his 1967 Playboy interview, we will not find ourselves one morning goose-stepping to work or awake one day to the posting of swastikas all over our communities. The change will be subtle, but nevertheless will be apparent to the vigilant observer and the dissenter.

The test in this case study will be what happens to those that dissent and confront powerful structures or agencies within our society, and how our media respond to their message. I submit the following test cases will reveal that we are no longer living in the country we were taught about in school.

The six parts of this series will consist of an essay on Gary Webb and Steven Kangas (Freedom of the Press); James Garrison ("Let justice be done though the heavens fall"); Colonel Fletcher Prouty (A question of honor); Abraham Bolden (Confronting the "unspeakable"); Oliver Stone (Confronting convenient fictions); and the witnesses and researchers of the assassinations of the 1960s.

Freedom of the Press
Part 1

Senator Frank Church and his fellow senate colleagues sat in stunned silence as witnesses within and outside of the CIA described **Operation Mockingbird**. The program was initially inspired by salient observations that journalists could gain better access to agents of foreign governments and acquire valuable information from contacts who ordinarily would not disclose to an intelligence officer employed by the Agency. This program was created in the 1950s by Frank Wisner, Allen Dulles and Richard Helms of the CIA who were joined by Washington Post publisher Philip Graham. The program was managed by CIA officer Cord Meyer whose wife, Mary Pinchot Meyer, would become a source of intrigue when it was discovered many years later that she had an affair with President Kennedy after her divorce. She was murdered in 1964 while walking in a park near her residence in Georgetown just outside Washington D.C. Her death has never fully been resolved and remains a mystery.

The CIA essentially recognized that to enhance its influence and access to vital information, not only abroad but domestically as well, required relationships with the media. These symbiotic alliances were formed to benefit the CIA and its propaganda objectives, and in return the journalists received intelligence briefings, and in some cases were financially compensated, for their cooperation with the Agency. The program continued to grow to enormous proportions until it reached its zenith when its existence was unveiled by the Church Committee Hearings in the mid-1970s. It was revealed through testimony that 25 media giants which included ABC, NBC, CBS, Newsweek, the Associated Press, United Press International, Reuters, Hearst Newspapers, Henry Luce's publications, as well as 400 journalists had been recruited by the CIA. Noam Chomsky of MIT reported that the list of reporters on the CIA payroll consisted of "who's who in journalism."

This relationship not only impacted on the objectivity of the media by disseminating misinformation to the public, but it also promoted myths that obfuscated the inner world of the CIA's clandestine services. The Agency also used this alliance as an instrument to perpetuate its fictitious image as a defender of democracy around the world while exaggerating the evil objectives of our adversaries to justify its existence. The reality was in stark contrast with this narrative. In fact, the CIA in many circumstances was actually engaged in defending its corporate allies by overthrowing democratically elected governments that threatened their profits and replaced them with brutal dictatorships.

The Church Committee eventually recommended sweeping reforms to discourage programs such as **Operation Mockingbird** to reign in the Agency that Senator Frank Church had described as a "rogue elephant" that was threatening our democratic institutions and our society. The modest reforms that were ultimately enacted would be partially swept away as future administrations in the name of national security engaged in policies that necessitated the CIA's complicity to advance nefarious programs that required secrecy and for the government plausible deniability.

Steven Kangas and Gary Webb would learn how potent this alliance between the Agency and the media had become when they both tried to pierce the veil of secrecy and expose the darkness that lay beneath the superficial reporting of our corporate media. The wrath they unleashed ultimately overwhelmed them. Not only was their work shoved down the "memory hole" by the mainstream media (MSM), but their character and credibility was also diminished by a constant barrage of journalistic assaults that eventually resulted in tragedy.

Steven Kangas

Steven Robert Fish who would later change his name to his mother's maiden name, Kangas, after his parents divorced was born in May 1961. His parents were devout conservative Christians. Because of their religious affiliation, he attended religious academies in South Carolina. After he graduated high school in 1979, he enlisted in the U.S. Army. After boot camp, he was sent to the Monterey School of Languages operated by the Army when it was determined he had a proclivity for languages. He attended classes for one year at that school learning several languages that included Russian. After his graduation, he was transferred to military intelligence. This scenario is reminiscent of Lee Harvey Oswald's experience before being co-opted by the CIA in their false defector program. He was politically very conservative and initially enjoyed the intrigue and excitement while fulfilling his duties as a military intelligence officer.

He was originally assigned to Goodfellow Air Force Base in Texas before being sent to Central America. In 1984, the military transferred him to West Germany where he engaged in electronic eavesdropping of Soviet military units stationed in Eastern Europe. His primary duties entailed transcribing transcripts that when completed he sent to NATO command. It was at this time that he began to question his political beliefs and the Cold War politics he was immersed in. He was well aware that Washington was exaggerating the threat of Soviet intentions to advance into Western Europe. He knew this because of the information he had access to through his electronic monitoring of their military units.

Two major incidents would change him forever and cause him to drift in another direction that his adolescent self would never have imagined or contemplated. The first incident involved the terrorist bombing of a Berlin discotheque in 1986 only a few blocks from his residence. Libya was immediately blamed and as a result President Reagan ordered the bombing of Libya as a consequence for their transgression. Steven knew at the time that the bombing was ordered before the administration had any empirical proof that Khadafy's Libya had been involved either directly or indirectly with the tragedy. The second event occurred while he attended the funeral of Major Arthur Nicholson an "intelligence compatriot" who had been assassinated. As he watched the funeral proceedings, his eyes fixated on Nicholson's 4-year-old daughter "clutching a cabbage patch doll throughout the entire service." Steven wrote that this image was "forever burned into my memory." He decided to resign from his intelligence work and pursue an alternative career.

He applied and was admitted to the University of California at Santa Cruz. It was an angelic campus situated on top of a small mountain of redwood forests overlooking 50 miles of Monterey Bay. It was known as a very liberal school with a significant contingent of peace activists among its academic staff and student body. He was considerably influenced by their progressive perspective to the extent that he would become a radical journalist that was known for his controversial articles that were critical of the establishment and the U.S. government's human right violations. More specifically, his research would focus on the top one percent and the CIA. After graduating from the university, he founded the website "Liberalism Resurgent" where he posted his articles and promoted his political activism. He wrote two significant articles in the 1990s that reverberated throughout the progressive community on the web.

His prominent and influential article entitled **"The Origins of the Overclass"** was published in 1998. He reported based on his research that the top one percent had begun their ascent in 1975 when the new right, corporate America and the CIA joined forces. Kangas alleged that business magnate, Richard Mellon Scaife, one of the richest men in the world operated "Forum World Features" which was a foreign news service "used as a front to disseminate CIA propaganda around the world." He used his wealth to influence elections and promote policies that provided further advantages to the elite in our society at the expense of the working and middle classes. Kangas added that Scaife was the leading financial supporter of a movement that would reshape American policies and perpetuate the inequitable realities of our present economy. It was reported that Scaife was very angry with Kangas' article and that he had hired a private detective to investigate the journalist.

Kangas' most salient work was his piece called **"Timeline of CIA Atrocities"** which he posted in 1996. This article was inspired by a study by the **Association of Responsible Dissent** that had concluded that the CIA as a consequence of its black covert operations and other nefarious programs were indirectly and directly responsible for six million deaths since its inception in 1947. A former State Department official, William Blum, indicated that this was akin to an "American holocaust." Kangas further wrote that the CIA justified these collateral consequences as necessary because of the threat that world communism posed to our nation and our allies. And yet, most coups sponsored by the CIA did not involve communist threats. The overthrow of the Iranian government in 1953 and the Guatemalan government in 1954 were democratically elected by their people. The threat the CIA was confronting was to its corporate allies not any threat from Moscow or Peking. In fact, the regimes that the CIA replaced these governments with were brutal dictatorships that oppressed their people and were infamous for their human right violations. Essentially, the article goes on to list all the CIA atrocities from 1947 through 1996. He concluded that the CIA should be abolished and replaced with a "true information gathering and analysis organization." He added that "the CIA cannot be reformed. It is institutionally and culturally too corrupt."

Kangas was probably unaware of the surveillance he was under. Although, he may have suspected that his work was attracting the attention of powerful opponents to his message, they did not intend to be casual observers while he continued to attack the heart of their political power. Kangas would be found dead in 1999 in a restroom on the thirty ninth floor of One Oxford Center Tower in Pittsburgh only several doors from the offices of Richard Mellon Scaife. Kangas was found by a maintenance worker named Don Adams who was making a routine check of the electrical circuit breakers located in the men's room. He indicated that he found Kangas lying face down in a pool of blood and that his head was protruding beneath a toilet stall. After he left to notify the authorities, he returned to find that Kangas' body had been repositioned on the toilet. This would be one of many unexplained facts in this case that troubled friends and family. Near Kangas' body was a 9mm pistol and 47 rounds of ammunition in his backpack and pockets. In addition, a copy of Hitler's **Mein Kampf** and a bottle of Jack Daniels were in his possession. He had no credit cards and only had $14.63 in his pocket.

Arnold Leonard of Salon Magazine wrote in March 1999 that there were a multitude of discrepancies between the police and EMT descriptions of the crime scene and the final conclusion of the medical examiner who had determined it was a suicide. The police and the ambulance attendants had all reported that Kangas had been shot on the left side of his head. The coroner wrote in his report that the bullet entered his brain through his mouth and that there was no exit wound. Leonard in his research further discovered that Kangas' computer drive had been erased shortly after his death. Friends and family had reported that he was working on a book about the CIA's covert activities. The reporter was also curious why Scaife had hired a private detective to investigate Kangas' past and pondered what this investigator had been doing prior to Kangas' death.

Just like the backyard photos of Oswald, the evidence found at the scene appeared to be contrived and excessive. What was he doing with a copy of Hitler's autobiography, and why did he have so much ammunition? His parents indicated that he was totally non-violent and did not have any affinity for guns. They also stated that their recent interaction with their son was positive and that there were no signs that he was depressed or suicidal. His close friends corroborated their statement. His parents added that he might have "been running scared" but suicide did not seem to be a plausible explanation for his death.

Gary Webb

Gary Webb was an award winning journalist that had a Pulitzer for his reporting on the 1989 Loma Prieta earthquake. He also had become somewhat of a local celebrity in San Jose by judging journalism contests and appearing on local television. He was employed as a journalist by the San Jose Mercury News which when compared to the LA Times, Chicago Tribune, San Francisco Enquirer and the New York Times was a minor paper in the media world. He nevertheless brought some positive notoriety to the small newspaper. He was considered by his colleagues as a hard working journalist who loved his job. He arrived early in the morning and stayed late on many evenings. In spite of his long hours, he was a family man who enjoyed his home life with his wife and three children.

His nightmare began ironically with his most successful and important story entitled **"Dark Alliance."** This series appeared in the Mercury News from August 18th through to the 20th of 1996. The main thrust of the story was about three individuals who were involved in selling large quantities of crack cocaine – primarily being distributed in African American neighborhoods of South Los Angeles. The money that was generated from the sales was used by the Contras in Nicaragua to purchase weapons and supplies for the purpose of overthrowing the leftist regime who had toppled Somoza. The Contras essentially were a counter revolutionary group supported by the CIA who were complicit in this alliance with the drug cartels in Central America.

The story initially was well received by the public. In fact, **"Dark Alliance"** expanded its following when Mercury News created a state of the art interactive website. On that site, Webb posted documents and updates on the story. The website became so popular that on one day over one million had logged in to read Webb's disturbing account of what the CIA was involved in while supporting the Contras. James DiEugenio who wrote **"Kill the Messenger: Rare Truth –Telling"** noted that Webb's expose for several weeks was unopposed on talk radio, cable television and the internet. This did not last long as the corporate media began to take notice of the story that they had ignored from the very beginning.

Before I can discuss the merits of Webb's series, it is important to recount the history that proceeded his discovery. He was not the first to implicate the CIA with drug trafficking to support its black ops and allies.

Robert Kirkconnell wrote a morose book that was published in 2013 entitled **American Heart of Darkness (Transformation of the American Republic into a Pathocracy)**. His tome covers a variety of subjects, including the Kennedy assassination. His discussion regarding his experience in Vietnam in 1972 as a staff sergeant in the Air Force assigned to the 603 Airlift Squadron is that portion of the book that is relevant. He was stationed in Okinawa, Japan on the Kadena Air Base as a transportation supervisor. His specific position was a non-commissioned officer in charge of flight data recovery and processing.

In December 1972, a large Air Force C-5 transport landed at the base carrying the bodies of soldiers killed in action (KIA). There were two military couriers that accompanied the bodies which was quite unusual. These two individuals immediately disappeared before the authorities could interview them. Japanese custom officers were promptly notified that there was "something suspicious about the individuals and their cargo" and were summoned to the base. Upon investigation, the custom officers discovered that the body cavities of the soldiers had been removed and filled with bags of heroin. An Air Force officer from the Office of Special Investigations (OSI) ordered Kirkconnell not to release any documents on the matter until further notice. He indicated that he would contact him with further instructions. Shortly thereafter an Army officer from their Criminal Investigation Division (CID) appeared demanding all relevant documentation on the matter. Kirkconnell refused as instructed by Special Investigations. The CID officer accused him of obstruction of justice and then left. He eventually was contacted by OSI and instructed to collect all relevant documents in his possession and send them to their office. After the initial investigation was completed, it was clear that the military couriers had fled when they suspected that Japanese custom officers were to be summoned to the scene because the Japanese had very severe penalties for smuggling drugs into their nation or territories.

There was an article in Time Magazine in 1973 that reported on the investigation that quickly faded into oblivion. In that article, it was reported that federal authorities suspected that an international drug ring had been transporting millions of dollars of heroin into the U.S. on transport planes emanating from Vietnam. The heroin was being produced in what was referred to as the Golden Triangle in Southeast Asia. Other than that article, there has been no follow up investigation, and all the documents provided to OSI have disappeared. As Kirkconnell pointed out, the operation required an extensive knowledge of U.S. Air Force shipping codes, regulations and procedures in order to accomplish what was referred to in the Time article. The logistics of such an operation necessitated a sophisticated organization that required contacts within military intelligence and possibly the CIA.

Kirkconnell indicated that many Americans and Vietnamese were involved in black market operations. It was an "endless war for endless profit." It was the GI's who were the sole losers, as well as the Vietnamese civilians. Kirkconnell further wrote that as a young officer he observed all these planes with "Air America" written on them. They seemed to fly everywhere in Southeast Asia. He finally decided to ask the "old timers…What was Air America and what were they doing there?" They nonchalantly responded as though it was common knowledge that Air America was the CIA airline. He further inquired "What were they carrying?" They stated that the CIA was transporting "prostitutes, drugs, weapons" among other classified materials.

While researching his book, Kirkconnell discovered articles on the internet written by a 25-year veteran in the Drug Enforcement Agency (DEA) named Michael Lavine. He later learned that Lavine had even published editorials in the New York Times, LA Times, Esquire and USA Today. Lavine had written that the CIA had prevented the DEA and other law enforcement agencies from destroying the Chang Mai Factory that was the source of massive amounts of heroin that was being smuggled into the United States. He further alleged that they were accomplishing this by hiding the drugs in the bodies and body bags of GI's killed in Vietnam. Lavine's unit was in charge of all heroin and cocaine smuggling cases through the port of New York. Lavine wrote, "We could not avoid witnessing the CIA protecting major drug dealers." He added "Not a single important source in Southeast Asia was ever indicted by U.S. law enforcement" during his tenure as squad leader. On many occasions, the CIA or the State Department would intervene to prevent an indictment. He also reported that "CIA owned airlines like Air America were being used to ferry drugs throughout Southeast Asia, allegedly to support our allies. The CIA's banking operations were used to launder the drug money." This of course confirmed Kirkconnell's recollection of his military service in Vietnam.

After President Nixon negotiated an accord with North

Vietnam in 1973 to end the war, the CIA would begin to transfer resources to other hot spots in the world. One of those hot spots was Nicaragua. The Somoza regime had been an ally of the United States ever since he took power. His human right violations were overlooked because of his staunch anti-communist record. He also did not interfere with corporate interests in his country even when his people suffered as long as he received his share of the profits. He was eventually overthrown by the Sandinista National Liberation Front (FSLN) in 1979 which was a leftist organization that vowed to retake Nicaragua's government and give it back to the people. As with most revolutions, the Sandinistas failed to adhere to their promises as they struggled to maintain power.

The Reagan administration was determined to remove the Sandinistas and replace them with a puppet regime. President Reagan assigned the task of accomplishing that goal to William Casey who was the Director of the CIA. The CIA quickly backed the Contras and began supplying them with weapons and resources to mount their assault against the leftist government. Contemporaneous with this Reagan initiative was an Iranian hostage situation in which the administration was seeking the release of American citizens through diplomatic means. As Reagan's second term began, these two projects began to merge. The Congress had imposed an arms embargo on Iran. Nevertheless, senior administration officials were secretly facilitating a sale of arms for hostages. The Congress had also approved the Boland Amendment which prohibited further funding of the Contras by the U.S. government. President Reagan who was known as the great delegator assigned his Vice President, George H.W. Bush, the task of addressing both problems. After all, Bush had been involved in intelligence since the 1950s and because of his oil companies was quite familiar with the Middle East. He had also been appointed the CIA Director by President Ford after Director William Colby was fired in January of 1976 – presumably for cooperating too much with the Church Committee.

To secure the release of several hostages, intelligence agents sold weapons to the Iranians. Lieutenant Colonel Oliver North of the National Security Council in 1985 modified the operation so that a portion of the proceeds generated from the sale of arms could be transferred to the Contras for the purpose of purchasing weapons to fight the regime in Nicaragua. The CIA facilitated this transfer and managed the logistics to effectuate the plan. The Iran-Contra Scandal became public in November 1986 when a Corporate Air Services transport plane was shot down by the Sandinistas. This plane was owned by Southern Air Transport which was linked to the CIA. Aboard that plane was not only weapons but a CIA contractor named Eugene Hasenfus. CIA Director William Casey would admit later to journalist Bob Woodward that he was aware of the program. He died of brain cancer before he was able to testify before Congress.

Reagan had defended his support of the Contras by comparing them to our founding fathers. The reality was that the Contras were committing atrocities within Nicaragua that caught the attention of many human rights organizations. The administration as a result was under a constant barrage of negative press for their support of the Contras and their handling of the hostage situation. As the scandal began to envelop the administration in ways reminiscent of Watergate, Reagan went on national television acknowledging that the administration did sell arms to Iran but not for hostages. He also denied any knowledge of funds being directed to support the Contra operation. Of course, this may have been partially true when you consider Reagan's lack of interest in the details of his policies. It was reported in the **Untold History of the United States** by Kuznick and Stone that on occasion Reagan would have a few jelly beans and then fall asleep during national security council meetings.[144] However, Vice President Bush in my opinion knew all about the details of the operation. Just as Nixon managed Operation Zapata against Cuba, and the CIA's solicitation of mafia assistance in the assassination of Castro during the latter part of Eisenhower's second term, Bush supervised the **Iran-Contra Operation**.

The consequence of the scandal was that all the funds were cut off compelling the Contras to tap into another source to generate the money they needed to maintain their operation. The end result was that the Contras formed an alliance with drug cartels with the CIA's knowledge to purchase narcotics and then sell them in the U.S. for profit. As revealed in the CIA's **Black Vault Encyclopedia Project**, the Attorney General and Director of the CIA had negotiated an agreement which excluded the CIA from reporting narcotic and drug related crimes to the Justice Department. This agreement was enforced from 1982 until 1995 which conveniently covered the period that the U.S. government was involved in Nicaragua.

Robert Parry and Brian Barger of the Associated Press in 1985 wrote a story that exposed the Contras involvement in drug trafficking to finance their war against the Nicaraguan government. President Reagan immediately attacked the journalists to discredit their reporting. The corporate media also was not impressed with the article which resulted in minimal coverage on the merits of their claims. A special senate subcommittee chaired by Senator John Kerry, however, was formed to investigate the matter. The result was a 1,166-page committee report on **US Operations in Latin America and the Caribbean**. Within that report, it was determined that "considerable evidence" was uncovered that affirmed that the Contras were linked to trafficking drugs and that the U.S. government was aware of their activities. The report concluded that "...Contras themselves knowingly received financial and material assistance from drug traffickers. In each case, one or another agency of the U.S. government had information regarding the involvement either while it was occurring, or immediately thereafter." In fact, the Chief of the CIA's Central America Task Force admitted "with respect to drug trafficking by resistance forces...it is not a couple of people. It is a lot of people." This is where Webb in the mid-1990s picked up the story and began his investigation.

"Dark Alliance" as pointed out earlier was primarily about three individuals who were involved in shipping cocaine to the U.S. This cocaine was sold as crack which was cheaper than the powder version. These sales, however, spurred a crack epidemic in Southern California which eventually spread to other regions. Meneses Cantarero, a powerful Nicaraguan player working with the Contras, recruited Oscar Denito Blandon Reyes who was the largest cocaine dealer in the U.S. Reyes distributed the cocaine to Ricky "Freeway" Ross who sold the crack cocaine in South Los Angeles. Webb through his sources was able to make the connection to the Contras who were backed by the CIA to these immensely profitable drug transactions that resulted in a horrific humanitarian crisis. In his reporting, he never alleged that the CIA was directly involved. But as further evidence was uncovered long after his expose was written, he did explicitly accuse the CIA of its complicity in these drug trafficking operations in interviews such as the one he gave to Len Osanic of Black Op Radio in 2002. The corporate media ignored the merits of the story and only several weeks after it was published began its assault on the credibility of Webb and his reporting.

The LA Times would assign 17 journalists whose mission was to "get Webb's team" and to "take away the guy's Pulitzer." The CIA as this media campaign began watched the developments closely and even corroborated and provided assistance to media outlets to challenge Webb's reporting. The CIA also actively discouraged other media outlets from publishing or covering Webb's story. In **"Managing a Nightmare: How the CIA Watched Over the Destruction of Gary Webb"** by Ryan Devereaux which was published in September 2014, he reported that only six weeks after Webb's story was released that the corporate media's onslaught supported by the CIA began to shift public opinion against Webb. The CIA's public affairs officer gave a great deal of credit for this sea change to the negative reporting on Webb by the Washington Post. The consequence of all these attacks according to Devereaux caused a "firestorm of reaction" against Webb's employer, the San Jose Mercury News. Devereaux further wrote that the editors of the paper began to distance themselves from their award winning reporter and eventually would shut down the website. By October 1996, the CIA with its corporate media allies had completely reversed what had begun as a public relations disaster for the Agency to another major success for its Public Relations Department.

Unfortunately for Webb, his reporting had flaws that the MSM were able to exploit to the extent that his character and credibility lay in ruins by the time they were done. Peter Kornbluh of Columbia Journalism Review wrote sympathetically that Webb's series was "problematically sourced" and "edited." In addition, he promised evidence that was not always forthcoming. He was also the victim of his own hyperbole and exaggerations. Nevertheless, according to Kornbluh, the overall thrust of his series was corroborated by declassified documents and other sources. The MSM ignored the evidence and never did correct the record. An LA Times reporter, Jesse Katz, admitted that their reporting did amount to "overkill." Katz further stated "We had this huge team of people at the LA Times and kind of piled on to one lone muckraker up in Northern California." In spite of this, most of Webb's reporting stood up to the scrutiny only to be buried by the national media.

The consequence was that Webb was forced to resign in disgrace from the San Jose Mercury News. He found it very difficult to find work as a journalist. He would eventually become destitute. His wife divorced him, and his house had to be sold before it went into foreclosure. He returned to his mother's home and wrote a book that received little publicity. As a result, the book did not generate much income.

He eventually seeped into a deep depression. Although he had suffered from clinical depression for years, Devereaux opined that his death was directly related to the major "smear campaign against him." Webb committed suicide in 2004. He did leave a suicide note for his estranged wife and three children. In that note, his ex-wife disclosed to the press that he had no regrets for writing **"Dark Alliance."** As an investigative journalist, he felt it was his duty to report on this horrific alliance that caused so much pain and suffering by those who became addicted to crack.

The CIA's response to Webb's demise was without humanity nor humility. Nicholas Dujmovic, a CIA Directorate of Intelligence staffer was quoted in the six page CIA document entitled **Managing a Nightmare** that was recently declassified, attributed the initial outcry over Webb's reporting by the public as "societal shortcomings" that are not present in the Agency. He added "As a personal post-script, I would submit that ultimately the CIA drug story says a lot more about American society … than it does about either the CIA or the media…We live in a somewhat coarse and emotional times-when large numbers of Americans do not adhere to the same standards of logic, evidence, or civil discourse as those practiced by members of the CIA community."

James DiEugenio observed in his above cited article that "In December 1996, after seeing Webb at his Midnight Special appearance with fellow journalist Robert Parry, I noted Webb's still confident attitude in both his story and the corporate structure above him. Having studied the assassinations of the 1960s, I didn't quite comprehend it. For like the assassinations, the link between CIA and drug running was a radioactive subject. It was on the short list of bête noires (black beast) of the MSM." Webb had failed to recognize the demons he had unleashed by his story, and the true objective of their campaign against him. By the time Webb recognized what was happening to him and his career, it was too late. Webb when discussing his downfall said at first he won awards and public accolades for his reporting "and then, I wrote some stories that made me realize how sadly misplaced my bliss had been. The reason I'd enjoyed such smooth sailing for so long hadn't been as I'd assumed, because I was careful and diligent and good at my job. The truth was that, in all those years, I hadn't written anything important enough to suppress."

A movie eventually was made of Webb and his important journalistic attempt at revealing the truth entitled **Kill the Messenger**. The movie was based on a biography of Webb written by Nick Shou which was released in theaters in the fall of 2014. It was an empathetic portrait of a hero. In the end, one hopes that his death was not in vain. Senator John Kerry wrote to his former employer the Sacramento News and Review, a job held briefly after he resigned from the San Jose Mercury News, that "Because of Webb's work, the CIA launched an Inspector General Investigation that named dozens of troubling connections to drug runners." Ironically, it would be CIA documents that were declassified shortly before and after Webb's suicide that would buttress Webb's claims that the Contras were implicated in criminal acts with the CIA's knowledge and support. All of this would be ignored by the MSM.

James Garrison
("Let justice be done, though the heavens may fall")
Part 2

As depicted in the movie **JFK (1991)** directed by Oliver Stone, Garrison played by Costner walked down the corridor of the court house through a sea of reporters launching questions at the

beleaguered District Attorney (DA) who was not only prose-
cuting a respected businessman in the city of New Orleans but
was confronting powerful dark forces within our government.
When he initiated his investigation into the murder of President
Kennedy, he naïvely assumed that the FBI and the Justice
Department, as well as other agencies, would assist his case in
search of the truth. He quickly learned that he and his
government would be on opposing sides. The press continued to
harass him as he turned a corner and began to ascend the stairs
to an upper floor when a reporter exclaimed that he was hurting
the country. Garrison turned and replied "Let justice be done,
though the heavens may fall."

I was impressed with the quote and the idealism it evoked
and began to research its origin. I would discover one night
through serendipity while watching television an individual
who may have popularized the quote but may not have been the
original source. I had randomly come upon a movie that caught
my attention entitled **Belle (2013)** that took place at the end of
the eighteenth century in Britain.

The film was about Dido Elizabeth Belle who was taken in by
her uncle the Earl of Mansfield when her father died. She was of
mixed race for her mother was of African descent. Her father was
the brother of the Earl and because of the mores of the time he
was obligated to assume the responsibility of raising his mulatto
niece. He was concerned initially how this arrangement would
impact his reputation in high society and his career as the Lord
Chief Justice in the King's court. As time passed, his affection for
Belle evolved to the point that he loved her as though she had
been born out of his marriage.

The Earl held some of the prejudices of the time but was not
an admirer of the institution of slavery. In his decision in the
Somersette case of 1772, he had ruled that there "was no legal
basis for slavery in England." The facts of the case pertained to
the legality of keeping slaves in Britain. He further pointed out

in his decision that "slavery had not been established by statute in Britain and was not supported by common law." It was a controversial decision that revealed an inner courage that enabled him to decide the case in a way that was consistent with his moral convictions. It, however, was not the case that catapulted him into the annals of history nor was it the focus of the film.

The case that was the central concern of the movie involved the Atlantic slave trade, and the horrible conditions suffered by the slaves, as well as the inhumane practices that were employed by the captains, attempting to secure a profit for the owners and a good reputation for themselves. The name of the infamous ship was the Zong. The ship was owned by the Gregson slave trading syndicate based in Liverpool. The tragedy that made this voyage an emblematic example of the dark side of human nature was simply referred to as the Zong Massacre. The captain and the crew had brought on 142 enslaved Africans to be transported to the Caribbean. It was a common custom at the time to fill the ship with as many slaves as they could cram into the bowels of the vessel. The conditions were fertile ground for disease and even death. It was also the practice of these shipping companies to take out insurance on their cargo so they could be indemnified if the ship sank or the cargo was lost. The slaves were treated no differently than tea, livestock or other types of cargo.[145]

The captain began throwing slaves overboard when it was determined that there was not enough food and water to reach their destination. By the time the crew had fully effectuated his order, 132 to 142 slaves had been left to drown in the Atlantic. The ship ultimately reached the port at Black River on the coast of Jamaica. Once the owners were notified, they filed their claim with their insurer for the loss of their cargo. The insurer refused to pay because it was their contention that the loss was the consequence of navigational mistakes by the captain. This repudiation of the claim resulted in the court case of Gregson v. Gilbert (1783).

The case implicated an important principle of "general averages" which allowed the captain to order the jettison of part of his cargo in order to save the rest without affecting his claim under the insurance policy. He could do this even if it involved the killing of human beings. It was a very significant principle when you consider the risk and expense that was involved in every voyage at that time.

The Earl presided over the legal dispute that was tried before a jury. The original verdict by the jury was in favor of the shipping syndicate. The jury determined that there was an "absolute necessity" that compelled the captain to throw the slaves overboard to save the rest of the cargo. As morally depraved as their verdict was, they had made the requisite findings that justified their verdict under the law.

The insurer refused to pay and requested that the verdict be set aside when new evidence surfaced. The parties presented their arguments to a tribunal which included the Earl. The new evidence established that there had been a significant rain storm during the second day of the killings which resolved the water shortage. In addition, it was determined that the captain had failed to stop at several ports that could have allowed the ship to replenish its supplies. It was clear the ship was overcrowded and some of the slaves may have become seriously ill which would severely impact the money they could obtain at market.

The decision as portrayed in the film was to kill the slaves and seek to be indemnified by the insurer. This was the captain's first voyage, and he wanted it to be a profitable one for his employer. The Lord Chief Judge (Earl of Mansfield), under the constant prodding of Belle and a young attorney she had become romantically involved with, decided in favor of the insurer. In his ruling, with a full appreciation of the powerful business interests he was impacting, had declared, "Let justice be done, though the heavens may fall."

The publicity generated by the case mobilized and inspired

the formation of many abolitionist groups. The following year Parliament passed the first law regulating the slave trade when they set limits on the number of slaves per ship. Eventually, the **British Slave Trade Act** of 1807 was enacted abolishing the African slave trade.[146] I imagined that Garrison as a legal scholar and practicing attorney was familiar with this history when he articulated the above mentioned quote, linking two tragedies that had occurred two centuries apart.

James Garrison was born in 1921. His family moved to New Orleans when he was a young child. His mother retained custody and raised him after his parents divorced. By the time he entered college, he stood 6 foot 6 inches tall and had a deep southern drawl when he spoke. In many ways, he reminded me of Gregory Peck when he portrayed Atticus Finch the protagonist in the film **To Kill a Mockingbird (1962)** that was based on the Pulitzer prize winning book written by Harper Lee.

He voluntarily joined the National Guard and honorably served his country in **World War II**. As he pointed out in his 1967 Playboy interview, "I was with the artillery supporting the division that took Dachau; I arrived there the day after it was taken, when bulldozers were making pyramids of human bodies outside the camp. What I saw haunted me ever since." He would remain in the National Guard for almost 20 years.

He eventually applied and was accepted to Tulane University Law School in which he received his law degree in 1949. After graduation, he was employed by the FBI for two years before joining the law firm of Deutsch, Kerrigan and Stiles in 1954. He became an assistant district attorney of New Orleans Parish in 1958. His attempt to become a criminal court judge was stymied when he lost the election in 1959. He was undeterred for in 1961 he would successfully be elected as the District Attorney (DA) of New Orleans even though he did not have any major political backing or money. His victory was attributed primarily to his performance in a televised debate with his opponent Richard

Dowling. His performance was reminiscent of the success of Senator Kennedy in his first televised debate with Vice President Nixon.

He was an energetic and aggressive DA who immediately cracked down on the rampant prostitution that was occurring on the streets and in the numerous brothels and strip joints located on Bourbon Street. The eight judges that were assigned to that district had ignored these transgressions and were not initially impressed by the bravado of the new DA. A conflict soon developed between the judges and Garrison that resulted in a war of words in the press. Garrison eventually accused the judges of racketeering and conspiring against him. The judges successfully charged him with a misdemeanor of defamation pursuant to a statute that he would later be convicted of. In 1965, the U.S. Supreme Court overturned the conviction by declaring the statute unconstitutional in that it violated Garrison's first amendment rights. Other than the above conflict, Garrison was well liked and admired in his district. His tenure as DA was refreshing considering the historical pandering and corruption that had embroiled many of his predecessors. It became clear to the local press and the political pundits that he had the potential as a political rising star to reach the heights of U.S. senator or governor of his state. This would all change after November 22, 1963.

He was an admirer of President Kennedy and supported much of his domestic legislative agenda which included Medicare, civil rights, education and tax reform, as well as equal pay for women to name a few. In addition, he was in favor of Kennedy's foreign policy and believed that he was taking the country in the right direction. Even though he was a libertarian who vehemently supported the rights of the individual as prescribed in the U.S. Constitution and was a staunch defender of individual liberty when encroached on by government action, he nevertheless still supported the idea that the government could play a vital role in making our society fairer, more equitable and humane. Thus, it is not surprising that he supported Roosevelt's New Deal or Kennedy's New Frontier.

As the fall of 1963 unfolded, the nation appeared on the cusp of resolving the Cold War and addressing the injustice of government sanctioned segregation in the South and racial discrimination throughout the country. President Kennedy had signed the Limited Test Ban Treaty after being ratified in the Senate in September. He was also able to get a wheat-grain agreement through Congress to assist the Soviet Union with a severe shortage that was due to austere weather conditions, as well as establish a direct communication link that allowed the Pentagon to communicate directly with the Kremlin. This was commonly referred to as the "red telephone." The President had signed the Equal Pay Act in June and his civil rights bill was moving through Congress. Most of the country was supportive of the President, and it appeared he was going to win the election in 1964 no matter who his opponent would be. This political atmosphere of hope was violently derailed by the assassination of Kennedy in Dallas.

The motives for his murder were obfuscated by a powerful cabal that not only covered up the conspiracy while blaming it on a patsy, but would also endorse myths that would distort the real legacy of Kennedy. The fact that he had decided to withdraw from Vietnam, seek rapprochement with Castro's Cuba and end the Cold War through negotiation was immediately removed from the public record as the "Ministry of Truth" incinerated his true policy objectives down the "memory hole."

Once Garrison became aware on the weekend of the assassination that Lee Harvey Oswald had spent the prior summer in New Orleans, he immediately launched a preliminary investigation to ascertain what Oswald had been up to and whether he had contacts that assisted him in the assassination. The first incident that was brought to the attention of the New Orleans

Police Department was an assault on Jack Martin by Guy Bannister in their office at 544 Camp Street. This assault had been witnessed by Bannister's secretary, Delphine Roberts. Martin indicated that they had been drinking the day of the assassination. Bannister became intoxicated which was unusual for him in the middle of the day. He appeared preoccupied and agitated. Martin further stated that when they entered Bannister's office they were standing in the proximity of where Bannister's secret files were kept. Bannister accused Martin of absconding with his files by hiding them in his coat. Martin sarcastically remarked "What are you going to do, kill me like you did Kennedy?" Bannister became so angry that he pulled out his pistol and began hitting him with the butt of the gun. He would have seriously injured him if Roberts had not intervened. Once you know the activities that Bannister and his associates were involved in that prior summer, the volatile reaction of Bannister in his drunken state no longer seem irrational. Martin also volunteered that David Ferrie had made a trip to Texas suggesting that he was the "get away pilot" for the assassins.

Ferrie had apparently travelled to Texas on the afternoon of the assassination driving 400 miles during one of the worst torrential rain storms of the fall for the purpose of going ice skating and goose hunting. He was accompanied by two young men. They initially went to Houston which was a strange place to go if you were planning to hunt geese. From Garrison's perspective as pointed out by James DiEugenio in his tome entitled **Destiny Betrayed – 2nd Edition (2012),** it was equivalent to someone travelling 400 miles to get a hamburger. Garrison found the whole story dubious and brought him in for questioning. By the time Garrison had finished his interrogation, Ferrie had conceded that he had failed to bring any skates and had forgotten his hunting rifle. Garrison would eventually learn from the proprietor of the Winterland Skating Rink in Houston that Ferrie stood next to a phone the whole time he was there.

Once the phone rang, he answered it and then left with his two companions. Ferrie also denied knowing Oswald even though he had worked with him in the Civil Air Patrol in the mid-1950s. Because Ferrie had been so nervous and evasive during his examination, Garrison suspected that he was lying and decided to notify the FBI.

The FBI asked Ferrie a few questions and then dismissed him without any further follow up. Garrison was informed that Oswald was a lone nut and was solely responsible for the shooting in Dallas. Garrison not having any reason not to trust the proclamations of his government accepted their report. After the **Warren Commission Report** (WCR) was completed in late September 1964 and submitted to posterity along with its 26 volumes of evidence that presumably convicted Oswald as the lone assassin, Garrison continued to be troubled by it all but accepted the Commission's verdict.

This would all change when by accident he was able to discuss the matter with Louisiana Congressman Hale Boggs who had been a member of the Commission. Boggs indicated that he thought the single bullet theory was a sham and that there were a multitude of disturbing facts that were left unanswered. He also told Garrison that the Commission had been poorly served by the FBI, Secret Service and the CIA. In short, he thought they were covering up something.[147] As an aside, Boggs' twin engine plane would disappear over a remote section of Alaska in 1972. The plane has never been located.

Garrison left the conversation very concerned and as a result he purchased three sets of WCR and its 26 volumes of supporting documents. He placed one set at home, one in his office and the other in his vehicle. As pointed out by colleagues, he not only was reading them but was becoming an expert on the Warren Commission's investigation. After he had completed reading it all, he recognized that the Commission's conclusions were not supported by the evidence and that most of it was irrelevant. As he stated in his Playboy interview, "To show you how cosmically irrelevant the Warren Report is for the most part...one of the exhibits is classified in the front as, 'A study of the teeth of Jack Ruby's mother.' Even if Jack Ruby had intended to bite Oswald to death, that still would not have been relevant."

He began his secret investigation of the President's murder in late 1966. He would uncover Oswald's connections to Guy Bannister the former head of the FBI's Security Division in Chicago who was running a private detective agency that was essentially a front for his intelligence work. He would also link Oswald to David Ferrie, a pilot for the CIA and mafia boss Marcello, as well as the CEO of the International Trade Mart, Clay Shaw. Shaw at the time was using an alias and was known on the street as Clay Bertrand. He had numerous witnesses that connected all of them, including some anti-Castro Cubans such as Sergio Arcacha Smith who was the head of the Cuban Revolutionary Council that had been formed by CIA Agents E. Howard Hunt and David Atlee Phillips. As Garrison probed further, he kept butting heads with the CIA and their domestic clandestine operations. He would even track down the name of the man that ordered Ruby to take out Oswald. He tracked a telephone number to a location in Las Vegas. And then a young ambitious reporter for the New Orleans States-Item, Rosemary James, discovered his investigation and wrote a story that changed history.

As reported in my article **The Patsy (A walk through the "wilderness of mirrors"),** most of the evidence was inconclusive or exonerated Oswald such as the paraffin test. Once his investigation became public, it did not matter what the evidence was because the cabal that he was confronting were not interested in resolving the crime. The reality was that the media and the CIA, as well as other government agencies, began to not only discredit his investigation as nothing more than a publicity stunt to advance Garrison's career, but also attacked his character and integrity by asserting that he was a corrupt narcissist that was trying to defame honorable individuals who were serving their country. Garrison responded to these allegations by the media in his Playboy interview when he stated, "I'd have to be a terribly cynical and corrupt man to place another human being on trial for conspiracy to murder the President of the United States just to gratify my political ambition." He added to the contrary "I was perfectly aware that I might have signed my political death warrant the moment I launched this case—-but I couldn't care less as long as I can shed light on John Kennedy's assassination." He defiantly concluded "I'm going to break this case and let the public know the truth. I won't quit before that day. I wouldn't give the bastards the satisfaction." As former CIA Agent Victor Marchetti, who was the highest ranking CIA officer to become a whistle blower on Agency misconduct, reported, the CIA Director Richard Helms had created the **Garrison Group** that discussed options available to the Agency to undermine Garrison's investigation and support the defense of their asset.

Garrison, after Ferrie died under suspicious circumstances, decided to indict Shaw before something happened to him. While Shaw was being booked at the police station by a young police officer who was not familiar with the case, Shaw had answered a routine question regarding the use of aliases. Without thinking, he answered that his alias was Clay Bertrand. His defense team during the trial would keep the document from the jury by successfully challenging it as a violation of their client's Fifth Amendment rights because the officer had failed to administer the Miranda warning. Garrison was dismayed and baffled by the judge's impetuous ruling that had significantly damaged his case.

The case was finally presented before a jury in 1969. The most compelling component of Garrison's case, other than the medical testimony, was Abraham Zapruder's 8mm film of the assassination. His opponents had long recognized its value and had compelled him to argue before the U.S. Supreme Court to secure its release in compliance with his discovery request. The presentation of the film was the first time the public had ever seen it. The Zapruder film was essentially locked in the archives of Life Magazine ever since the publisher had purchased the rights to it in late 1963. The most significant segment of the film was the headshot and Kennedy's reaction after he had been struck. Garrison in dramatic fashion repeated this sequence several times while simultaneously describing Kennedy's movement as "back and to the left." Other than an occasional gasp, the court room was completely still and silent. It was obvious to everyone that observed that segment of the film that day that Kennedy had been shot by an assassin that was positioned in front of the motorcade not behind it. If the rest of Garrison's case had been as provocative and compelling as the film, we would be living in a different reality influenced by an amended history.

The jury after deliberating for a brief period found the defendant not guilty. However, Mark Lane, a renowned critic of the WCR, who was working with Garrison as a consultant discovered after he interviewed the jury that Garrison had proven to them that there was a conspiracy, but he was not able to prove beyond a reasonable doubt that Shaw had been involved. In spite of this, the press reported that the matter had been settled and that the verdict had affirmed the conclusions of the Warren Commission. The reality, if one wanted to examine the facts, was far different than their superficial pronouncements. In fact, Garrison's investigation had been smeared by the media and thoroughly sabotaged by the federal government.

Oliver Stone and Zachary Sklar wrote in their article **"Yes, there was a cover up" (2013)** that "Everyone of Garrison's attempts to extradite witnesses from other states were rejected – something that had never happened in his six previous years as district attorney. His routine requests for important evidence such as x-rays and photos from the President's autopsy, and tax records and intelligence files on Oswald, were denied. Federal prosecutors refused to serve subpoenas on CIA officials such as Allen Dulles and Richard Helms. Garrison's office phones were tapped, and Garrison and his staff were followed by FBI agents. Key witnesses were bribed or died under mysterious circumstances. And the district attorney's files were stolen and turned over to Shaw's defense counsel before the trial began." They further stated "We know now, as a result of released Freedom of Information documents, that the defamatory and false articles about Garrison were planted in the mainstream press as part of a smear campaign orchestrated by the CIA to discredit critics of the Warren Commission."

Stone indicated that he worked closely with Garrison for several years while directing **JFK**, and it was his observation that Garrison was an honest, highly intelligent and courageous man. As Vincent Salandria, a prominent defense attorney in Philadelphia and a known pacifist, observed, these are not the actions of an innocent government.

The federal government even after the trial continued its assault on Garrison to ensure that he was completely discredited and that his capacity to continue his investigation was destroyed. Federal prosecutors in 1973 filed charges against Garrison for accepting bribes to protect illegal pinball machine operators. They further alleged that he was receiving $3,000 every two months. Garrison successfully defended himself when a jury found him not guilty. After the trial, the IRS in 1974 filed additional charges claiming that he had failed to report the income that he received from the bribes. He was eventually found not guilty of those charges as well.

Even though he was exonerated in both cases, the press continued to portray him as a corrupt narcissist that the nation should ignore and allow him to fade into the past. As a result of these cases and the continued attacks on his character, Garrison lost his bid for re-election in 1973 to Harry Connick, Sr. His wife, Elizabeth, also filed for divorce. He appeared to be losing everything he cared about. Reverend Martin Luther King, Jr. said, "The ultimate measure of a man is not where he stands in moments of comfort, but where he stands at times of challenge and controversy." Garrison refused to give up and become an "unperson." He triumphantly rebounded in 1978 by winning a special election as a judge for the fourth Circuit Court of Appeals. A position he held until his death in October 1992.

Garrison never relented in his quest to solve the murder of the century. He read everything he could get his hands on and followed the Church Committee Hearings and the House Select Committee on Assassinations (HSCA) very closely. When the HSCA reluctantly declared because of acoustic evidence it could not ignore that Kennedy's death was "probably" the result of a conspiracy, Garrison was still denounced as a conspiracy nut. John Barbour, a script writer, producer and a journalist, telephoned to congratulate him because of the HSCA's conclusion. Barbour exclaimed when he got Garrison on the phone "that you must feel vindicated." He also added that the media must be constantly badgering "you" to get a response. Garrison replied, "John, you are the only one who has called." He indicated further that he was fine with that.

Garrison would write three books on the assassination. The first was about the Shaw trial called the **Heritage of Stone** which was published in 1970. The second book was a fictional account of the assassination of a president entitled **The Star Spangled Banner**. His most successful tome was published in 1988. This book was titled **On the Trail of the Assassins** which made the New York Times best seller list. This was also the book that inspired Oliver Stone to write the script for **JFK**.

As a result of an NBC attack in 1968 on his investigation, Garrison was allowed to respond when the FCC ruled that under the Fairness Doctrine NBC had to grant him time on their network. He was allowed 30 minutes outside of primetime. Garrison stated, "One of the stated objectives of the Warren

Commission was to calm the fears of the people about a conspiracy. ... There is no room in America for thought control of any kind, no matter how benevolent the objective. Personally, I don't want to be calm about the assassination of John F. Kennedy. I don't want to be calm about a president of my country being shot down in the streets."

In his book **On the Trail of the Assassins**, he proffered his view on why the CIA preferred Johnson over Kennedy. "In retrospect, the reason for the assassination is hardly a mystery. It is now abundantly clear ... why the CIA's covert operations element wanted John Kennedy out of the Oval Office and Lyndon Johnson in it. The new President elevated by rifle fire to control our foreign policy had been one of the most enthusiastic American cold warriors. ... Johnson had originally risen to power on the crest of the fulminating anti-communist crusade which marked American politics after World War II. Shortly after the end of the war, he declaimed that atomic power had become 'ours to use, either to Christianize the world or pulverize it' – a Christian benediction if ever there was one. Johnson demonstrated enthusiasm for American military intervention abroad... earned him the sobriquet 'the senator from the Pentagon'."

Garrison was interviewed only several months before he died by his friend John Barbour for three hours in July 1992. This award winning interview would be known as the **Garrison Tapes**. Garrison was asked by Barbour if he could do it all over again would he? He replied that while he was terribly disturbed about what happened to John Kennedy he was not sure he would do it, considering the "emotional price I paid."

Garrison was a veracious reader. He read poetry and classic novels, as well as biographies. One of his favorite writers was Shakespeare. He also was significantly influenced by George Orwell's novel **1984**. The novel had a lasting impact on his concern for the individual and the awesome power that a state could exercise over its citizens if its power was unchecked as he observed when witnessing the horror of Dachau and the colossal carnage of war. He was not particularly concerned that it could happen in America until his investigation of the assassination placed him "in an incongruous and disillusioning battle with agencies of my own government." He warned "I'm afraid, based on my own experience, that fascism will come to America in the name of national security."

He, in many ways, identified with the America Kennedy envisioned, and the hope he inspired for a future that would never come. Instead, we marched into the jungles of Vietnam with little comprehension of what we were getting ourselves into. We had no knowledge of Vietnamese culture, tradition or history. We assumed that the awesome fire power of our weapons would insure our success in preventing an imagined communist foe from consuming all of Southeast Asia. The result of their hubris and ignorance was the worst foreign policy debacle in our history. In addition, we maintained a policy of hostility towards Cuba for over 50 years, as well as perpetuated an adversarial posture against the Soviet Union that fueled the Cold War until the late 1980s. He nevertheless consoled himself with the thought that in the end his government would be held accountable by the people and would be compelled to make amends for the transgressions of the past. He, therefore, was optimistic that the secrets of Dallas would eventually be revealed and that our republic could begin to heal.

As to Garrison the man, he was an articulate, intelligent and compassionate person whose sole motivation was to seek the truth. If he could find the truth, he could achieve justice not only for Kennedy but the nation as well.

John Barbour in his documentary entitled **The Last Word on the Assassination (2014)** told a story about Garrison to demonstrate what kind of man he was. Barbour indicated that his children were visiting him while he was relegated to a bed because of cancer and a severe heart condition in late 1992. He knew he did not have long to live. He ordered them to get their mother and bring her to him. When she arrived, he told her they needed to remarry. She replied that she already had married him once and had no intention of doing that again. He pleaded with her until she agreed. He died a short time later because of heart failure, leaving behind his wife and five adult children. Barbour stated that the reason he had forced his wife to remarry him was so that after his death she would receive his pension. Her second husband had bankrupted her, and she was without the means to meet her financial obligations. Barbour concluded, "that was the kind of man he was."

Barbour further added that a poll (1992) indicated that 51% of the public believe that the CIA was involved in the conspiracy to murder the President. In 1967, only one man accused the CIA of murdering the President and that man was James Garrison.

Colonel L. Fletcher Prouty
(A question of honor)
Part 3

Colonel Leroy Fletcher Prouty was in a unique position within our national security apparatus in that he was privy to some of the most secret and highly classified covert operations during the Eisenhower and Kennedy years. He worked closely and formed friendships with Allen Dulles, James Jesus Angleton, Major General Ed Lansdale, the military brass and most of the cabinet members.

President Eisenhower in March 1954 signed National Security Council Directive 5412 that in essence formalized an ever expanding program for covert operations in Asia and around the world. The 5412/2 group created by Eisenhower later that year included the Director of the CIA, Secretary of Defense or desig- nated representative, the Secretary of State or designated repre- sentative, the National Security Advisor, Chairman of the Joint

Chiefs of Staff, the Vice President and the President. Eisenhower's goal was not only to expand and enlarge covert operations but also to provide some supervision of the CIA's activities. The President was not always present during the meetings and on many occasions had Nixon participate on his behalf. Because of the need to maintain plausible deniability not only for the government but the President as well, the orders from the Commander-in-Chief were very general and in some cases were not memorialized in writing.

Prouty was assigned to the United States Air Force Headquarters in 1955 to organize a worldwide military network to support the clandestine operations of the CIA. From 1955 until 1964, he was essentially the liaison for the military and the CIA for all black ops and paramilitary operations. During the Kennedy administration, he was specifically assigned as the Chief of Operations for the Joint Chiefs of Staff. He was awarded the Legion of Merit from the U.S. Air Force as a result of a CIA Commendation for his work. He retired in 1964 from the Air Force to join the private sector with profound concerns he initially kept to himself regarding what happened in Dealey Plaza on November 22, 1963. Upon his exit, General Maxwell Taylor, the Chairman of the Joint Chiefs of Staff (JCS), awarded Prouty the Joint Service Commendation Medal as recognition for his diligence and hard work.

Prouty had served in **World War II** as a pilot. He ultimately was assigned to British West Africa in February 1943 as a pilot with Air Transport Command. In time, he became the personal pilot of General Omar Bradley, General John C.H. Lee and General C.R. Smith who after the war would become the founder and President of American Airlines. He also served in the legendary mission that concerned the evacuation of British commandos involved in the Battle of Leros. This operation was immortalized by the novel the **Guns of Navarone** by Alistair MacLean which later became the basis of a famous film that featured Hollywood icons Gregory Peck, David Niven and Anthony Quinn. He was transferred at the end of the war to the Pacific theater under the command of General Douglas MacArthur. From 1952 through to 1954, he served in the Korean War in Japan as the Military Manager for Tokyo's International Airport during the U.S. occupation.

He had a stellar and honorable career in the U.S. Air Force that included service in two wars. And if Kennedy had not been assassinated, he would have remained a celebrated part of the early years of the **Cold War**. This would not be his fate for his knowledge of assassination projects compelled him to become an antagonist of those agencies he had valiantly served and as a consequence would be dismissed as another conspiracy theorist.

He intuitively had surmised from the reported evidence, his professional experience and his own observations that Kennedy was murdered by a conspiracy. The conspiracy Prouty contemplated included individuals he had worked with intimately on projects that only a select few within the inner sanctum of the executive branch were privy to that he referred to as the **Secret Team**. As an agent of that team, he was implicated in these covert projects and as a result was very familiar with the modus operandi of intelligence when executing these operations. Although his duties were primarily concerned with logistical support for CIA paramilitary operations around the world, he was a trusted insider that was privy to dark projects that included their assassination program. The CIA had a protocol that to the trained observer was their signature. He knew it well and immediately spotted remnants of it as the events in Dallas unfolded.

When Kennedy was inaugurated on January 20, 1961, there was a great deal of enthusiasm not only domestically but around the globe that this young President would usher in an era of enlightenment and idealism. The developing world was elated with his views on nationalism and the attempts by many nations to sever the bondage of colonialism and become independent sovereign countries. His speeches on Vietnam (1951) and Algeria (1957) were not the only basis on which this hope was founded. The candidate had also affirmed that the era of colonialism was over and that the United States must be a catalyst for peaceful change that supported the emergence of many nations that wanted autonomy. He stated that to ignore this great tide of transformation by defending the status quo would be a major mistake and would place the United States on the wrong side of history. In addition, he avowed to address civil rights, as well as other progressive programs such as his proposal for health insurance for the elderly.

Initially, he would not disappoint his admirers. His inaugural address was inspiring and is still considered one of the best speeches of the twentieth century. His call to public service was enthusiastically received by a generation that traveled to Washington in numbers not witnessed since the early days of FDR's administration. He immediately announced his program to establish a **Peace Corps** that was inspired by his brother-in-law Sargent Shriver who also became its first director. In addition, he proposed to change the relationship that the United States had with Latin and South America by announcing the **Alliance for Progress**. His honeymoon period was truncated by policies he inherited from Eisenhower regarding Vietnam, Laos and Cuba. He was also entrapped by some of the hawkish rhetoric he had unleashed during the campaign. The reality of the time was that you could not get elected if you were perceived to be soft on communism.

When meeting with outgoing President Eisenhower, he was apprised of the developments in all three countries. Eisenhower told him that Laos was the most critical and that he may have to interject combat troops into that impoverished land-locked nation to prevent a communist takeover by the Pathet Lao. He also reported, as had Allen Dulles the Director of the CIA (DCI), that there was a plan to assist Cuban exiles in overthrowing the communist regime in Cuba. His advice on Vietnam was to support Diem as best he could to maintain South Vietnam's independence.

President Kennedy was distressed by what he had been told because his agenda was to lessen the tensions of the Cold War not enhance them by pursuing a comprehensive test ban treaty with the Soviets that had eluded Eisenhower. He outlined this agenda in his book entitled a **Strategy for Peace** he had published during the campaign. These leftover policies would initially derail Kennedy's desired initiatives, but more importantly would eventually divide his administration. The consequence of this division imposed significant stress upon the President's relationships with the Joint Chiefs, his national security advisors and the covert sector of the CIA. In fact, 1961 would be one of the most intense and traumatic years that any President had confronted. He was advised to send combat troops by his military and civilian advisors to resolve predicaments in Laos, Vietnam, Berlin and Cuba. He resisted these provocative recommendations while seeking peaceful solutions that were consistent with his broader goals much to the dismay and consternation of his national security team.

The **Bay of Pigs** fiasco in April 1961 was a harsh introduction to the internal politics and intrigue within the executive branch. Kennedy had become a target of the CIA in their attempt to entrap him into committing U.S. armed forces in Cuba. The CIA and the Joint Chiefs thought they could intimidate the young President and place him in the undesirable position of having to choose between total defeat and humiliation or war.

Allen Dulles, in notes that were discovered by researchers, had indicated that he was convinced once the operation began to fail the President would be compelled to introduce combat forces and invade Cuba to save the operation. President Kennedy prior to the invasion had repeatedly told the CIA that the trained

Cuban exiles would have to succeed on their own for he was not under any circumstances going to involve the United States in a war in the jungles of Cuba. He required that U.S. support had to be limited in such a way as to maintain plausible deniability.[148]

The CIA leadership which included the CIA Director Allen Dulles, Richard Bissell and General Charles Cabell assured Kennedy that this was a viable plan and that the Cuban Brigade of 1400 exiles had a good chance of success. They indicated further that the invasion would spark an internal uprising by anti-Castro militants that would eventually cause the termination of Castro's regime. The CIA had purposely omitted important information and intelligence that contradicted their rosy assessment of their plan.

Castro, ever since the Eisenhower administration had ignored his proffer to establish diplomatic relations while visiting the United Nations, was concerned that the United States might attempt to reverse the revolution and reinstall another dictator beholden to the U.S. and its corporate interests. Because of this, he had turned to the Soviet Union for protection from the goliath that confronted him just 90 miles north of Cuba. The Soviets provided him with military equipment which included some MiG fighter jets, as well as Soviet military advisors. He also began rounding up all the counter revolutionaries that threatened his newly formed government and incarcerated them in Cuban prisons. When the anti-Castro rebels were informed of the CIA plan, they reported that their numbers had been so decimated by Castro's policies that they were in no position to provide any support to Brigade 2506. This was never reported to the President. In addition, the President had been told that the exiles could flee to the mountains if necessary and mount their offensive against Castro. The reality was that the Escambray Mountains were 80 miles away and that enormous mosquito infested swamps had to be crossed to reach them.

The President was also not apprised of the fact that the

individuals who prepared the plan had anticipated U.S. military involvement that included airstrikes that would render Castro's air force impotent. In addition, he was not informed of the assassination plots against Castro, his brother and the charismatic revolutionary Che Guevara. The President without this information tacitly approved a plan that he was not very enthusiastic about. After all, President Eisenhower, the Joint Chiefs, his National Security Advisor and the CIA had all endorsed it. He would later regret trusting the CIA and his military advisors.

After the **Bay of Pigs** debacle, the President at a press conference took full responsibility for the disaster. Privately, he set up a commission to study the operation to ascertain what went wrong. He assigned General Maxwell Taylor as the Chairman. The other members consisted of Admiral Arleigh Burke, DCI Allen Dulles and the President's brother Robert Kennedy who was the Attorney General. The findings of the committee were that the plan was poorly designed and that the Cuban exiles' chances of success without U.S. military support was minimal which was contrary to what the President had been assured by the CIA. The President was furious and felt betrayed when he was apprised of the committee's conclusions. He famously exclaimed "I would like to splinter the CIA in a thousand pieces and scatter it to the winds." Prouty indicated that he almost succeeded in doing just that before he was assassinated. Supreme Court Justice William Douglas, a close friend of Kennedy, recalled "This episode seared him. He had experienced the extreme power that these groups had, these various insidious influences of the CIA and the Pentagon, on civilian policy, and I think it raised in his own mind the specter: Can Jack Kennedy, President of the United States, ever be strong enough to really rule these two powerful agencies? I think it had a profound effect...It shook him up!"

The first action the President implemented in his goal to reform and in some ways tame the CIA was to fire Dulles, Bissell and General Cabell. He did allow Dulles to resign in November but everyone within the beltway knew the truth. Dulles and Cabell were humiliated and never forgave Kennedy for his decision to allow the operation to fail and for ending their illustrious careers on such a sour note. The Joint Chiefs' assessment of Kennedy's actions were not much kinder.

The Chairman of the Joint Chiefs of Staff, General Leminitzer, indicated that Kennedy's failure to send in the Marines was criminal if not an act of treason.[149] Leminitzer was eventually reassigned as commander of NATO because of his staunch support for false flag projects such as **Operation Northwoods** which annoyed Kennedy. This top secret document that was unanimously supported by the JCS advocated for a pretext that could be used to galvanize public approbation for an invasion of Cuba. Some of the scenarios listed in the document included the sinking of a U.S. ship, the shooting down of a jet liner or detonating bombs in Guantanamo and blaming it on Castro. He was replaced by General Maxwell Taylor.[150]

Others like General Curtis LeMay felt that the President had lost his nerve and did not have the guts to follow through with the program to the end. Former Vice President Nixon had a similar appraisal and even reported to Kennedy that he would have authorized the military to respond and invade Cuba. There was talk of impeachment by the hawks in Congress and in the Pentagon. Kennedy in a speech wisely rejected this concept of preemptive war that would become the **Bush Doctrine** several decades later when he stated that it was not in the American tradition to invade a country that had not attacked us first.

The other actions that were initiated by Kennedy to reign in the power and influence of the CIA was to reduce its budget by 20 percent by 1963 and his signing of National Security Action Memorandums (NSAM) 55, 56 and 57. Prouty said that NSAM 55 was a very significant act because it stripped the CIA of its large paramilitary operations. The Joint Chiefs were now in charge of these operations with the CIA relegated to a supportive role. Under Eisenhower, it was reversed. Kennedy also created the **Defense Intelligence Agency** (DIA) whose first director was a former FBI agent named Joseph Carroll. The purpose of this agency was not only to assimilate intelligence collected by other agencies but also to reinforce NSAM 55 and insure that the CIA's clandestine operations were under strict military control. By 1963, the power struggle being waged between the President and the CIA may have caused concerns within the hierarchy at Langley that their survival was at stake if they did not prevail in this battle.

The President in Laos negotiated a neutral coalition government that would include the communist. As to Vietnam, he stubbornly refused on numerous occasions to send combat troops and thereby Americanize the war. In a meeting with all his national security staff held on November 15, 1961, Kennedy, as described by Professor Blight of Brown University in his documentary **Virtual JFK,** brilliantly defused and refuted his advisors' rationale for sending combat troops to Vietnam. The result of the meeting was NSAM 111 which did not authorize combat troops, but it did increase the number of military advisors to 16,000 and included some planes and helicopters to be used to train South Vietnamese pilots in what would be called **Operation Farm Gate**.

Eventually, the President decided to withdraw from Vietnam completely. He would sign NSAM 263 on October 11, 1963. Prouty had helped write the document that was the U.S. policy when Kennedy died. Kennedy announced that one thousand unnecessary personnel would return from Vietnam in December. The second part of the withdrawal plan would remain secret for decades. In paragraph two of NSAM 263, it referenced relevant sections contained in the **McNamara – Taylor Report** which recommended that the rest of all U.S. personnel in Vietnam would return no later than December 1965. Prouty said that the term "U.S. personnel" as opposed to "military personnel" was intentional. By using this language, he was including the CIA agents as well.

The **Cuban Missile Crisis** of October 1962 was the closest the two super powers ever came to a nuclear war. Once again the young President trying to avoid a war – that Premier Khrushchev had aptly described as a war in which "the living would envy the dead" – was in a major confrontation with his military advisors and the CIA. Both had advised him to bomb the missile sites and invade Cuba. Kennedy repeatedly refused seeking desperately to find a solution that would allow Khrushchev to withdraw the missiles without being humiliated.

In order to buy time, he decided to place a quarantine around the island to prevent the Soviets from shipping more equipment and supplies to complete the installation of the missiles. He could not call it a blockade because that would be an act of war. After a U2 had been shot down by Cuban forces, the President was under tremendous pressure to respond.

As the Soviet supply ships approached the gauntlet of U.S. Naval vessels that encircled Cuba, President Kennedy decided to send his brother on a back channel mission and speak with the Soviet Ambassador Anatoly Dobrynin of whom he had a cordial relationship. According to the Ambassador in a cable he sent to Moscow on October 27, 1962, he noted that the President's brother looked like he had not slept in days. He wrote that Robert Kennedy had emphatically pointed out that his brother was under tremendous pressure by the military to bomb Cuba and launch an invasion. Kennedy's brother added that he did not know how much longer the President could maintain control of his government before the military took over.[151] Upon receiving this message, Khrushchev knew he had to help Kennedy. He sent a memo indicating that he would withdraw the missiles if Kennedy would pledge not to invade Cuba. Upon pressure from the hawks in his government, he quickly sent a second letter which included the demand that Kennedy remove the U.S. Jupiter missiles in Turkey. Kennedy upon receipt of the letters decided to act upon the first and ignore the second. However, he did promise through back channels that the Jupiter missiles would be removed from Turkey in six months.

These missiles were obsolete, and Kennedy had discussed their removal prior to the missile crisis. The advent of the Polaris missile that could be launched from a nuclear submarine was a far better deterrent to Soviet aggression than stationary land based missiles such as those placed in Italy and Turkey.

Once an accord had been reached, Khrushchev ordered the ships to return to their home base and instructed his military to begin the arduous process of dismantling the missiles.

At a conference held in 1992 which was the thirtieth anniversary of the October crisis, U.S. and former Soviet military and civilian personnel gathered to discuss and share information regarding this seminal event. The U.S. contingent which included former Secretary of Defense McNamara were informed that the Soviets had placed over 94 tactical nuclear weapons in Cuba. They also indicated they were prepared to use them if the United Stated had invaded. This was unknown at the time by the CIA or military intelligence. McNamara was shocked by the disclosure. This revelation enabled him to appreciate even more the measures taken by both leaders to restrain their militaries from instigating a war that would have resulted in 150 million deaths in the span of an hour. Because of President Kennedy's determination to prevent a war and his willingness to trust the discretion of his adversary, the crisis had been diffused and the missiles were withdrawn.

After it was over, Kennedy invited the Joint Chiefs to the Oval Office to thank them for their advice and support. Based on their vitriolic and bellicose performance, this was simply a courteous gesture by Kennedy for he clearly was dismayed by their lack of judgment and counsel during the crisis. The response he received startled the President. General LeMay said this was a major defeat and that we had been fooled. He demanded that the President rectify the matter immediately and order the invasion of Cuba. He added that this political solution was no different than what happened in Munich in 1938. The other Joint Chiefs agreed.[152] Back at the Pentagon, Daniel Ellsberg said that after the crisis there was a coup atmosphere that permeated throughout the building.

As the fall of 1963 unfolded, the President was clearly on a path towards detente with the Soviet Union and rapprochement with Castro's Cuba. Prouty surmised, however, that it was the President's decision to withdraw from Vietnam that was the straw that broke the camel's back. It was this policy that instigated the fermentation of a plan that would lead to a military coup d'état. The conspirators had recognized that the hope of getting rid of this radical President by the electoral process was probably non-existent. It would require something more dramatic and drastic. The idea of assassinating the President as pointed out in the movie **JFK** was something that was discussed in the "wind" until a few high ranking CIA officers came up with a plan which was supported by the military brass.

Major General Ed Lansdale was the individual that ordered Prouty to be part of a military escort for a group of international VIPs to the South Pole to activate a nuclear power plant for heat, light and sea water desalination at the U.S. Naval Base at McMurdo Sound only 11 days before Dallas. Lansdale was designated as an Air Force officer as a cover for his work as a CIA employee. His expertise within the Agency was in psychological warfare and propaganda. He was attributed with the overthrow of the Philippines' government in the early 1950s. He also was instrumental in Diem's rise to power in South Vietnam. During the latter part of 1961 until November 1962, he was appointed by Kennedy as the chairman of the special augmented group that was in charge of **Operation Mongoose** which coordinated efforts to undermine Castro's government through sabotage, propaganda and other nefarious activities.

Prouty indicated that this trip could have been handled by anybody for it certainly was not part of his normal duties. As it was reported to him, this was in reality a paid vacation. He suspected that the actual objective was to prevent him from performing his customary duties to coordinate additional security for the President's trip to Texas.

On his trip back, he briefly stopped on November 23, 1963, in New Zealand. It was at this time as he was reading the Christchurch Star that he learned of the President's assassination in Dallas. He noted that the paper had a complete biography of Lee Harvey Oswald that even included a studio picture of him wearing a suit. The story also contained information on his defection to the Soviet Union among other interesting facts that depicted him as a communist. What immediately puzzled Prouty was how did the paper obtain all this information on an allegedly unknown 24-year-old? It must be noted that there was no internet or computer technology that was affordable at the time. The computers that existed were extremely expensive and required a large room to house their components. In order to develop a story with all the information as reported, the journalist would have taken days, if not longer, unless you already had a file on the individual being investigated. Of course if he was an unknown lone nut, this clearly was not the case. The whole thing according to Prouty appeared to be a cover story.

The paper also had pictures of the Texas School Book Depository (TSBD) where Oswald was employed and where the sniper's nest was reportedly located. Prouty quickly noted that many of the windows in the upper floors were open at a location during the motorcade where the President would be most vulnerable to an assassin as the large Lincoln navigated the sharp turn onto Elm. He clearly surmised that this was a major breach in the President's security.

When he returned to Washington, he noted that offices in the Pentagon that were shutting down before he left as Kennedy's withdrawal plan from Vietnam was incrementally being implemented were buzzing with activity when he returned. The first official meeting Johnson held was on Sunday, November 24, 1963, and the subject he discussed with his national security staff was Vietnam not the President's murder. In fact, President Johnson authorized NSAM 273 on November 26 only four days after the assassination. The language used in NSAM 273 was deceptively subtle in that it appeared to be consistent with Kennedy's policy but a closer review, as pointed out by Professor Peter Dale Scott, revealed commitments and operations that had reversed Kennedy's Vietnam program. More specifically, Johnson had reaffirmed our commitment to defend South Vietnam and cancelled the one thousand personnel that were to be brought home in December. He also authorized OPLAN -34A which was an offensive covert operation that involved the sabotage and destruction of military targets in the Gulf of Tonkin. The U.S. Navy would provide support to South Vietnamese saboteurs who were trained by the CIA.

In December, Johnson told the Joint Chiefs that "If you help me get elected, I will give you your damn war." The President approved NSAM 288 in March 1964 which set forth the bombing targets in Vietnam and the military strategy that would be invoked when U.S. forces were deployed. As Johnson pointed out to his National Security Advisor Bundy, he now just needed congressional support to go forward with his policy in Vietnam. He would get that support in August of that year when U.S. Naval vessels were attacked by three North Vietnamese Navy torpedo boats defending their territorial waters.

There were two reported incidents. The first resulted in one 50 caliber bullet hole sustained by the U.S. Cruiser Maddox. According to declassified documents, the second incident was a result of false radar readings. Johnson never told Congress that the U.S. Navy was patrolling in North Vietnamese waters while supporting South Vietnamese operations in the Gulf. Instead, he had led Congress to believe that we were innocent victims of North Vietnam's unprovoked aggression. The result was the **Gulf of Tonkin Resolution**. By 1965, the first combat troops landed in Vietnam.

Prouty began to investigate on his own the events in Dallas. He discovered that the security provided the President was lax. Dallas was a breeding ground for extreme conservative militant groups such as the John Birch Society and followers of General Edwin Walker who had been fired by Kennedy for indoctrinating his troops in violation of the Military Code of Conduct. In addition, the Ku Klux Klan (KKK) were also a prominent and influential organization that permeated within most of the city government, including the Dallas Police Department. There were also numerous threats directed at the President that included a flier that was posted all over the city that had a picture of President Kennedy with the caption "Wanted for Treason." Lastly, when the U.S. Ambassador to the United Nations, Adlai Stevenson, had visited the city just two months prior to the President's scheduled visit, he was verbally assaulted and had objects thrown at him. Consequently, the city of Dallas posed serious security problems that should have warranted a comprehensive plan that would have included as many resources as possible.

Contrary to what he expected, Prouty learned that there were no secret service or police monitoring the crowds. He indicated that the 112 Intelligence Group at the Army Headquarters at Fort Sam Houston in San Antonio had been told to "stand down" that day over the protest of their commanding officer. He also learned that the resources at the Secret Service Office in Fort Worth were informed that they would not be needed in Dallas. In addition, Sheriff Deputy Roger Craig reported that his department was instructed by the Sheriff not to participate in the security of the

President and that their role that day were merely as spectators. This clearly was a lot of man power that was not being utilized. This not only perplexed Prouty but reaffirmed his initial instincts that the President was not gunned down by some anonymous lone nut using an antiquated Italian rifle with a defective scope. Prouty indicated that whenever the government does not follow basic protocol this is a red flag that something is wrong.

Prouty stated that there should have been snipers assigned to some of the roof tops to watch the buildings and the crowd. There should have been numerous agents scattered along the motorcade and where possible all the windows in the high rise buildings should have been shut or at minimum closely monitored. In the past when he was involved in preparing the security for the President, they would have studied the motorcade route in advance and determined what were the most vulnerable areas that presented potential opportunities for assassins. He would have many officers on the ground equipped with radio communication capability. To Prouty's astonishment, none of this was done. And if ever there was a city that required it, it was Dallas.

Prouty wrote that Oswald was specifically selected by the CIA from a targeted group of military personnel intended to give support to CIA operations. It was a program that Prouty had helped to establish in 1955. The CIA's **False Defector Program** started shortly thereafter. In order to have been selected, the CIA would have vetted him, and the FBI would have conducted a background check. The claim by these agencies that they did not know Oswald was clearly a fabrication.

According to Prouty, "Oswald was only the cover story designed to lead people away from what really happened." It is a common practice by intelligence to employ misdirection and diversion that draw attention away from the assassins. Thus, the cover story is very important to the success of the operation. Every contingency needs to be considered so that this story can survive intense scrutiny and continue for years if not decades. Prouty pointed out that the cover story employed in Dallas was "fantastic." People have been writing and debating about who Oswald was and what was his role, if any, in the assassination since its inception rather than focusing on who benefited and why the President was assassinated.

The other part that was important involved controlling the investigation after the fact so that any imperfections of the plan can be covered up. This is why Prouty did not believe the Mafia did it because they did not have the power to cover it up. He believed they played a role in the assassination, but it was a minor role with exception to Ruby's murder of the patsy. If Oswald had lived, there never would have been a **Warren Commission** because murder, even if the victim was the President of the United States, in 1963 was a state crime. The investigation and the eventual jury trial would have occurred in Texas. It was after Oswald's death that the formation of a commission to investigate the President's murder was suggested to Johnson. The appointment of Allen Dulles, who should have been a primary suspect, to the Commission was an indicator to the rest of the world that the Commission would not seek the truth but rather would obfuscate and bury it under a pile of deception that would allow the perpetrators to escape punishment. It was only the U.S. citizens that naïvely assumed that their government would tell the truth.

If the cover story is properly crafted, the professional mechanics simply fade into the crowd and disappear. As long as the coup is successful, "no one will be prosecuted." If the target is terminated, there will be a change in the government but more importantly a new policy will emerge. Prouty asserted this is how a military coup d'état works. "Anybody that doesn't realize that isn't using their head."

Prouty would write **The Secret Team – The CIA and its allies in control of the world** after his retirement from the Air Force.

The book was published in 1973 with details that caught the attention of not only the media but the intelligence community as well. Since Prouty was never employed by the CIA, he never signed a secrecy oath that would have prevented him from writing the book. Because of his prior position within the national security state, it was difficult to refute his assertions and claims. The CIA resorted to its standard tactic by labeling him a conspiracy nut that was hoping to make a lot of money by defaming the Agency. Fortunately for Prouty, the Agency had bigger matters to attend to as the decade progressed; revelations of assassination attempts on Castro and programs that targeted U.S. citizens and associations took center stage which resulted in the creation of the **Rockefeller Commission,** the **Church Committee** and the **House Select Committee on Assassinations.**

However, Prouty over the years would provide the mainstream media and the CIA with plenty of gifts to use against him to smear his reputation. He not only was labeled as a conspiracy nut because of his well-known views on the Kennedy assassination, but he was a member of the **Church of Scientology** which promotes many controversial if not bizarre opinions. He also surmised that the secret team was involved in the death of Princess Diana, and was a critic of the theory of evolution. Prouty also did not assist his cause when he inadvertently was a featured speaker at the 1990 convention for the **Liberty Lobby** which is a known anti-Semitic organization. He was also named to their advisory board, the **Lobby's Populist Action Committee**. In addition, Prouty had his book reprinted by the Noontide Press which is the publishing arm for the **Historical Review,** a holocaust denial organization.

When Oliver Stone intended to use Prouty as a consultant for his film **JFK**, he confronted the retired Air Force officer with this history. He told Prouty he could not have a racist associated with his film. Prouty defended himself by asserting that he was unaware of the political beliefs of these organizations and assured Stone that he was not anti-Semitic nor was he a denier of the Holocaust. Stone accepted his protestations as sincere and not only used him as a consultant but modeled the character Mr. X after him. Unfortunately for Prouty, the mainstream media and the CIA would not be so gracious. When his second tome was published in 1992 entitled **JFK, The CIA, Vietnam and the Plot to Assassinate John F. Kennedy**, he was pummeled by an avalanche of anti-Semitic allegations. In addition, his controversial views listed above were also mentioned repeatedly which allowed the corporate press and the CIA to avoid discussing the facts presented in his book.

I do not think it is proper to assign guilt by association or defame a person's reputation because of a few mistakes of judgment. It would be fortunate if Jesus would come forward and reveal the truth. But since we know that is not going to happen, we must accept that human beings with all their frailties must stand in his place. Prouty served his country with integrity and with pride. He was one of the few that resigned his post as a matter of honor after Dallas. He was not going to participate in a government that murdered his president.

Abraham Bolden
(Confronting the unspeakable)
Part 4

President Kennedy's description of courage was "A man does what he must – in spite of personal consequences, in spite of obstacles and dangers and pressures – and that is the basis of all human morality." Abraham Bolden fit perfectly within that definition of courage when he had spoken out against the lack of professionalism he observed while a member of the Secret Service's elite squad often referred to as the presidential detail. But his courage was never more evident when he refused to remain silent about an assassination attempt in Chicago, and the

Secret Service's complacent approach to the President's security that he firmly opined were relevant to what happened in Dallas on that dark day when the torch of the New Frontier had gone out. He could not have known at the time that his effort to speak the truth would cause him to confront what Thomas Merton had called the "unspeakable"; an evil so vast and powerful that it would have intimidated most of us to cower and fade into the abyss of silence. His refusal to be intimidated initially resulted in the loss of his liberty, but in time provided him with an awareness of how power in our nation truly works. His story is disturbing in many ways, but it is also an example of hope and redemption.

Bolden was interviewed in 2012 on the Canadian radio show **Night Fright** by Brent Holland to discuss Bolden's book **The Echo from Dealey Plaza** that was published in 2008. Bolden suitably initiated the conversation by quoting an Irish statesman who lived in the eighteenth century, Edmund Burke. Burke said "The only thing necessary for the triumph of evil is for good men to remain silent." This quote may have been the inspiration for Dr. Martin Luther King's famous admonition that "It's not the repression of the bad people that hurts, it's the silence of the good." Bolden after stating how evil can prevail over justice began to describe his path into history.

In the 1950s, he had become a patrol officer for the Illinois State Police. He would by chance get an opportunity to take a civil service exam that if he passed would allow him to become a member of the Secret Service. He unfortunately failed that examination by two points. He was told, however, that because he was a state trooper he could still join the agency under what they termed a schedule A appointment. He essentially would be placed on probation for two years. If he got through that period, he would become a full-fledged agent of the Secret Service. This is the path he chose to take.

It was at a thankyou dinner for Mayor Richard Daley on April

28, 1961, which was held at the McCormick Convention Center in Chicago that his place in history would be secured. Most of the agents were assigned to the banquet room where President Kennedy would join Mayor Daley for his celebratory dinner in appreciation for his contribution to Kennedy's narrow victory that prior November. Bolden was directed to guard a basement rest room that had been set aside for the President's exclusive use. Bolden who was an ardent admirer of the President initially was disappointed with his assignment because he assumed that he would not have an opportunity to see or meet him. As he was standing guard, he heard a commotion at the top of the stairs. To his surprise, the President followed by Mayor Daley and their security came down the stairs and approached Agent Bolden. The President then stopped directly in front of him and "looked me in the eye." He asked "Are you a Secret Service Agent or one of Mayor Daley's finest?" Bolden responded "I'm a Secret Service Agent, Mr. President." He then asked if there ever has been a "Negro" agent on the Secret Service White House Detail. One of Bolden's superiors standing behind the President said there had not been one. The President smiled and asked "Would you like to be the first?" Bolden enthusiastically replied "Yes sir, Mr. President!" This is how Bolden became a member of the presidential detail.

Bolden told his wife when he got home that they were moving to Washington. He could not wait to be part of an elite group of agents whose responsibility was to protect the president of the United States. More importantly, he had been given the opportunity to protect John Kennedy. He stated in the Holland interview that "I thought he was a wonderful President and a most gracious man." Just like James Garrison, he supported much of Kennedy's agenda and was inspired by the President's words and his leadership through that difficult time. A time that was especially harsh if you were an African American.

He joined the White House detail on June 6, 1961. Bolden

remembered that on one occasion while he was guarding the Oval Office he reached in to close a door when he heard the President call out his name with that familiar accent and invited him in. The President welcomed him to the White House and inquired about his living arrangements and his family.

Although he clearly admired the President, his experience in Washington did not meet his expectations. He was very disturbed by the lack of professionalism and the reckless conduct of his fellow agents who on many occasions showed up for duty with a hangover. Most of the agents were from the South and ignored him. They conversed about things as though he was not even in the room. He overheard them fraternize about parties they were involved in and all the alcohol they were consuming. They also discussed the prostitutes and other chicanery they participated in while on assignment.

He observed that they were lax while performing their duties, but even more disturbing to him was their open hatred of the President because of his civil rights agenda. They also thought he was a coward and a communist sympathizer because of the way the President handled the **Bay of Pigs** and the **crisis in Berlin.** In addition, they also complained and joked about his religion. His initial thought was the President was in "immediate danger" with this lot who were in charge of his security. On one occasion, he heard his colleagues admit that if someone tried to assassinate the President that they would not protect him – never mind take a bullet on his behalf.

Bolden concluded that the agents that surrounded the President had lost their focus and had misconstrued their constitutional oath that they had been sworn to uphold. They were not there to protect a man, but the office that he had been elected to by the people. Not all the agents were implicated in this conduct. Bolden had conceded that some of them like Clint Hill were honorable public servants. Hill, however, was assigned to protect the First Lady not the President. Bolden reported much of the above to his supervisor Chief James Rowley who promised to look into his allegations but apparently never did.

When the President and his family relaxed at the Kennedy compound in Hyannis Port in Massachusetts, Kennedy on many occasions headed out into the bay on the Presidential Yacht named after his maternal grandfather, the *Honey Fitz*. The President noted that Bolden was always assigned the difficult duty of following the yacht in speed boats that provided security for the family as they enjoyed their outing. The President spoke with Bolden's supervisor and requested that Bolden be allowed to join him on the presidential yacht. Bolden could not believe his assignment. He stood guard by a cabin door just 20 feet from where the President and the First Lady enjoyed the company of their children, Caroline and John. He marveled at how beautiful a family they were. As he was enjoying this moment, a man in a white naval uniform provided him a chair to sit in and then to Bolden's astonishment told him that the President thought he might be hungry. He then had lunch brought to him. He remembered that it was the best clam chowder that he had ever had in his life. As they got off the boat, President Kennedy introduced him to his brother Bobby as "the Jackie Robinson of the Secret Service." He then introduced him to the rest of his family, including his parents. As he was enjoying the moment, his immediate supervisor on that day, Harvey Henderson from Mississippi, who had been drinking beer while watching Bolden's interaction with the first family – called Bolden over to have a few words. Harvey while placing his finger into Bolden's chest said "I want to tell you something and don't you ever forget it. You're a nigger; You were born a nigger; You're going to die a nigger; You will never be anything else but a nigger. So act like one!"

Bolden decided that it would not be good for his health or his career to remain in Washington. He indicated that the racism of many on the detail at the White House at some point would have resulted in a physical altercation between himself and one of his colleagues. He placed his written request with his supervisor to transfer back to the Chicago field office in July 1961. He agonized over his decision because he feared for the President's life. He knew he was not leaving Kennedy in a good situation as it related to his security. When he returned to Chicago with his family, he joined the Secret Service's counterfeiting investigation squad. He became quite proficient at it and was eventually awarded two commendations by the Secret Service for "cracking counterfeiting rings." In 1962, he was ranked second in the nation in solving counterfeit and check forging cases.

The year 1963 initially inspired hope that peace was not some unreachable ideal that would be forever just beyond our grasp. It was the year that an American president had equated segregation to a moral crisis that our country had to confront if we were to live up to the ideals that founded our nation. The most comprehensive civil rights bill since the end of the Civil War was sent to Congress that summer. At home in Chicago, Bolden's career continued to prosper until a plot in Chicago on November 2, 1963, to assassinate the President was thwarted by an anonymous tip to the local FBI office by a man named "Lee." Bolden did not realize it at the time, but this assassination plan that had been prevented by luck would begin a period of tribulation that would result in him serving three years in a federal prison.

Upon receiving the tip, the FBI notified the local Secret Service office immediately. Kennedy was scheduled to arrive in Chicago on November 2, 1963, to watch with friends the Army-Navy game being played at Soldiers Field. His motorcade much like Dallas would have to slow down at a location surrounded by tall buildings as the large vehicle made the sharp turn off the Northwest Expressway ramp onto West Jackson.

In one of the buildings was located the patsy, Thomas Arthur Vallee, who was an ex-Marine who had served at Camp Otsu in

Japan which was a U2 base operated by the CIA. While serving in Korea, he had sustained a traumatic brain injury (TBI) when a mortar shell exploded near him. He also had trained Cuban exiles for the CIA to assassinate Fidel Castro. The Chicago Police Department based on intelligence that Vallee had threatened Kennedy's life would stop and search Vallee's vehicle. When they opened the trunk, they found rifles, ammunition and explosives. Vallee reported to the officers that he worked for the CIA. He was eventually released.

In addition to the patsy, there were four suspicious males that had high powered rifles in their hotel room as reported by a female witness who was aware of the President's trip. She stated that she suspected two of them were of Cuban descent and the other two were Caucasian. Two of the alleged assailants were arrested by the Secret Service and brought in for questioning. The other two got away when an officer inadvertently botched a surveillance operation. Because the two presumed assailants remained at large, the President's visit to Chicago had been cancelled.

These events in Chicago were never reported to the agents that were assigned to the President's trip to Texas where a second plot had been prepared to assassinate the President. This plan was not going to fail for the plotters had accounted for every contingency.

There was another investigation that occurred in Chicago regarding a Cuban exile involved in gun running named Echevarria. There were rumors that money had been gathered to pay assassins to murder the President. The Secret Service had been investigating him since October 1963. It was reported that the FBI and CIA were obstructing the investigation for some obscure reason. On November 26, 1963, agents returned to Chicago to revise these reports by advancing the dates to make it appear as though the investigation had taken place after the assassination.

At the same moment that these events were taking place in the second city, Diem and his brother were being assassinated in South Vietnam as a result of a military coup d'état that had been instigated and promoted by the CIA. Their murders were carried out contrary to the explicit order of the President that they be safely escorted out of the country.

Gerald Blaine in his book **The Kennedy Detail (2010)** co-authored by professional writer Lisa McCubbin had stated "There wasn't a thing we could have done to stop it." He of course was referring to the assassination of President Kennedy in Dealey Plaza in Dallas on November 22, 1963. This has been the view supported by the mainstream media for decades but is it true. Bolden vehemently disagreed with that position.

Much of the commentary in **The Kennedy Detail** and supported by the media is the assertion that it was President Kennedy's interference in his security in Dallas that contributed to his death. The standard claim is that he ordered the hard top of the 1961 Lincoln to be removed and that he had made it clear he did not want any agents on the back of the vehicle. Bolden said that the claims that the President interfered with his security were never mentioned when he was a member of the presidential detail. These allegations only surfaced after his death.

In an article entitled **The Dirty Secret of the Secret Service: President Kennedy Should Have Lived** written by Jacob Engels in October 2014, he cites a plethora of evidence that not only contradicted the allegations that Kennedy often interfered with his security but also disputes Blaine's defensive assertion that there was nothing the Secret Service could have done that day to save Kennedy. Engels initially points out that he was one of the supporters of that position until he read Bolden's book and Vincent Palamara's tome **Survivor's Guilt: The Secret Service and the Failure to Protect President Kennedy** which was published in 2013. Palamara had interviewed dozens of agents that reported that Kennedy never meddled in his security. They confided that the President was always very courteous and differential to the agents and their responsibilities.

It was reported by Engels that two Secret Service Chiefs for Kennedy, U.E. Baughman and James Rowley, who had 50 years of experience between them indicated that the Secret Service is in charge of presidential security not the president. As pointed out by Engels, Baughman conveyed this in his 1962 book, as well as his testimony before the Warren Commission. Baughman testified "No President will tell the Secret Service what they can and what they cannot do." Engels added that this view was shared by Presidents Truman and Johnson. In fact, an article in the Associated Press had reported one week prior to Kennedy's death that, "The Secret Service can overrule even the President where his personal security is involved." Even Blaine's co-author admits that she discovered evidence when researching for their book that contradicted what Blaine was telling her, but she deferred to him because he was the expert. It is true, however, that on many occasions the President wandered into crowds against the wishes of those in charge of his security, but as Engels aptly observed the President was not killed at a crowded "rope line" but rather in his "special limousine driven by a Secret Service agent on a motorcade route designed by Secret Service agents ... and with security invoked by Secret Service agents."

It becomes very apparent as you research the history that the Secret Service falsely blamed President Kennedy for his own murder when it was their own professional negligence that resulted in his assassination. The first major error was the motorcade route that was ultimately agreed to by Mayor Cabell that unnecessarily exposed the President to risks that could have easily been avoided. For example, most motorcades are designed so that the presidential limousine does not go below 30 miles per hour. This means that whenever possible sharp curves or turns are avoided when designing the motorcade route. The original route had the presidential motorcade traveling through the center of Dealey Plaza on Main Street. Agent Blaine misled his readers when he wrote that there was only one way to get to the Trade Mart off of Main Street where the President's luncheon was scheduled.[152] As pointed out by journalist and author, Jim Marrs, they could have reached their destination by remaining on Main Street.[154]

The other issue was who ordered the bubbletop's removal that day. Special Agent Sam Kinney was adamant that he was solely responsible for that decision. The other major contention is why there were no agents placed on the back of the vehicle. There is a video on YouTube that clearly shows Special Agent Emory Roberts ordering an agent off of the back of the President's Lincoln at Love Field. The agent appears perplexed and even raises both arms into the air in disbelief over what he is being instructed to do. In fact, he is left behind and appears not to be involved in the President's security after that point. Even Blaine in his book states "...the only way to have a chance at protecting the President against a shooter from a tall building would be to have agents posted on the back of the car."

Palamara discovered while researching for his book that on many occasions prior to Dallas multi-story buildings were closely monitored and in some cases guarded by agents just as Colonel Fletcher Prouty had recommended. In Dallas, not only was the Texas School Book Depository (TSBD) not guarded but none of the tall buildings along the whole motorcade were monitored or guarded as well. Engels writes that Chief Inspector Michael Torina who was the author of the Secret Service's manual confirmed that guarding tall buildings was a matter of routine protocol.

Another important matter had to do with the motorcycle formation that was employed that day. In other cities, there was a wedge formation that was utilized to protect the President but not in Dallas. All the motorcycles operated by law enforcement were situated behind the President's vehicle. If the wedge formation had been implemented in Dallas, the assassin's line of fire from the front may have been obstructed enough to prevent the head shot that mortally wounded the President.

There was also the issue regarding the placement of the press vehicle. This vehicle usually was situated behind the President's limousine, and in some cases in front, so the media could record and obtain photographs of the President responding to the crowds. In Dallas, the press vehicle was two cars back behind the Vice President's vehicle in a position where they were unable to photograph the assassination. The photos and films we have regarding the events in Dealey Plaza that day were primarily taken by amateurs.

The other significant concern related to Bolden's observations of his fellow agents when he was assigned to the White House. Agents who were designated on the night of November 21, 1963, to guard the President's hotel room left their post to go drinking at a bar in Fort Worth Texas. The individuals they assigned to cover for them were two volunteer fireman.[155] These agents did not return to their hotel rooms until 2:00am that night. It was reported that several of them had hangovers while they were engaged in protecting the President during that fateful motorcade. In my opinion, the performance of the agents that day reflect their incapacity to fulfill their duties or their complicity in the conspiracy to murder the President.

The driver of the limousine when the first shots are heard does not accelerate the vehicle as protocol demands but rather slows it down to approximately 9 mph. He was traveling at this sluggish speed when the President was struck by the mortal shot to the head.

Whether you believe there were three, five or more shots fired that day, the sequence of events as timed by the Zapruder film is 5.6 seconds which is an eternity for a Secret Service agent. And yet, no one reacted to the gunfire with exception to two agents. One of those agents was assigned to the Vice President. He was in the front seat of the vehicle that had Vice President Johnson. Upon hearing the first shot, he jumped over the seat and pushed Johnson to the floor behind the front seat. The other agent that responded – jumped off of the vehicle behind the President's Lincoln and climbed onto the trunk of that car – was Clint Hill. Hill was assigned to the detail that protected the First Lady not the President.

Hill was not originally scheduled to be a part of the security for the Texas trip. He was in effect looking forward to a rare weekend with his family. It was Mrs. Kennedy that had significant concerns and anxiety about the upcoming political trip to Texas, and especially Dallas, who had specifically requested that Clint Hill be assigned to her security. If Agent Hill had not been there, the Zapruder film would have depicted a disturbing portrayal of the Secret Service that seemed paralyzed and confused as the tragic event transpired. Essentially, there would have been no reactions by any of the agents assigned to protect the President and his wife that day. The agent that was in the front seat of the limousine did nothing which when contrasted with the actions of the agent that protected Johnson is astounding. When you consider the reaction of security agents that protected President Charles De Gaulle of France from assassins armed with machine guns in 1962, our security detail appeared grossly incompetent.

Bolden was very distressed when he heard what happened to President Kennedy in Dallas. He probably regretted that he chose to remove himself from Kennedy's security team. As Brent Holland aptly observed that if Bolden had been part of the President's detail on that dark day, he might have been saved. Bolden certainly would not have been out drinking the night before. It also must be noted that when the Assassination Records Review Board (ARRB) was set up by President Clinton in compliance with the JFK Records Act of 1992, all agencies, according to ARRB member Doug Horne, were instructed not to destroy documents relevant to Kennedy's presidency or his assassination. The Secret Service in blatant disregard of that order inexplicably shredded their security records from September through to November 1963. This, to steal a line from Attorney Vincent Salandria, is not the act of an innocent agency. What is even more appalling is that no one was prosecuted for violating a congressional act.

Bolden was deeply troubled by the events in Dallas, not only because of what he witnessed as a member of the presidential detail, but also the events in Chicago just three weeks prior to the assassination. He decided that he would offer his testimony to the Warren Commission (WC) and travelled to Washington to contact them. While he was in a phone booth, he noted an individual next to him that was acting suspicious. He decided to hang up and seek out another phone.

According to the Chicago Tribune in May 1964, the WC was considering Bolden's offer to testify before their committee. They were interested in his allegations regarding the drinking habits of the Secret Service. Before he could testify, he was advised by his superiors that he needed to return to Chicago immediately. Upon his arrival, he was arrested by federal agents for conspiracy to sell a government file to Joseph Spagnoli, Jr. in exchange for $50,000. The file that Spagnoli was seeking was related to evidence that implicated him in a counterfeiting ring.

Bolden was arraigned on May 20, 1964, on federal charges that he had solicited a bribe from the ring he had successfully broken. Bolden protested to the press that he had been framed by the government to prevent him from testifying before the WC. Chief James Rowley, when given his opportunity to testify and confront Bolden's allegations against his agency, stated "The fact is he never informed me.... I think the record shows, Mr. Chairman, that we were never advised that he wanted to testify..." Rowley defiantly concluded that there was "no truth to the charges of misconduct." He added that his investigation had uncovered no evidence to substantiate Bolden's claims that agents were in violation of Secret Service regulations. The matter was swept aside and forgotten by the mainstream media.

The primary witnesses against Bolden, Frank Jones and Joseph Spagnoli, were both facing felony charges that emanated from the Secret Service investigations that Bolden had participated in. Their jury trials were to be conducted by the same Chicago court that was hearing Bolden's case. Bolden was not accused of receiving the money, for federal investigators were never able to locate any illicit funds in his possession or accounts.

The first jury trial ended in a deadlock. The jury was 11 to 1 in favor of conviction. The Presiding Judge, Joseph Sam Perry, issued an Allen charge in an attempt to get an agreement. When this was unsuccessful, Judge Perry decided to employ a seldom used judicial prerogative to inform the jury of his assessment of the evidence that supported a guilty verdict. He further advised them that they were free to disregard his opinion before sending them back to deliberate. The lone juror refused to budge, and the jury remained deadlocked. The judge decided to declare a mistrial on July 11 and set the second trial for August 3, 1964.

Judge Perry would surprisingly be the presiding judge for the second trial as well. Upon the conclusion of the evidence, the judge decided to clear the court room and discontinue the jury's deliberations for the day and excused Bolden and the attorneys. He then locked the courtroom and instructed the jury to continue their deliberations without notifying the attorneys. In a verdict that had been apparently sealed overnight, the defendant would be informed the following morning of their guilty verdict. Judge Perry at his sentencing hearing ordered that Bolden be held in a federal penitentiary for six years. As a result, he was fired by the Secret Service.

While Bolden's appeal was pending, the primary witness against him, Spagnoli, was found guilty on counterfeiting charges and sentenced to 15 years. At his trial, he had testified that he had lied at Bolden's trial that "his mother supported him." He also lied about times and dates, and asserted that his testimony was coaxed by the government in order to enhance his veracity with the jury. On the basis of this testimony and the sworn affidavit of Attorney George C. Howard in which Spagnoli conceded that Bolden had been framed with the assistance and knowledge of U.S. Attorney Richard Sykes and the U.S. Secret Service, Bolden's attorneys would amend his briefs to support his appeal to overturn his conviction. In spite of this compelling evidence, Bolden's appeal was denied by the Seventh Circuit Court because they determined that Spagnoli's perjured testimony was "merely cumulative."

Bolden was ordered to begin his sentence in June 1966. He served over three years in prison and upon his release was placed on probation for two and half more. He primarily served his time at the prison camp located at the Federal Medical Center in Springfield, Missouri. On July 6, 1967, Bolden was inexplicably transferred to the 2-1 East Psychiatric Ward that was designed for the criminally insane. Bolden was fearful that the government was trying to destroy his mind so that he could never testify in the future and tell his story. They forced him to ingest psychotropic medications that were ordered by Chief of Classification and Parole, Julius Nichols, who later committed suicide while Bolden was at that facility.

Bolden described his experience in dire terms. He thought he would never leave that institution alive. He became so despondent as he stared at the cement walls that surrounded him each day which seemed to last for an eternity. And then one night, he heard a voice coming from his cell. His initial thought was they had finally caused him to lose his mind. He turned in his bed and saw a bright light in the upper corner of his room. He immediately felt calm and at peace. The voice had even attracted a guard who came down the hall and flashed a light into his room to ascertain what he was doing. He was convinced he had been visited by Jesus whose presence he surmised was to alleviate his despair by providing him with hope, as well as reassuring his faith that he had not been abandoned by God. From that day forward, he knew he would survive his ordeal and would be given the opportunity to be reunited with his family. He was eventually returned to the camp and released. He rejoined society emotionally drained, relieved and humbled but not defeated.

In 1975, Edwin Black, a syndicated columnist and journalist, investigated Bolden's allegations for eight months regarding the Chicago plot that the FBI and Secret Service claimed never happened. After interviewing numerous witnesses and reviewing government documents, he wrote a story that confirmed Bolden's narrative of events that were ignored by the mainstream media. Bolden would not give up his quest to speak out and tell his important narrative. He testified before the **House Select Committee on Assassinations** (HSCA) that were charged with investigating the murders of President John F. Kennedy and Dr. Martin Luther King, Jr. The HSCA was also responsible for evaluating the conduct and performance not only of the CIA and FBI but the Secret Service as well. The committee after its investigation was completed had determined that the "Secret Service was deficient in the performance of its duties" and that it "possessed information that was not properly analyzed, investigated or used by the Secret Service in connection with the President's trip to Dallas."

Bolden believes that President Kennedy was murdered by a conspiracy, and he would not be surprised if some of the agents in 1963 participated in that tragic event that had effected so many lives and more importantly reversed a policy of hope. Upon reflection, Bolden said his brief period in the Secret Service was special because of who Kennedy was. He said "Here's a man I had thought so much of when he was running for President, because the things he said and the improvements he wanted to make resounded with me deep in my heart, as it did with many African-American people."

Kennedy represented those ideals that made America great and unique among powerful nations. He inspired us to think of things bigger than ourselves and to reach for ideals long dismissed as unobtainable. He said at his American University speech in June 1963 "Our problems are manmade; Therefore, they can be solved by man. And man can be as big as he wants. No problem of human destiny is beyond human beings."

Bolden continued that "We loved President Kennedy because of the potential we saw and the fairness that he spoke about and the love for America he had. He just seemed like a very rich man who was out of place who should have been among us – a leader among our people." Bolden added that he was kind and gracious to him. He concluded that he always treated him with respect and that is what he will think of when he recalls those brief encounters with a man who has become part of the ages.

Bolden did rebuild his life with his wife Barbara after his prison sentence and acquired employment as a quality control supervisor in the automotive industry until he retired in 2001. He was never again accused of any wrong doing and was always highly regarded by those who knew him. His beloved wife died in 2005 only three years before Bolden's important memoir **The Echo from Dealey Plaza** was published. While writing his book, he tried to locate the transcripts of his two trials. They apparently were taken and were never returned to the National Archives. In fact, he could not obtain them in Chicago as well. It would seem that a powerful cabal was insuring that dark secrets remain secret so as to retain power in the present in order to continue to control the past. Bolden was undaunted by these efforts and would continue to fight to redeem what had been taken from him when he had been found guilty of charges he did not commit. Unlike James Garrison, he did not have the good fortune of being exonerated by a jury. The variable that probably had prevented him from obtaining justice may have been simply his race.

We do not have to reflect on the past for this reality can be seen in the recent incidents of police brutality that too often culminate in the victim's death. These men were all presumed guilty by those whose primary duty was to protect their fundamental rights as prescribed in our Constitution for the sole reason that they resided in poverty and were born black. How else can you explain the circumstances that befell Freddie Gray in Baltimore when the only act he was accused of was having eye contact with a police officer and then running away? This according to their union representative constituted probable cause that he had committed a crime because he lived in what was designated by law enforcement as a high crime neighborhood.

It was this same type of police indifference to the citizens they were charged with protecting in Oakland during the 1960s that gave rise to the **Black Panther Party for Self Defense**. It was this world view by those in power that desperately wanted to retain the status quo that led to the assassination of Fred Hampton by police and FBI in 1969 while he was sleeping in his apartment in Chicago. He was the charismatic chairman of the Illinois chapter of the **Black Panther Party** who had risen to national prominence at the young age of 21 because of his passionate oratory and his unique organizational skills. His only crime was his commitment to attain justice for the people he represented. As the cliché goes, the more things change the more things remain the same.

Bruce Watson, a critic for the Washington Post, while reviewing Bolden's memoir described his ordeal as "a shocking story of injustice." I would add that it was also a story of perseverance and courage against an evil so cosmic that like the universe is beyond human explanation. It is simply best described as the unspeakable.

The use of the word "unspeakable" to describe the evil behind the assassination was brought to my attention when I read the masterful tome on the Kennedy tragedy by James W. Douglass. (JFK and the Unspeakable – 2008).

Oliver Stone
(Confronting convenient fictions)
Part 5

Oliver Stone was born in New York City in 1946. He spent his youth in Manhattan and Stamford, Connecticut. He was born into a wealthy Republican family that vehemently opposed President Franklin Roosevelt and his New Deal. His father had achieved his wealth as a stockbroker on Wall Street and was a strong supporter of President Eisenhower and Vice President Richard Nixon. His parents were obviously very conservative in their politics and naturally he was initially influenced by their political views on the Soviet Union, China and the communist threat.

As a teenager, he spent his summers in France with his maternal grandparents and became fluent in French. Although his father was a non-practicing Jew and his mother was a Roman Catholic, he would eventually get involved in Buddhism. His parents would divorce in 1962 while he was attending a college preparatory school named the Hill School located in Pottstown, Pennsylvania. After he graduated from high school in 1964, he was admitted to Yale University and was part of the same class as George W. Bush. John Kerry was a senior during his freshman year. He was ambivalent on what course he wanted to take his life and decided to drop out and "see the world." He eventually taught English to high school students for six months at a staunch anti-communist school in South Vietnam called the Pacific Institute. He would later learn that the school was a CIA funded program that was part of their propaganda efforts to stem the rising tide of communism in that country.

He returned to the states to re-enroll at Yale University to complete his college education. As the term began, he recognized that he was not completely comfortable in that elite setting and for the most part felt like an outsider. He remained, however, an anti-communist conservative. And as the war in Vietnam became hot during the Johnson administration, he decided to leave Yale again and enlist in the army in 1967. He was determined to serve his country as his father had done in **World War II**. He believed in the cause and accepted his government's justification for sending combat troops to that poor beleaguered nation. He opined that it was an essential effort we were engaged in to confront communism before it consumed all of Southeast Asia. After all, the national media such as Time Magazine and the New York Times all supported the domino theory promulgated originally by Secretary of State John Foster Dulles and accepted by Presidents Eisenhower and Johnson as an accurate forecast of the consequences of Vietnam falling to the communists. President Kennedy never fully accepted this theory and refused to send combat troops and Americanize the war which infuriated his national security staff, including the Joint Chiefs and the CIA. This, as pointed out by Stone, was unknown to his generation at the time. The media, as well as President Johnson, repeatedly declared that his policy of military intervention was consistent with the martyred President's objectives. Even Barbara Tuchman in her book, **The March of Folly**, wrote that the war was inevitable because of the political paradigms that were dominant in the 1950s and 1960s. She too, as were many other historians, was completely oblivious to the reality that on the day Kennedy was assassinated the policy of the United States was to withdraw from Vietnam by December 1965.

Stone would discover in combat while trying to serve his country that the effort was not as noble as pronounced by the media and our leaders in Washington. He stated, "We were not fighting the enemy. We were fighting ourselves." He witnessed the mass killing, and the suffering of civilians and the desensitization of killing itself.

While he served for the 25th Infantry Division and the First Calvary Division, he earned a Bronze Star for heroism in combat. He also received a Purple Heart with an Oak Leaf Cluster after being wounded twice in battle. In addition, he was awarded an Air Medal for participating in more than 25 helicopter combat assaults which included missions near the Cambodian border. Lastly, he received the Army Commendation Medal for his service which was from September 1967 until November 1968.

He had served his country honorably and was discharged to civilian life that no longer seemed familiar to him. He indicated that there were no trumpets or parades when he returned. The anti-war movement was growing and many were marching in the streets. 1968 witnessed two more assassinations of prominent figures who were against our continued involvement in Vietnam. He returned politically confused and emotionally "very mixed up and very paranoid and very alienated." Unlike John Kerry, he did not immediately denounce the war or join the movement. He remained conflicted on the meaning of it all for years.

He entered New York University under the GI Bill and graduated in 1971 with a Bachelor of Fine Arts in Film. After graduation, he worked for New York City's sanitation department and as a taxi driver until the late 1970s. He wrote the script for **Platoon** in 1976 which was semi-biographical in that it integrated many of Stone's combat experiences. Although many were impressed with his script, none of the major studios were interested in a film on Vietnam that was a morose critique of America's war effort. The movies on the Vietnam War that were being filmed and produced at the time were **Rambo, The Deer Hunter** and **Apocalypse Now**. These movies did not reassess our war policy but rather continued to blame the liberal media and the student demonstrations for losing the war. Consequently, these films still portrayed the enemy as inhuman and our intervention as a righteous cause to defend our ally, South Vietnam. President Reagan supported this view that the war was a noble effort as his administration attempted to reshape the American image at home and around the world. The thoughtful reflections of a policy that was driven by fear and pride with a complete misunderstanding of Vietnamese culture and history that doomed our effort from the start would come later.

Platoon was finally presented to the American public in 1986. It was his first major success as a director. He followed up this film with another anti-Vietnam movie entitled **Born on the Fourth of July** which was an autobiographical film about a U.S. Marine turned peace activist, Ron Kovic. Although these films were critical of our establishment and our disastrous Vietnam policy, he did not become known as a controversial director until he directed **JFK** in 1991. This movie featured Kevin Costner as James Garrison, the District Attorney of New Orleans, who had the temerity to indict and prosecute the CEO of the International Trade Mart, Clay Shaw, for allegedly participating in the conspiracy to murder President Kennedy. This was the beginning of a very difficult period for Stone in which he found himself constantly defending his film to the national media, historians and the CIA.

JFK was nominated for 8 academy awards and would win two. The cast included, in addition to Costner, John Candy, Kevin Bacon, Tommy Lee Jones, Joe Pesci, Sissy Spacek, Donald Sutherland, Ed Asner, Jack Lemmon, Walter Matthau and Jim Garrison as Chief Justice Earl Warren. Stone was inspired to make the movie after reading Jim Garrison's book **On the Trail of the Assassins** which was published in the late 1980s. He not only interviewed Garrison, but he also consulted with other experts and historians such as Robert Groden, Jim Marrs, John Newman, James DiEugenio and Colonel Fletcher Prouty. He also interviewed witnesses, law enforcement personnel, retired FBI and CIA agents, as well as journalists. In addition, he read multiple books on Kennedy and the assassination before he started writing the script and selecting the all-star cast. His investigation and research spanned over two years.

Before the accolades by the public and the academy, he was attacked mercilessly. In fact, the first draft of his script was stolen which was unprecedented at the time according to Stone. This draft was disseminated to the media who used it as the basis for their harsh critiques of the film's premise that Kennedy was murdered by a domestic conspiracy that was sponsored by CIA agents who vehemently opposed his policies towards the Soviet Union, Cuba and Vietnam. Liberal polemicists such as Noam Chomsky and journalists at the Nation, the Chicago Tribune, the Washington Post and the New York Times to name a few all wrote articles bashing Stone's interpretation of Kennedy and how his movie was providing a false history to a whole generation of Americans. Their articles also proclaimed his movie as another conspiracy theory based on paranoia and poor historical research. The CIA also unleashed its media assets to defend the Warren Commission and encouraged the publication of tomes that reinforced the lone nut theory.

This frenzy led to books such as **Cased Closed** by Gerald Posner reestablishing in the minds of the public that Oswald committed the crime and that the single bullet theory was not as magical as reported by the conspiracy nuts. In addition, there were tomes written to smear Kennedy's character and legacy in an attempt to undo the image of peacemaker as portrayed in Stone's movie such as **The Dark Side of Camelot** by Seymour Hersh. This specious tome was partially debunked because Hersh naively used false testimony and forged documents in his haste to support his claims against Kennedy. In addition, Thomas Reeves wrote **A Question of Character** (1997), and Nigel Hamilton assaulted Kennedy's younger years in **JFK: Reckless Youth** (1993) in which he diagnosed Kennedy as manifesting symptoms consistent with a narcissistic personality disorder. These characterizations of Kennedy were unfamiliar and fabricated to those who knew him. During this period, there was a concerted campaign to insure Stone did not receive the academy award for best director or best film. He even had a difficult time getting support from the studios for future projects. In fact, he had to eventually establish his own company to produce his films.

Clearly, Stone had hit a nerve in his attempt to capture the essence of a tragedy that continued to captivate the public. The primary attacks on his film concentrated on two major artistic techniques used by directors and script writers to condense a story that is extremely complex. He did this with his use of Mr. X who was played by Donald Sutherland. In the movie, Garrison travels to Washington to meet Mr. X who informs him he is on the right track and that he must continue until the conspiracy begins to crack open and reveal itself. This character was modeled after "deep throat" who was the anonymous and shadowy figure that guided Woodward and Bernstein while reporting on the Watergate scandal that would eventually bring down the Nixon administration. Mr. X, however, was a compilation of two individuals named Colonel Fletcher Prouty and military intelligence officer Richard Case Nagell while FBI Agent Mark Felt was in actuality "deep throat."

The other issue the media and the critics focused on was the closing argument that Costner gave at the end of the Shaw trial. Stone acknowledged that this speech was a culmination of different statements that Garrison had given which were combined with his actual closing argument. He was not distorting the facts but was seeking efficient ways to convey a complex story in a three-hour format. His explanation did not appease the media critics whose version of Kennedy and the assassination had been etched into their resume and legacy. If their version of the martyred President as a cold warrior and a cautious politician was not correct, their reputation and credibility on a number of issues would be questioned. Even worse, if the Warren Commission was fiction and Stone's movie was reality, the public would question their integrity for promoting an untruth for so long and never really investigating the contorted and fabricated evidence that was proffered by their government. The stakes were high, and they were determined not to let the cat out of the bag. Instead, Stone and his movie had to be discredited and more importantly future directors needed to be discouraged from challenging the elite's version of the truth. They were partially successful in the latter objective. When Emilio Estevez was asked by the press why he did not confront the growing controversy that encircled the assassination of Robert Kennedy in his movie **Bobby**, he responded that he had observed what they had done to Stone. Anybody who knew the struggle Stone had endured needed no further explanation.

Stone's movie at the very end indicated that thousands of documents were still in the government's possession not scheduled to be released for decades. This inspired the public to write to Congress to demand the release of all the classified papers related to the assassination. The result was that Congress in 1992 passed the JFK Assassination Records Recovery Act which was presented to President George H.W. Bush who signed it. He left the enforcement of that law to President Clinton who commissioned the Assassination Records Review Board that helped facilitate the declassification of millions of pages of documents over a period of four years. As researchers and historians waded into this treasure trove of history, the Kennedy that had been hidden for decades began to reemerge. In short, Stone's version of Kennedy was supported by the documents, as well as his portrayal of what happened to Kennedy in Dealey Plaza. The Warren Commission at this point lay in shambles as was demonstrated in tomes written by researchers and historians such as Gerald McKnight of Hood College who wrote **Breach of Trust**

(How the Warren Commission failed the nation and why) in 2005.

Stone had the last laugh in that the revelations exposed in these declassified documents were not very gracious to his critics. He would slowly rehabilitate his reputation and his career. And yet, he is still viewed as a radical and arrogant director that is casually dismissed as a heretic in some circles. Even so, he eventually produced other historical and controversial films such as **Nixon** and **Natural Born Killers** undaunted by his detractors.

In many ways, Stone has become one of the elders trying to preserve the "true past" for future generations so that their understanding of our time will be placed in a proper perspective, as well as accurately understood by those in the future. In the fall of 2013, he co-authored a book with historian Peter Kuznick entitled **The Untold History of the United States** which was accompanied by a 13-hour DVD that was directed and narrated by Stone. He has come a long way from his conservative youth to the controversial progressive director we all know today. On many occasions, he has criticized President Obama for not standing by the principles and policies that motivated his base. He has supported Julian Assange and Edward Snowden, as well as joined forces with Michael Moore to defend the freedom of the press.

In an interview with his friend and former CBS anchor, Dan Rather, he stood by the factual accuracy of his films such as **Nixon** and **JFK**. Rather asked if he thought he was primarily a dramatist, an entertainer or a historian. He responded that he was none of those. He said his films "poche history" which is a French word that means to make a rough sketch. In spite of his characterization, he clearly researches the events and the people he portrays in his films with a tenacious attention to detail. His next project will be about Edward Snowden, and the classified documents he released to The Guardian and the Washington

Post. He believes it is an important story that needs to be told on the big screen.

In the Rather interview, there were signs of resentment and anger as a result of what he had endured and suffered after the release of **JFK**. He indicated "Part of me wants to fit in and would love to get Oscars but there's another part that says. 'I'm fucked.' I'm on the other side of history." He clearly does not use the same paradigms as his contemporaries when interpreting the social constructs or power struggles within our society that make up our history. His rough sketch of the Kennedy assassination inspired a whole generation to re-evaluate this tragic event. I know it did for me.

Witnesses to the truth and the researchers that risked everything to tell their story (Assassinations of the 1960s) Part 6

The assassinations of the 1960s wiped out a whole generation of charismatic progressive leadership whose vision for the country was to end the Cold War through negotiation, to cease the madness in Vietnam and to compel the nation to fulfill the promises made at our founding. Their deaths silenced the most dynamic voices that any generation at any time could hope for and that generations since have not witnessed. The assassinations of President John F. Kennedy (1963), Malcolm X (1965), Dr. Martin Luther King, Jr. (1968) and Senator Robert F. Kennedy (1968) have left a void in our national spirit that has not been entirely ameliorated. Their deaths five decades later are still mired in controversy in that the official verdicts by the government regarding their murders are not consistent with the eyewitness testimony and the forensic evidence.

Elizabeth Woodworth in her article published in 2013 by Global Research entitled **JFK, MLK, RFK, 50 Years of**

Suppressed History wrote, "50 years of research shows that three humane visions of global peace were thwarted by three covert operations." She concluded "In each case eyewitness accounts were written out of history. In each case the lone gunman fiction denied society a true understanding of the deep politics of history. In each case propaganda masked truth and undermined the public good."

The perpetrators of these heinous crimes against society were allowed to avoid punishment by a powerful cabal that through deception, misdirection and fabrication were initially able to convince the public that these men were victims of random acts of violence. Below I intend to present several witnesses that I believe demonstrate why we should be skeptical of the government's explication for the deaths of these visionary leaders. The unanticipated deaths of the witnesses are also fraught with inconsistencies and contradictions that do not provide much confidence in the conclusions proffered by the investigating authorities. Former legendary CIA asset Bill Corson, who had substantial knowledge of CIA black projects, said "Anybody can commit a murder, but it takes an expert to commit a suicide."

In addition, I must underscore the gratitude we as a nation owe a small band of citizen researchers that refused to be intimidated from telling the stories of those witnesses that were privy to the truth. It is because of their persistent efforts that we have been able to declassify documents long suppressed by our government through the **Freedom of Information Act**. And as a result of their diligent pursuit of the facts and evidence that was capriciously dismissed by the mainstream media and our government, we are in a superior position to understand the true nature of these tragic events.

Dorothy Kilgallen

Dorothy Kilgallen was a nationally syndicated columnist who wrote a gossip column read by millions each day. She was also a regular on the popular television game show called **What's My Line?** She was a very ambitious journalist and after the Kennedy assassination, unlike most of the mainstream media, was using her articles to criticize the government's version of what transpired in Dallas.

Jack Ruby was an admirer of Kilgallen and granted her an exclusive interview shortly after his arrest for murdering Oswald. She returned from Dallas with information that she told friends would "bust this case wide open" and vowed that she would "crack this case." She, however, did not disclose the intelligence that she had obtained from her extensive interview with Ruby in his jail cell. She was intending to include it in her anticipated blockbuster book she titled **Murder One**. A version of her book would be published posthumously after her death without the JFK material.

Kilgallen was aware of the untimely and suspicious deaths of journalists Bill Hunter and Jim Koethe who were tracking down and interviewing witnesses to the assassination. Because of this, she made a copy of her copious notes and gave them to her close friend fellow journalist Flo Pritchett. She was very engrossed with her upcoming book, and the impact it would have on her career. She kept teasing friends with comments such as "I'm about to blow the JFK case sky high." In one of her columns, she announced to her readers that "In five days, I'm going to bust this case wide open." But before she could complete her investigation, she had scheduled a trip to New Orleans to close up some loose ends. She would never get a chance to make that trip. She was found dead on a bed in her apartment on November 8, 1965, by her hair dresser who was also a close friend. The official verdict of the medical examiner was "acute ethanol and barbiturate intoxication." He further listed her death as a suicide or accidental overdose. He did note that there were "circumstances undetermined." Her friends and family disagreed with the coroner's conclusions and pointed to a number of factors that they believed supported a homicide.

Prior to her death, Kilgallen had disclosed to friends that she knew she was under surveillance but she was not sure who were the culprits. She had also told those close to her that she had received death threats if she revealed what she knew about the JFK murder. In addition, there were a multitude of suspicious factors associated with the crime scene and where the body was found. She was discovered in a bed that she never used in a "bolero-type blouse over a night gown" that according to those who knew her she would never have worn to bed. In addition, her body was found with her makeup and false eyelashes still on. By her body was a book, she had already reported to friends she had read. And even if she decided to reread it, her reading glasses were not located near her body.

There was also physical evidence that caused more questions than provided answers. For instance, she had apparently had an alcoholic drink before taking a lethal "cocktail" that included three types of barbiturates and yet only traces of one barbiturate was detected on her glass. In addition, the authorities could only locate one bottle of medication. Evidence regarding the other two barbiturates could not be located in her apartment even after a diligent and thorough search had been conducted by law enforcement. Lastly, the air conditioner was on which was an oddity because her apartment at night got quite cold. It was reported that she turned it off before she started her nightly ritual. In essence, the crime scene appeared to be staged by someone who was not familiar with the daily habits of Kilgallen when preparing to retire to bed for the night.

There were other disturbing developments that strengthened the case for a homicide as opposed to a suicide or accidental death. The autopsy had also concluded that that her body had been propped up in the bed and her head tilted after her death. The purpose of positioning the body in that particular pose was to make it look like an accidental death. Friends also pointed out that Kilgallen was a very intelligent woman and would not have used that barbiturate cocktail with alcohol. As others have noted, there were too many pills consumed to be an accident and too few to be consistent with a suicide.

The other major revelation was that her notes regarding the JFK assassination could not be located and have never surfaced since her death. If her death was accidental, why would notes that friends had fervently indicated to investigators were so important that she always had them with her wherever she went would now be missing? Another coincidence or factor supportive of foul play was that her friend Flo Princhett would die just 24 hours later of a cerebral hemorrhage apparently as a result of her leukemia. If her death was of natural causes, the same perplexing question could be asked in that the copy of Kilgallen's JFK notes could not be located at her home as well.

John Garrett Underhill

The second witness is John Garrett Underhill who was a graduate of Harvard. He served in **World War II** as a military intelligence officer while working for the Office of Strategic Services (OSS) and would be given special assignments by the CIA after the war. He was also a consultant for Henry Luce – the owner of **Time, Fortune and Life Magazine.** His expertise was in limited warfare and small arms weaponry. These two areas of specialty would be in large demand when the CIA would expand its clandestine operations under the stewardship of Allen Dulles in the 1950s.

James DiEugenio provided the most cohesive explanation of what Underhill claimed he witnessed and what he reported to friends before his alleged suicide in his book **Destiny Betrayed**

2nd edition (2012).

In the evening of November 22, 1963, Underhill, in fear of his life, left Washington in search of refuge. He eventually appeared at the door of his close friends, Robert and Charlene Fitzsimmons, who resided on Long Island. Charlene's husband was still asleep when Underhill walked into their home in a panic. Charlene skeptically listened to her distraught friend who had clearly been frightened by something or someone. He normally was a very calm and rational person and because of this his behavior had her quite concerned.

She initially told him that they were preparing that day to travel to Spain for a month. Underhill responded "You're going to Spain? That's the best thing to do. I've got to get out of the country, too. This country is too dangerous for me now." He continued to ramble. "I've got to get on a boat, too. I'm really afraid for my life." Charlene inquired if he had been drinking in which he insisted he had not.

He then disclosed to her why he was so nervous and excited. He stated it was about the "JFK assassination" the day before. She still was confused and asked him to clarify how this was relevant to his present emotional condition. He answered, "Oswald is a patsy. They set him up. It's too much. The bastards have done something outrageous. They've killed the President! I've been listening and hearing things. I couldn't believe they'd get away with it. But they did." Charlene interrupted and asked who "they" were? Underhill excitedly responded, "WE, I mean the United States. We just don't do that sort of thing! They've gone mad! They're a bunch of drug runners and gun runners – a real violent group. God, the CIA is under enough pressure already without that bunch in Southeast Asia. Kennedy gave them sometime after **Bay of Pigs**. He said he'd give them a chance to save face."

Charlene remained unconvinced but continued to listen. Underhill continued, "They're so stupid. They can't even get the right man. They tried it in Cuba, and they couldn't get away with it – right after the Bay of Pigs. But Kennedy wouldn't let them do it. And now he'd gotten wind of this, and he was really going to blow the whistle on them. And they killed him!" He paused and then added "But I know who they are. That's the problem. They know I know. That's why I'm here. I can't stay in New York. Can you put me up?" She reminded him that they were leaving for Europe on a plane later that day. He then exclaimed "Well, maybe I can go with you." Charlene was now very frustrated. She did not want him ruining their long awaited vacation. She assuaged him by suggesting that when Robert got up he might agree to allow him to spend a few days at their home while they were gone. Underhill decided to leave indicating that he would return. She would never see him alive again. Years later she would write to James Garrison to apprise him of her conversation with her distraught friend.

Underhill was not an irrational raving lunatic. He was a Washington insider who knew most of the military brass and upper echelon of the CIA. He had previously expressed reservations about these power brokers secretly operating within the bowels of our government hidden from the public to his friend Asher Brynes who was a writer for **The New Republic**. This in essence was an individual who was connected with the black secrets of the government and knew the people he had tried to enlighten Charlene about. When he returned to Washington, he began to investigate further the assassination of Kennedy. On May 8, 1964, Brynes visited his friend's apartment and found him lying in bed. As he approached, he observed a bullet hole behind the left ear of his friend's head. The gun was also located underneath the left side of his body. His first thought was that something was suspicious because Underhill was right handed. If he committed suicide, it was done in an extremely awkward position. He promptly notified the police.

The coroner eventually concluded that the cause of death was suicide. Brynes was dismayed by the findings in the autopsy report. His estranged wife, Patricia, initially refused to talk about the circumstances of her husband's death. In fact, she never released any of the papers on his investigation of the assassination. Years later she would reveal that she was threatened by government agents to keep her mouth shut.

Other than what is reported above, there is no other information to flesh out the meaning of what he had disclosed to Charlene. It could be that the drug trafficking in Southeast Asia and the assassination projects of the CIA were connected. It also could be these were separate operations that the President had become aware of and was going to use that information to abolish the CIA. For instance, the President may have obtained reliable intelligence that the CIA was attempting to assassinate Castro which was contrary to his stated policy and that they were involved in drug trafficking to pay for their black ops.

Lt. Commander William B. Pitzer

The tome written by Richard Belzer and David Wayne entitled **Hit List** which was published in 2013, and James Douglass' ground breaking volume **JFK and the Unspeakable (Why he died and Why it matters) (2008)** are the sources for my essay on Lieutenant Commander William B. Pitzer of the United States Navy.

There has been a substantial amount of evidence and witness testimonials regarding the alteration of President Kennedy's wounds at Bethesda Naval Hospital in Maryland. David Lifton was one of the first to conduct an objective comprehensive assessment of the allegations of surgical alterations, the two caskets and the doctored x-rays and photographs taken during the official autopsy at Bethesda. The evidence he gathered was included in his eye opening tome **Best Evidence (1981)**. The mainstream media dismissed his work as paranoid speculation by another conspiracy theorist. However, Doug Horne of the Assassination Records Review Board participated in a thorough examination of the declassified medical records that were made available to the public as a result of the **JFK Records Act** of 1992. He also partook in numerous depositions of those who were involved or witnessed the autopsy. He concluded that Lifton's assertions are clarified and supported in the record. Lifton's book was also buttressed by CIA veteran John Stockwell's study in which he determined that "The evidence was extensively tampered with. The President's body was altered: The photographs of the autopsy were altered; Over 100 witnesses were killed or died mysterious or violent deaths."

Pitzer was the head of the Audio-Visual Department of the Naval Medical School. In that capacity, he worked closely with Bethesda Naval Hospital. During the Kennedy autopsy, he was used as an x-ray technician whose responsibility was to film the autopsy. He would later be debriefed by military intelligence. During that debriefing, he was advised to remain silent about what he witnessed. They further indicated that he would suffer severe consequences if he breached his promise to remain silent. He reported to friends that the experience was "horrific." He added that he was visited by military personnel repeatedly who reminded him for reasons of national security he had to honor his promise not to reveal what he had observed that evening.

On that following Monday or Tuesday after the assassination, Pitzer was visited at his office by his good friend First Class Hospital Corpsman Dennis David. David observed that Pitzer was editing a film when he arrived. Pitzer asked him to come closer because he wanted to show him what was on the film. David immediately recognized that it was President Kennedy's body. After reviewing the film and observing the wounds, they both concluded that the President had been shot from the front. More specifically, they noted a small entrance wound in Kennedy's forehead and a large exit wound in the occipital (back) region of the skull. Both had seen numerous bullet wounds and were quite familiar with injuries caused to the body by gunshots. David would later state that his friend's film clearly contradicted the Warren Commission Report and the photos and x-rays that would eventually be made public.

Pitzer was looking forward to his retirement from the Navy which was to begin on October 29, 1966. He had lucrative offers from the networks that his friend David speculated may have been prompted by his classified film. He was more thrilled, however, by the prospect of teaching at Montgomery Junior College. In fact, on the day he was murdered, he had gone to his office to prepare a speech he was to deliver at that college. His body would be discovered on the floor of the TV production studio at the National Naval Medical Center which was his work area. He had been shot in the head by a 38 caliber revolver that was found close to his body. His head was beneath the lower rung of two aluminum step ladders that were propped up against a foundation post. It was alleged by friends that he may have stored the JFK film in the false ceiling in his production studio. This may have accounted for the ladders and the ceiling tile that was found slightly ajar from its normal position. The JFK film was never located and remains another mystery associated with the assassination. The medical examiner would determine that the cause of death was suicide.

As in the other cases, there was evidence that was more indicative of a homicide than a suicide. The paraffin test did not detect nitrates on his hands that would be an indication that he had discharged a pistol that day. The test further established that he was shot from a distance of approximately three feet. Unless his arms were abnormally long, the claim that he shot himself did not seem feasible. Although Pitzer had signed the gun out, he had a notation on his calendar to return it which was odd if you were planning to kill yourself. In addition, the FBI was never able to determine how the ammunition for the weapon had been obtained. Friends had also stated that he was a very meticulous person and yet there was no suicide note found at the scene. In addition, there was no proof according to friends and family that he was suicidal. In fact, on the day he died, it was reported that he was in a good mood. The government would eventually assert that he was having marital problems and may have been involved in an extra-marital affair. They also argued that they had located documents that were two years old that stated he had been depressed. Of course, all these documents that allegedly supported the government's position that Pitzer had committed suicide were all destroyed by the Navy.

Pursuant to a lawsuit filed under the **Freedom of Information Act** in 1997, the FBI released documentation that supported the claim that he had been murdered. The documents contained information that a heel print had been made near the body that was not consistent with the shoes the victim was wearing. In addition to all the evidence, the government's behavior and conduct was consistent with an individual who had something to hide. They refused to release the autopsy report to the family. The government also denied the request of Pitzer's wife to have his wedding ring returned to her. To be more specific, they had claimed his left hand was too mangled to pull it off. And yet, the injuries reported by the government did not include severe injuries sustained to his hands. In fact, there was no mention of this type of injury in the autopsy.

The case became more complicated in 1993 when a former Green Beret had watched a documentary that included the death of Pitzer. In August of 1965, U.S. Army Special Forces Lieutenant Colonel Daniel Marvin was approached by CIA agents to solicit his participation in a black project they were planning. They asked him if he would assassinate a Naval officer who had become a threat to our national security. Marvin indicated that the CIA told him that this individual was planning to divulge classified material to the public after his retirement. They added that this material was related to the JFK assassination. He declined their request to terminate the Naval officer. This all would be clarified when he attended the **Special Warfare School at Fort Bragg** in North Carolina. The training that elite forces and intelligence officers received at that school related to guerrilla warfare, assassination and terrorism. At the time, he supported the notion that extreme measures were sometimes necessary when our national security interests were involved. He no longer supports that view.

His bizarre narrative, however, does not end there. He continued that he and his Green Beret classmates were then taken to "a different building that had a double barbed wire fence, surrounded by guard dogs." They were then brought into a large class room. The CIA instructors than began to discuss the JFK assassination. They even had a highly detailed model of Dealey Plaza to refer to during their presentation. They informed the group that what happened in Dallas was a "classic example" on how to eliminate a nation's leader, while blaming a lone assassin. He added that they were provided with details on how it worked and why it had been successful. They showed them multiple photos and films of the assassination that he had never seen before or since. The instructors even pointed out on the scale model where the shooters were located. During a coffee break, he and his friend overheard one of the CIA facilitators tell the other instructor that "things really did go well in Dealey Plaza, didn't they?" After it was over, he rationalized at the time that the killing of Kennedy had to be in our national security interest. Otherwise, it would have never been done because we are not in the business of assassinating our own leaders.

By watching that documentary on the JFK assassination, he now knew who the CIA had wanted murdered that day. After he declined to participate, they must have located another willing participant that actually committed the crime. Since watching that documentary, he telephoned Pitzer's wife to apprise her of what he had been requested to do by CIA agents in 1965 to her husband. He also has testified and written extensively about this episode in his military career, including testimony he gave to the Assassination Records Review Board. Because of his coming forward, he has been marginalized by the government and the national media as a nut. In addition, he was summarily dismissed from the **Special Forces Association of Retired Soldiers**. His family has repeatedly pleaded with him to stop discussing this matter to avoid further retribution. It is no wonder none of his classmates have come forward to confirm his memory at Fort Bragg.

Dr. Thomas T. Noguchi

Senator Robert F. Kennedy had just completed a victory speech in a large banquet room at the Ambassador Hotel to his jubilant supporters after winning the important California primary when he left the podium to attend a press conference. He was escorted by his family, his campaign staff and his personal security which included Los Angeles Ram Rosey Grier and Olympian Rafer Johnson down a long narrow corridor that led through the hotel's pantry. After being fatally wounded in the pantry of the hotel by alleged assailant Sirhan Bishara Sirhan, he was transported to the Good Samaritan Hospital in Los Angeles. His life would expire at 1:44am on the morning of June 6, 1968, just 24 hours after the shooting. The Chief Medical Examiner for the county of Los Angeles, Dr. Thomas T. Noguchi, was promptly notified of the Senator's death.

Upon hearing the tragic news, Dr. Noguchi was determined to avoid the controversy and intrigue that had surrounded the autopsy of President Kennedy. He contacted his fellow practitioner Dr. Cyril M. Wecht for advice before he commenced his examination of the body. He meticulously gathered all the evidence he could and carefully documented everything he did.

To his dismay based on the witness accounts of where Sirhan had been standing in relation to Senator Kennedy, he ascertained that the gunshot that had caused the death of the Senator had entered his skull just below the right earlobe. The gun had discharged the bullet only 1.5 to 2 inches away from Kennedy's head. It travelled in an upward trajectory into the center of the brain. The other wounds in Kennedy's back and other locations were also created by a gun that was very close to the body and behind the Senator. By all witness accounts, Sirhan was two to four feet in front of Kennedy.

In an article written by Frank Morales, dated, June 6, 2012, entitled **The Assassination of RFK: A Time for Justice**, it was reported that Dr. Cyril Wecht and Dr. Robert K. Joling had reviewed the autopsy and the documented evidence used to support its conclusions. Both doctors concurred that the shot that killed Robert Kennedy had emanated approximately 1.5 inches from the right earlobe and that the shooter had to have been standing just behind and to the right of Kennedy. There were witnesses that saw a second gunman but were ignored and dismissed by the Los Angeles Police Department (LAPD). There were also witnesses that indicated that they heard more than eight shots fired that night in the pantry. In addition, several witnesses remember Sirhan being escorted into the building by a young woman in a red polka dotted dress and an unidentified male. In spite of all this, LAPD concluded its investigation by assigning blame on another lone nut.

A freelance newspaper reporter Stanislaw Pruszynski by providence inadvertently left his audio recorder on during the assassination. He was unaware at the time that he was recording evidence that would establish the presence of two shooters that night. This recording would become known as the **Pruszynski Tape**. The technology to analyze his tape that could remove the noise sufficiently to determine the acoustic sounds that were consistent with gunshots would not be available until 2005. The experts that examined the tape utilized the Spangenberger-Analysis test. They were able to identify 13 acoustic sounds that were made by gunshots. "The conclusion is inescapable that there was a second shooter during the shooting that resulted in the death of Robert F. Kennedy, and that the five shots fired from the second gun were fired in a direction opposite the direction in which Sirhan fired."

Attorney William F. Pepper filed briefs on behalf of Sirhan requesting that the court reopen the case based on this evidence. It was proffered by Attorney Pepper that at the time of Sirhan's original trial the prosecution had suppressed the conclusions of the autopsy; they had not provided copies to defense counsel nor did the defense request it; there were efforts by the DA to have the coroner falsify the results of the autopsy; and there was criminal coercion and persecution by LA authorities upon the coroner. The case is awaiting a decision by the court.

David Sanchez Morales

Another witness may have been involved in the murder of both Kennedys or at a minimum knew who did it. His name was David Sanchez Morales. He was a CIA officer who was up to his neck in black projects for the CIA. One former agent reported that if you saw David in town you knew someone was going to be kidnapped or assassinated. He was the one the CIA would turn to when they needed an operative who was willing to do anything requested of him to defend the CIA or his country. He was involved in the training of Cuban exiles who landed at the **Bay of Pigs** and was implicated in the assassination of Che Guevara in Bolivia. He also became part of the notorious **Phoenix Program** in Vietnam that was attributed with murdering 26,000 Vietnamese.

One evening, he was drinking with his attorney Robert Walton. Walton casually mentioned that he was considering working for the reelection of Senator Edward Kennedy. Morales went into a tirade about JFK and RFK that lasted several minutes. He then calmed down and said, "I was in Dallas when I, when we got the mother fucker, and that I was in Los Angeles when we got the little bastard."

David Talbot the founder of Salon.com interviewed Morales' lifelong friend Roben Carbajal to confirm what Attorney Walton had stated. Carbajal was very devoted to his friend that he had grown up with in the city of Phoenix. He said that Morales was very patriotic and loyal to the CIA. He felt that the CIA assignments that his friend had accepted were very "courageous missions" that he did for his country. He added, "When some asshole needed to be killed, Didi (nickname for Morales) was the man to do it." He conceded that Morales may have been in Dallas and Los Angeles during the two assassinations but would not reveal anything beyond that. He shared the same animosity towards the Kennedys that his deceased friend had. He stated "JFK disserved what he got because of what he did at **The Bay of Pigs**." He added in any event "The Kennedys were giving the damn nation to the blacks." He did reveal, however, that he had been told by Morales and CIA colleague Tony Sforza that the CIA was involved in the assassination of President Kennedy.[156]

RFK confided to a friend while campaigning in Washington DC that "I'm afraid there are guns between me and the White House." The anguish that Kennedy had gone through before he announced his candidacy for President of the United States was more fraught with peril than anyone at the time recognized. Consequently, the media mistakenly accused him of being an opportunist for announcing his intent to run in March 1968 after Senator Eugene McCarthy had exposed the vulnerabilities of the incumbent President, Lyndon Baines Johnson, by his strong performance in the New Hampshire primary. The decision to run was more complicated and personal for Kennedy in ways not even fully appreciated by those in his inner circle. The animosity between himself and the President was well known, and he did not want the election to digress into a battle of personalities that would overshadow the central issues of the time such as the Vietnam War. The other concerns he contended with he settled in private in discussions with his family.

Because of his prior service as Attorney General and his secret investigation into the death of his brother, he was familiar with the dark side of the government and fully comprehended the brutality of his opponents that would unite to prevent his ascension to the presidency. When he had made his decision to enter the race, he had accepted death as a possible consequence for his quest to not only finish his brother's work but to heal a nation that was torn asunder by the powerful tides of poverty, racism, injustice and violence. If he succeeded and survived, he might also attain justice for his slayed brother.

In the last speech Bobby delivered, he said "Fear not the path of truth for the lack of people walking on it." The closer you examine the assassinations of the 1960s the more disturbing the picture becomes.

We stand today – several decades later – in a nation that has lost its moral compass, and its purpose as the guardian of liberty that we valiantly earned by the sacrifices our nation endured in **World War II**. Instead, we have become a nation that is enforcing a "Pax Americana" on the rest of the world by our weapons of war. If we truly are an exceptional nation, we should be committed to the righteous aspiration of the Greeks "To tame the savageness of man and make gentle the life of this world."

Conclusion

There is no whistleblower defense to a charge brought under the Espionage Act of 1917. As former NSA analyst Edward Snowden proclaimed, there is no distinction between the release of classified documents to serve a public interest, and those documents disseminated to a foreign government for personal benefit such as financial compensation. Because of this, he submits he would be unable to receive a fair trial. Thus, he remains in Russia as a dissident of the United States that has been granted political asylum by President Vladimir Putin. He, in essence, has been compelled to reside in a nation whose government does not endorse the individual liberties he risked everything to protect.

When the documents were first made public by The Guardian and The Washington Post, the response from President Obama and Secretary of State Kerry was that he was a traitor and a threat to our national security. Although the mainstream media was divided on the issue, there were large segments that supported the government's contention that he needed to be immediately extradited to the U.S. and tried as a traitor. Paradoxically, the programs he unveiled were more of a threat to our liberty and national security than his act of absconding with classified documents that were eventually disseminated to the public.

The second allegation levied against Snowden was that he did not avail himself of internal mechanisms within the NSA to address his concerns regarding the legality of these surveillance programs. This internal program for NSA employees apparently does not exist and is a fictitious argument asserted by those who are unfamiliar with how intelligence organizations work or worse they are lying.

This outcry has somewhat softened since a U.S. appellate court has ruled that the metadata collection programs that are compiling telephone calls, e-mails, texts and other forms of communication by U.S. citizens were not supported by the statute the government was citing to legally justify the NSA programs. The court unfortunately did not have to confront the second argument presented by the American Civil Liberties Union that these programs were in violation of the U.S. Constitution, more specifically the first, fourth, fifth and fourteenth amendments. Snowden is a recent example of how the media and the government respond to those who are objecting to the status quo and are attempting to inspire the public to demand a change in the law or in this case to amend or abolish a secret government program.

Another excellent modern example would be Julian Assange, an Australian journalist and founder of WikiLeaks, and his release of documents that were given to him by Private Bradley (Chelsea) Manning whose motives were similar to those of Snowden. Her trial resulted in a guilty verdict. Manning is presently serving a 35-year sentence for revealing corruption and actions by U.S. military personnel that constituted war crimes under international law and the Geneva Convention.

In Assange's case, he has been charged with committing rape and molestation on two Swedish women that resulted in an arrest warrant being issued. He immediately sought refuge in Ecuador's embassy in London where he has remained since 2012 as a prisoner to avoid being arrested and extradited to Sweden. He adamantly denies these allegations and has asserted that this legal fiction is an attempt to discredit his character to undermine his public support that U.S. authorities are hoping will eventually lead to his extradition to the United States to face the charge of espionage. Whether the merits of the case against him prove to be accurate or not, this should not obfuscate the core issue related to his release of the documents and their relationship to the fundamental concept of freedom of the press.

Former CIA Agent, Jeffrey Sterling, was sentenced to 3.5 years in a federal penitentiary on May 11, 2015, for allegedly distributing classified documents to New York Times reporter James Risen regarding a covert plan called **Operation Merlin** developed in 2000 by the CIA. The primary purpose of the operation was to forestall Iran's nuclear program by providing them with defective nuclear plans. James Risen included this material in his book **State of War** that was published in 2006.

Risen concluded that it was a poorly thought out plan that ironically would have enhanced Iran's nuclear program.[157]

Sterling was convicted in 2011 of 9 felony counts which included an espionage conviction that was the impetus for the sentence that was imposed by a federal court. The prosecutors had recommended that he serve 20 years for his acts against his country. Sterling's attorneys have filed an appeal.[158]

Sterling contends that he was not the source of the leak that supplied Risen with those documents and adamantly denies that he has done anything illegal. He added that he was the first African American to file a racial discrimination case against the CIA. He submitted that the charges that resulted in his conviction were filed as retribution to his lawsuit.[159]

He indicated after 9/11 he eagerly wanted to get involved in the response by intelligence agencies to that seminal event. He told his CIA superiors he would be willing to drop his lawsuit if they allowed him to be reinstated and participate in CIA operations. The response he received was short and sweet. "You're fired!" In fact, John Brennan, who is presently the Director of the CIA, had a meeting with Sterling to tell him to his face that he was "fired." One of his colleagues remarked when you "pull on Superman's cape" this is what happens.[160]

He affirmed that he had concerns about the operation against Iran and had informed the Senate Intelligence Committee about the potential collateral consequences with this plan, but he was not Risen's source.[161]

This is another example of our government clamping down on citizens trying to reign in government programs that are cloaked in claims of national security when in fact they are jeopardizing it. The Obama administration's record in this area is an abomination when you consider that he promised during his 2008 campaign to pursue a more transparent and open government. His administration has prosecuted more whistleblowers than any administration in our history. His intent seems to be to discourage this activity by imposing severe sanctions on those who do it – regardless of their motivations or even the merits of their concerns that prompted their willingness to jeopardize their liberty.

We do not have to look to the past to appreciate the threat that our national security state represents to our liberty and our republic. As William Faulkner wrote, "The past is never dead. It's not even past." The past is reflected in everything we do and believe in. It is an intrinsic part of everyday life whether we are willing to accept it or not. The slow undoing of the objectivity and the independence of the press for instance is not something that appeared one day against our will.

The transformation of the mainstream media as a guardian of liberty to a mouth piece of corporate power and an instrument of government propaganda developed over decades as a consequence of the cumulative acts of our elected representatives which we allowed to occur by our passive indifference. It will take a concerted effort not only from the public but our public officials to reverse this incestuous alliance. Until this is done, most of our citizens will be brainwashed and ignorant of that knowledge that is essential to effectively participate in a democracy.

If the corporate media cannot be reformed because we cannot summon the political will to change it or because the hidden power behind it refuses to cooperate, it will be necessary to fervently support programs such as net neutrality and the formation of a variety of diverse cable stations that are not beholden to advertisers or government censors such as Free Speech TV. The internet poses a complex challenge for those who wish to manipulate and control the flow of information that is disclosed to the public. These new technologies may present certain hazards but also may be our salvation.

The examples of the dissenters I presented in this six-part series I believe established a clear and disconcerting pattern on how the power centers in our society confront those that contradict the reality that they want us to uncritically accept. If they cannot discredit your message, their tactics become more ominous such as allegations of sexual deviant behavior or the commission of criminal acts. If this does not achieve their objectives, they will in some circumstances resort to murder. The number of suicides and deaths by natural causes to witnesses to the Kennedy assassination are astounding and beyond the reasonable probabilities that one would be willing to accept as mere coincidence.

If we want to save our republic, we first need to arm ourselves with knowledge. A people that expect to be ignorant and free are living in a dream world. In addition, we need to establish a whistleblower exception or defense to the Espionage Act of 1917. We also must reform the classification program we have developed since **World War II** that is so broad almost anything can be kept secret no matter how tenuous it is to our national security. If we hope to maintain our basic freedoms, we must revise our national security laws and abolish the **Patriot Act**. As Patrick Henry stated, "The liberties of a people never were, nor ever will be, secure, when the transactions of their rulers may be concealed from them." Also, the assassinations of the 1960s unequivocally taught us that secrecy is the main factor that allows for corruption and extremism to not only survive, but it is the necessary sustenance that allows it to thrive.

Sissela Bok, a Swedish philosopher, stated in 1982, "I believe that a guarantee of public access to government information is indispensable in the long run for any democratic society...If officials make public only what they want citizens to know, then publicity becomes a sham and accountability meaningless." If secrecy remains the foundation of our national security, how are we as citizens supposed to competently exercise our right of franchise and hold our elected officials accountable not only for their conduct, or the policies they support, but all the actions of the agencies that constitute our government? The answer is that we can't.

The CIA, for example, submits a budget that is so secret the Congress has no idea where the money is spent. The Senate and House Intelligence Committees are supposed to provide some oversight to this powerful agency and yet they are dependent upon the good faith of CIA officials and their willingness to divulge all intelligence necessary for their supervision to have meaning. Many inside the beltway mockingly refer to those groups as the overlooked committees not the oversight committees. This is not something we should take lightly. The CIA, for instance, has done significant damage to our nation's reputation and credibility. They are considered by the developing countries as the largest secret police force in the world. If you are familiar with how they define "secret police", it will be self-evident that this is not a compliment.

The CIA in many ways acts like an organized criminal organization that operates under its own set of regulations and laws. It has murdered many people in the past, and it is still killing people allegedly on our behalf in support of our nation's national security. Senator Frank Church when referring to all the weapons, chemical and otherwise, being developed by the CIA warned, "I don't want to see this country ever cross the bridge...I know the capacity that is there to make tyranny total in America, and we must see to it that this agency and all agencies that possess this technology operate within the law and under proper supervision, so that we never cross over the abyss. That is the abyss from which there is no return."

In my opinion, the CIA must be reformed and transitioned into an intelligence gathering and analysis agency as originally intended by President Truman when he created it in 1947. Its clandestine operations should be terminated. If this cannot be accomplished, the CIA should be abolished.

Epilogue

The news reports of drone attacks around the globe, the bombing of a hospital in Afghanistan, the ongoing violence in Iraq, Syria and Guatemala, the drug cartels in Mexico, the killing of children in Palestine, the Saudi's bombing of civilians in Yemen and the millions of refugees are all emblematic of mankind's inability to elevate our common humanity above the sovereign interests of the state whose primary purpose is to establish a new balance of power not create a new world of law. In most instances, this impulsive penchant to resort to military solutions to perceived threats only benefits the most powerful and affluent in our societies. Although the United States is not the singular cause of these tragedies, it has played an instrumental role in instigating these atrocities by attempting to impose its will on the rest of the world by our weapons of war. In many cases such as Iran, Cuba and Guatemala, their turbulent past and the suffering of their citizens can be directly attributed to the covert actions of the CIA to defend its corporate allies cloaked in claims of advancing democracy in order to enhance our national security. All of this is possible because of the classification system we have developed that promotes secrecy while diminishing transparency in government policy that allows for this nonsense to be protected under the ambit of national security.

The prosecution of individuals attempting to defend our liberty under the Espionage Act of 1917 – who should be treated as whistleblowers if not heroes – and the audacious investigative journalists who reported on the documents not only has a chilling effect on future efforts to expose government actions that curtail our liberty, but it is also an assault on our fundamental concept of freedom of the press.

It is absurd that the British taxpayers during a period of government imposed austerity have spent $19 million dollars to pay for agents to maintain constant surveillance of the Ecuadorian Embassy, waiting for Julian Assange to venture out far enough for them to descend upon him and arrest him. It is also disturbing when the power of government is used to intimidate journalists to compel them to divulge their sources as was done to James Risen. The media and the whistle blower have an important role to play in the safeguarding of our liberty from government actions that are hidden from us. This occurs even though it is supposed to be working for the people. As Jesse Ventura pointed out, a democratic government by its nature is supposed to be of us, for us and by us. The present system that is dominated by our national security complex has been turned on its head. The government treats us as children who cannot handle the truth so they instead provide us with fairy tales. Can you imagine if an employee told his employer that he did not have the requisite security clearance to know what was happening in his business? The employee would be fired.

It is anticipated that the declassification of over 1,100 documents that pertain to agents that are prime suspects in the Kennedy assassination and others are scheduled to be released in 2017 in compliance with the JFK Records Act. I suspect the information that will be discovered in these secret documents will allow the research community to supplement pieces of our mosaic that will not only reaffirm and enhance what we know about the Kennedy assassination, but will also reveal intelligence that will expose additional nefarious activity by our government that caused other dark events in our history.

I am presently a case manager in a drug court. In order for addicts to heal, they must first admit their addiction and confront their past behavior that caused so much damage to themselves, their families and their communities. By constantly telling their stories at recovery meetings, they not only help others but also assist their journey of recovery by reminding themselves of their past and the power of their disease. It seems to me that the government should do the same and begin to make amends for the transgressions of the past by reconciling our censored history with reality. In order to allow our nation to heal and begin the process of rebuilding our democratic republic, the government needs to tell the truth.

Endnote References

1. Dead Wrong by Belzer & Wayne pgs. 1-16
2. Ibid pgs. 2,5,6
3. Ibid pg. 6
4. The Devil's Chessboard by Talbot pgs. 74-93
5. Ibid pgs. 268-286
6. Ibid pgs. 74-93
7. Ibid pg. 198
8. "Allen Dulles 'Indonesia Strategy' and Assassination of JFK" by Edward Curtin
9. Ibid
10. Ibid
11. Ibid
12. "The Mysterious Death of UN Hero" by Lisa Peace
13. "New Inquiry is Sought in 1961 Death of U.N. Leader Dag Hammarskjold" by Alan Cowell
14. Ibid
15. "World: Africa UN Assassination Plot Denied" BBC News
16. Ibid
17. Betting on the Africans by Muehlenbeck pg. 32
18. Ibid pg. 5
19. Ibid pg. 6
20. Ibid pg. 6
21. The Brothers by Kinzer pg. 282
22. JFK: Ordeal in Africa by Mahoney pg. 70
23. The Brothers by Kinzer pgs. 292-293
24. Betting on the Africans by Muehlenbeck pg. 35
25. JFK: A President Betrayed
26. JFK and the Unspeakable by Douglass pgs. 109-110
27. Ibid pg. 112
28. Ibid pg. 111
29. Virtual JFK

30. "How the Agency Killed Trujillo" by Norman Gall
31. Ibid
32. Ibid
33. Ibid
34. "LBJ's Other War" by Ray Fanning
35. Ibid
36. Ibid
37. Ibid
38. Ibid
39. Ibid
40. Ibid
41. Flawed Giant title of Dallek's biography of LBJ
42. House of War by Carroll pgs. 349-353
43. Ibid pg. 351
44. Ibid pgs. 354-355
45. Ibid pgs. 349-353
46. Ibid pg. 385
47. Ibid pg. 375
48. The Untold History of the United States by Kuznick & Stone pg. 434
49. Ibid pg. 436
50. Ibid pg. 436
51. Ibid pg. 447
52. Ibid pgs. 450-451
53. Ibid pg. 451
54. Ibid pg. 451
55. Ibid pg. 454
56. The Devil's Chessboard by Talbot pgs. 167-177
57. House of War by Carroll pgs. 454-455
58. Interview of Seymour Hersh, Democracy Now, 5/12/15
59. Interview of Jeremy Scahill, Democracy Now, 5/3/16
60. Interview of Farea Al-Muslimi, Democracy Now, 7/9/15
61. "Virtual JFK 3" by DiEugenio quoting from In Retrospect by McNamara pgs. 96, 261

62. Lessons in Disaster by Goldstein pg. 46
63. Why CIA Killed JFK & Malcolm X by Koerner pg. 26
64. Ibid pg. 26
65. Ibid pg. 48
66. Ibid pg. 41
67. Ibid pg. 43
68. Lessons in Disaster by Goldstein pg. 47
69. Why CIA Killed JFK & Malcolm X by Koerner pg. 48
70. Ibid pg. 49
71. Lessons in Disaster by Goldstein pg. 60
72. Ibid pg. 61
73. Ibid pg. 63
74. Ibid pg. 64
75. Virtual JFK
76. Lessons in Disaster by Goldstein pg. 66
77. Ibid pgs. 65-66
78. JFK and the Unspeakable by Douglass pgs. 128-131
79. Ibid pgs. 128-131
80. Ibid pgs. 128-131
81. Lessons in Disaster by Goldstein pg. 235
82. JFK and the Unspeakable by Douglass pg. 187
83. Ibid pg. 187
84. Death of a Generation by Jones pg. 314
85. JFK & Vietnam by Newman pg. 347
86. Ibid pg. 351
87. JFK and the Unspeakable by Douglass pg. 182
88. JFK: A President Betrayed
89. Brothers by Talbot pg. 67
90. Ibid pg. 67
91. The Untold History of the United States by Kuznick & Stone pg. 303
92. Ibid pg. 309
93. House of War by Carroll pg. 267
94. Ibid pg. 263

95. American Heart of Darkness by Kirkconnell pg. 280
96. JFK and the Unspeakable by Douglass pg. 236
97. Ibid pgs. 238-242
98. Brothers by Talbot pg. 37
99. House of War by Carroll pgs. 269-270
100. "Exit Strategy" by J. Galbraith
101. "JFK vs. the Military" by Dallek
102. JFK and the Unspeakable by Douglass pgs. 342-343
103. Ibid pg. 195
104. Lessons in Disaster by Goldstein pg. 227
105. "John F. Kennedy's Vision of Peace" by RFK, Jr.
106. JFK and the Unspeakable by Douglass pg. 109
107. "General Giap Knew" by Kang
108. "John F. Kennedy's Vision of Peace" by RFK, Jr.
109. JFK: A President Betrayed
110. "The Truth as I see it" by Schlesinger, Jr.
111. "John F. Kennedy's Vision of Peace" by RFK, Jr.
112. Ibid
113. JFK and the Unspeakable by Douglass pgs. 351-355
114. Reclaiming Parkland by DiEugenio pgs. 196-198
115. Ibid pg. 57
116. Ibid pg. 58
117. Ibid pg. 58
118. Ibid pg. 58
119. Ibid pg. 58
120. Ibid pg. 58
121. Ibid pgs. 58-59
122. Ibid pgs. 60-61
123. Ibid pgs. 62-63
124. Ibid. pg. 176
125. Ibid pg. 177
126. Ibid. pg. 192
127. Ibid pgs. 69-70
128. Ibid pg. 70

129. Into the Nightmare by McBride
130. Reclaiming Parkland by DiEugenio pgs. 88-89
131. Ibid pgs. 101,103
132. JFK and the Unspeakable by Douglass pgs. 260, 265-266
133. Ibid pgs. 262-265
134. Ibid pg. 448
135. The Last Word on the Assassination
136. JFK and the Unspeakable by Douglass pg. 266
137. Full document on CTKA website
138. Reopen the Kennedy Case by DiEugenio
139. Bury My Heart at Wounded Knee by Brown pg. 446
140. Ibid pg. 448
141. Buck v. Bell, Democracy Now, 5/17/16
142. Ibid
143. The Devil's Chessboard by Talbot pg. 16
144. The Untold History of the United States by Kuznick & Stone pg. 423
145. The Zong Massacre by Spilman
146. Ibid
147. The Last Word on the Assassination – comments made by Joan Mellen
148. Brothers by Talbot pg. 46
149. Ibid pg. 50
150. JFK and the Unspeakable by Douglass pg. 98
151. "Did US Military Plan a Nuclear First Strike for 1963?" by Galbraith & Purcell
152. JFK and the Unspeakable by Douglass pg. 30
153. The Kennedy Detail by Blaine pg. 98
154. The Last Word on the Assassination-comments made by Jim Marrs
155. Ibid
156. Brothers by Talbot pgs. 396-401
157. Jeff Sterling, Democracy Now, 5/12/15
158. Ibid

159. Ibid
160. Ibid
161. Ibid

Bibliography

Belzer, Richard & Wayne, David, **Hit List** (New York: Skyhorse Publishing, 2013)

Belzer, Richard & Wayne, David, **Dead Wrong** (New York: Skyhorse Publishing, 2012)

Blaine, Gerald & McCubbin, Lisa, **The Kennedy Detail** (New York: Gallery Books, 2010)

Brown, Dee, **Bury My Heart at Wounded Knee** (Canada: Holt, Rinehart & Winston, 1970)

Carroll, James, **House of War: The Pentagon and the Disastrous Rise of American Power** (New York: Houghton Mifflin Company, 2006)

DiEugenio, James, **Destiny Betrayed – Second edition** (New York: Skyhorse Publishing, 2012)

DiEugenio, James, **Reclaiming Parkland** (New York: Skyhorse Publishing, 2013)

Douglass, James, **JFK and the Unspeakable** (Maryknoll, New York: Orbis Books, 2008)

Fiester, Sherry P., **Enemy of the Truth** (Southlake, TX: JFK Lancer Productions & Publications, Inc., 2012)

Garrison, James, **On the Trail of the Assassins** (New York: Sheridan Square Press, 1988)

Goldstein, Gordon, **Lessons in Disaster** (New York: Times Books, 2008)

Jones, Howard, **Death of a Generation** (New York: Oxford University Press, 2003)

Kinzer, Stephen, **The Brothers (John Foster Dulles, Allen Dulles, and their Secret World War)** (New York: Times Books, Henry Holt and Company LLC, 2013)

Kirkconnell, Robert, **American Heart of Darkness** (USA: Xlibris, 2013)

Koerner, John, **Why the CIA Killed JFK and Malcolm X: The**

Secret Drug Trade in
Laos (Winchester, UK: Chronos Books, 2014)

Mahoney, Richard, **JFK: Ordeal in Africa** (New York: Oxford University Press, 1983)

McBride, Joseph, **Into the Nightmare** (Berkeley, CA: Hightower Press, 2013)

Muehlenbeck, Philip E., **Betting on the Africans** (New York: Oxford University Press, 2012)

Newman, John, **JFK and Vietnam** (New York: Warner Books, 1992)

Newman, John, **Oswald and the CIA** (New York: Skyhorse Publishing, 2008)

Orwell, George, **1984** (Brawtley Press-St. John, reprinted in 2014)

Palamara, Vincent, **Survivor's Guilt: The Secret Service and the Failure to Protect**
President Kennedy (Trine Day, 2013)

Porter, Gareth, **Perils of Dominance** (Berkeley, CA: University of California Press, 2005)

Stone, Oliver and Kuznick, Peter, **The Untold History of the United States** (New York:
Gallery Books, 2012)

Talbot, David, **Brothers: The Hidden History of the Kennedy Years** (New York: Free Press, 2007)

Talbot, David, **The Devil's Chessboard** (New York: Harper Collins Publishers, 2016)

Trento, Joseph L. **The Secret History of the CIA** (New York: MJF Books, Fine Publications, 2001)

Periodicals

Aguilar, Gary, JFK, Vietnam, and Oliver Stone, History Matters, Nov. 2005

BBC Online Network, World: Africa UN assassination plot denied, BBC News, 8/19/98

Cowell, Alan, New Inquiry is Sought in 1961 Death of U.N. Leader Dag Hammarskjold,

The New York Times, December 16, 2014

Curtin, Edward, Allen Dulles' "Indonesia Strategy" and the Assassination of John F. Kennedy,

LewRockwell.com, 2016

Dallek, Robert, JFK vs. the Military, The Atlantic, 2013

Devereaux, Ryan, Managing a Nightmare: How the CIA watched over the destruction of

Gary Webb, The intercept, Sept., 2014

DiEugenio, James, 'Kill the Messenger': Rare Truth-telling, Consortium News, 10/6/14

DiEugenio, James, Reopen the Kennedy Case: Tom Hanks, Gary Goetzman, and

Bugliosi's Bungle (Comprehensive review of Reclaiming History),

Part 6, August 8, 2012

DiEugenio, James, Virtual JFK: Vietnam if Kennedy had lived, CTKA, 2008

DiEugenio, James, Virtual JFK 3: Review of Lessons in Disaster, CTKA, 2008

Engels, Jacob, The Dirty Secret of the Secret Service: President Kennedy should have

Lived, October of 2014

Fanning, Rory, LBJ's Other War, 2015

Fuchsman, Ken, Evidence Points to JFK's Post-War Stress, op-ed Hartford Courant, 2012

Galbraith, James K., Exit Strategy, Boston Review, October/November 2003

Galbraith, James & Purcell, Heather, Did US Military Plan a Nuclear First Strike in

1963? The Prospect, Sept. 21, 1994

Gall, Norman, How the Agency Killed Trujillo, The New Republic, June 28, 1975

Glanz, James & Garshowitz, Irit Pazner, Moshe Yaalon, Israeli Defense Minister, Resigns, New York Times, May 20, 2016

Garrison, James, Interview in Playboy, October 1967

Garrison, James, Closing Argument, JFK Lancer, Sept. 1, 1967

Josephs, David, The Evidence is the Conspiracy, CTKA, 8/21/14

Kangas, Steven, The Origins of the Overclass, 1998

Kangas, Steven, Timeline of CIA Atrocities, 1996

Kennedy, Jr., Robert F., John F. Kennedy's Vision of Peace, Rolling Stone, 12/5/13

Minor, Linda, Creature of the CIA, 2011

Morales, Frank, Assassination of RFK: A Time for Justice, June 6, 2012

Pease, Lisa, President Kennedy's Foreign Policy, Progressive Historians, March 30, 2008

Pease, Lisa, James Jesus Angleton and the Kennedy Assassination, Probe, July – August 2000 (Vol. 7 No. 5)

Pease, Lisa, The Mysterious Death of UN Hero, Consortiumnews.com, September 16, 2013

Reitz, Dave, The Mysteries of Dealey Plaza, CTKA, 9/15/14

Schlesinger, Jr., Arthur, JFK: The Truth as I See It, Cigar Aficionado, December 1998

Scott, Peter Dale, The Kennedy Assassination and the Vietnam War (1971), Excerpts

From text, History Matters

Spilman, Rick, The Zong Massacre, General Averages and Abolition, Old Salt Press, 11/29/13

Stone, Oliver & Sklar, Zachlary, Yes, there was a Cover-Up, Chicago Tribune, 9/18/13,

Posted on CTKA 9/20/13

Woodworth, Elizabeth, JFK, MLK, RFK, 50 Years of Suppressed History, Global Research, 2013

Documentaries and Films

Barbour, John, **The Last Word on the Assassination**, John Barbour Production in
Association with Wordsmith Media, Inc., 2014
Belle, Directed by Amma Asante, Fox Searchlight Pictures, 2013
JFK, Directed by Oliver Stone, Le Studio Canal + Regency Enterprises, Warner Bros., 1991
JFK: A President Betrayed, Directed by Cory Taylor, Agora Productions, 2013
Virtual JFK, Directed by Koji Masutani, Docuramafilms, 2008

Television, YouTube and Radio

Goodman, Amy, Democracy Now: The War and Peace Report, History of Black Panther
Holland, Brent, interview of Abraham Bolden, Night Fright, 2012
Horne, Doug, 6-hour presentation on JFK cover-up, You Tube, 2014
Osanic, Len, interview of Barry Ernest, author of **The Girl on the Stairs**, Black Op Radio, 2014
Osanic, Len, interview of Gary Webb, Black Op Radio, 2002
Party for Self Defense, the coup in Brazil and story on former CIA Agent Jeffrey Sterling, and the drone program, 2015
Rather, Dan, interview of Oliver Stone, 2014
Scott, Peter Dale, interview of Dallas Police Chief Curry, YouTube, 1977
Steinberg, Jeff, interview of Col. L. Fletcher Prouty, YouTube, Nov. 11, 1992
Ventura, Jesse, Simulation of Assassination, YouTube
Williams, Brian, interview of Edward Snowden on NBC, May 28, 2014

Internet

BrainyQuote
Great-Quotes.com
Wikipedia

Documents

Captain Fritz's of DPD notes on interrogation of Lee Harvey Oswald

CIA memorandum on how to confront the Warren Commission critics

Dewi Sukarno's letter to President Gerald Ford in 1975

FBI memorandum by Agent DeLoach (4/4/67), CTKA

Ho Chi Minhs letter to President Lyndon Johnson in 1967

Ho Chi Minhs letter to President Harry S. Truman in 1946

Katzenbach Memorandum

Kennedy's American University speech on June 10, 1963

Kennedy's Washington University speech in Seattle on November 16, 1961

MLK's Riverside Church speech on April 4, 1967

Operation Northwoods

NSAM 55, 56, 57, 263, 271, 273, 288

Veciana Affidavit (His contact "Maurice Bishop" was CIA officer David Atlee Phillips.)

Chronos Books
HISTORY

Chronos Books is an historical non-fiction imprint. Chronos
publishes real history for real people; bringing to life people,
places and events in an imaginative, easy-to-digest and accessible way - histories that pass on their stories to a generation
of new readers.
If you have enjoyed this book, why not tell other readers by
posting a review on your preferred book site. Recent
bestsellers from Chronos Books are:

Lady Katherine Knollys
The Unacknowledged Daughter of King Henry VIII
Sarah-Beth Watkins
A comprehensive account of Katherine Knollys' questionable
paternity, her previously unexplored life in the Tudor court and
her intriguing relationship with Elizabeth I.
Paperback: 978-1-78279-585-8 ebook: 978-1-78279-584-1

Cromwell was Framed
Ireland 1649
Tom Reilly
Revealed: The definitive research that proves the Irish nation
owes Oliver Cromwell a huge posthumous apology for wrongly
convicting him of civilian atrocities in 1649.
Paperback: 978-1-78279-516-2 ebook: 978-1-78279-515-5

Why The CIA Killed JFK and Malcolm X
The Secret Drug Trade in Laos
John Koerner
A new groundbreaking work presenting evidence that the CIA
silenced JFK to protect its secret drug trade in Laos.
Paperback: 978-1-78279-701-2 ebook: 978-1-78279-700-5

The Disappearing Ninth Legion
A Popular History
Mark Olly
The Disappearing Ninth Legion examines hard evidence for the
foundation, development, mysterious disappearance, or
possible continuation of Rome's lost Legion.
Paperback: 978-1-84694-559-5 ebook: 978-1-84694-931-9

Beaten But Not Defeated
Siegfried Moos - A German anti-Nazi who settled in Britain
Merilyn Moos
Siegi Moos, an anti-Nazi and active member of the German
Communist Party, escaped Germany in 1933 and, exiled in
Britain, sought another route to the transformation of
capitalism.
Paperback: 978-1-78279-677-0 ebook: 978-1-78279-676-3

A Schoolboy's Wartime Letters
An evacuee's life in WWII — A Personal Memoir
Geoffrey Iley
A boy writes home during WWII, revealing his own fascinating
story, full of zest for life, information and humour.
Paperback: 978-1-78279-504-9 ebook: 978-1-78279-503-2

The Life & Times of the Real Robyn Hoode
Mark Olly
A journey of discovery. The chronicles of the genuine historical character, Robyn Hoode, and how he became one of England's greatest legends.
Paperback: 978-1-78535-059-7 ebook: 978-1-78535-060-3

Readers of ebooks can buy or view any of these bestsellers by clicking on the live link in the title. Most titles are published in paperback and as an ebook. Paperbacks are available in traditional bookshops. Both print and ebook formats are available online.

Find more titles and sign up to our readers' newsletter at
http://www.johnhuntpublishing.com/history-home

Follow us on Facebook at
https://www.facebook.com/ChronosBooks
and Twitter at https://twitter.com/ChronosBooks